A NICKEL AND A PRAYER

ReGENERATIONS
AFRICAN AMERICAN LITERATURE AND CULTURE

VOLUME TWO

Also in this series:
Hearts of Gold *by* J. McHenry Jones

Regenerations is a new series devoted to reprinting editions of important African American texts that have fallen out of print or have failed to receive the attention they merit. *Regenerations* encourages research that develops and extends the understanding of African American literary and cultural history, by promoting regional and local research that represents the complex dynamics of African American experience.

"[*Regenerations: African American Literature and Culture*] has the potential to be a vital, exciting series that will make available neglected texts that can help us to rethink African American literary and cultural traditions."

—*Robert S. Levine, Distinguished Scholar-Teacher,*
University of Maryland

"[This] series will expand the scholarly discussion about the ways in which such texts help us to rethink the field and insure that the books will be taught in the classroom and thereby be sustained for the next generation."

—*Sharon Harris, Director, Humanities Institute and Professor of English,*
University of Connecticut

SERIES EDITORS

John Ernest — *Eberly Family Distinguished Professor of American Literature,*
West Virginia University

Joycelyn K. Moody — *Sue E. Denman Distinguished Chair in American Literature,*
University of Texas at San Antonio

A Nickel and a Prayer

The autobiography of **Jane Edna Hunter**

Edited by **Rhondda Robinson Thomas**

with a Foreword by Joycelyn Moody

WEST VIRGINIA UNIVERSITY PRESS • MORGANTOWN

West Virginia University Press, Morgantown 26506
© 2011 by West Virginia University Press. All rights
reserved.

Published 2011. Printed in the United States of America
19 18 17 16 15 14 13 12 11   1 2 3 4 5 6 7 8 9
ISBN-13 (cloth): 978-1-933202-65-5
ISBN-10 (cloth): 1-933202-65-3
ISBN-13 (cloth): 978-1-933202-64-8
ISBN-10 (cloth): 1-933202-64-5

Library of Congress Cataloguing-in-Publication Data
Hunter, Jane Edna, 1882–1971.
A nickel and a prayer / Jane Edna Hunter; edited by
Rhondda Robinson Thomas.
p.   cm.

Regenerations: African American literature and culture;
vol. 2
Originally published: Nashville, Parthenon Press (Elli
Kani Publishing Co.), 1941. With new foreword and
introduction.
Includes bibliographical references and index.

ISBN-13: 978-1-933202-64-8 / ISBN-10: 1-933202-64-
5 (alk. paper)
1. Hunter, Jane Edna, 1882-1971. 2. African Americans—Charities. 3. African American women—Biography. 4. Phillis Wheatley Association—History. I.
Thomas, Rhondda Robinson. II. Title.
HV3181.H8 2011
362.84'96073092—dc22
[B]

Library of Congress Control Number: 2010031964

Book and cover design by Than Saffel

Special thanks to the Phillis Wheatley Association, Cleveland Ohio:

JACQUELYN BRADSHAW, *Director*
THOMAS HARRINGTON, *President of the Board of Directors*
THE BOARD OF DIRECTORS
THE STAFF

You have maintained Jane Edna Hunter's commitment of service through your dedication to honoring her legacy of racial and community uplift by providing an array of services and programs for young and old alike. Thank you for giving me and my undergraduate researchers access to Ms. Hunter's papers and the PWA facilities, for sharing your insights about the PWA experience, and for your gracious hospitality each time I visited Cleveland.

RHONDDA ROBINSON THOMAS

PHILLIS WHEATLEY HOME
HUBBELL & BENES CO., Architects
REAUGH CONSTRUCTION CO.
Contractors
Date July 19·27

PHILLIS WHEATLEY HOME, JULY 19, 1927. Phillis Wheatley Association, 4450 Cedar Avenue, Cleveland (ca. 1927). Used by permission of the Phillis Wheatley Association of Cleveland, Ohio.

Nothing ever comes to one, that is worth having,
except as a result of hard work.

—Booker T. Washington

Others, Lord, others.
Let this my motto be.
Help me to live for others,
That I may live like Thee.

—Anonymous[1]

CONTENTS

xi   **Foreword**

xv   **Acknowledgments**

1   **Introduction**

25   **A Nickel and a Prayer**

164   **Appendix A**
         Letters between Jane Edna Hunter,
         Booker T. Washington, and George A. Myers, 1914 and 1921

171   **Appendix B**
         The PWA Employment Office
         and Sarah C. Hills Training School

174   **Appendix C**
         Capital Campaign for the new
         Phillis Wheatley Association, 1926–27

176   **Appendix D**
         Sample of Hunter's Manuscript
         for A Nickel and a Prayer

179   **Appendix E**
         Book Reviews of A Nickel and a Prayer

185   **Appendix F**
         Jane Edna Hunter's Personal
         Correspondence with Family and Friends

192   **Appendix G**
         Jane Edna Hunter's Resignation Letter from the PWA

196   **Notes**

248   **Bibliography**

261   **Index**

JANE EDNA HUNTER (1882-1971), CA. 1912, founder of the Phillis Wheatley Association. Phillis Wheatley Association Papers, Phillis Wheatley Association, Cleveland. Used with permission.

FOREWORD

J ane Edna Hunter would be in good company were she alive in
the current era of rampant African American conservatism—the
election of Barack Hussein Obama to the US presidency notwith-
standing. She would surely find many ideological soul-mates today. And
yet, as the painstaking research of Rhondda Robinson Thomas illuminates
in this vibrant edition of the autobiography *A Nickel and a Prayer*, Hunter
was not an unequivocal, dyed-in-the-wool reactionary. She was by midlife,
rather, a woman who deployed complex and sometimes contradictory
strategies for the socioeconomic and political welfare of black women like
her younger self: itinerant and undereducated, unprotected and unworldly,
and thus vulnerable in the early twentieth-century Midwest.

Hunter, emerging from impoverished origins in the rural US South,
rose to the pinnacle of leadership among Cleveland's black elite. In 1940,
she chronicled that arduous journey, and the later story of her development
of the Phillis Wheatley Association, in the pages of her autobiography—a
narrative at once self-effacing and self-promotional.

With this edition of *A Nickel and a Prayer*, Rhondda Robinson Thomas
remembers and revitalizes Jane Edna Hunter for contemporary readers.
John Ernest and I, coeditors of the series Regenerations: African American Literature and Culture, are privileged to present this meticulously re-
searched portrait of the autobiographer. The Hunter who emerges in Thomas's volume is both more complex and more complicated than the carefully

constructed figure Hunter herself devised. Thomas's diligence and her skillful excavation of early twentieth-century black archives in South Carolina (where Hunter was born), Virginia (where she studied nursing), and Ohio (where she worked indefatigably for and among transient young black women) has yielded a complete study of a formidable if also confounding leader. Here, Thomas adds *A Nickel and a Prayer* to the growing body of African American women's autobiography recovered and recontextualized for a new generation of readers.

Until now, *A Nickel and a Prayer* has been neglected, but it has always been worthy of scholarly and public attention. Thomas's expert attention to the details of its origins, its milieu, and its significance highlights its value today. Thomas situates the autobiography within several remarkably diverse scholarly contexts to demonstrate that *A Nickel and a Prayer* constitutes a compelling example of the irrepressible vitality of African American autobiography and of black women's subjectivity and their insightful interpretations of their sociopolitical milieus.

Representative of mid-twentieth-century African-American women's autobiography, *A Nickel and a Prayer* challenges persistent myths about US black women of the pre-Civil Rights era as thoroughly oppressed and downtrodden, as lacking the internal fortitude, to say nothing of the academic background, to author a book. Hunter articulates an informed and complex black female subjectivity, and chronicles the development of her geographical, psychological, and professional movements from a poor, overworked farm girl in 1880s and 90s Pendleton, South Carolina, to the founder and general secretary of the esteemed Phillis Wheatley Association in Cleveland (begun as the Working Girls Home Association in 1911). From beginnings made miserable chiefly by the socioeconomic ramifications of her gender, color, and caste, Hunter went on to provide not only shelter and guidance but also empowering conditions for numerous women among those who flocked to US urban centers—Cleveland, Chicago, Boston, New York City, Philadelphia, and others—as part of the early twentieth-century great black migrations.

A Nickel and a Prayer contributes significantly to the body of first-person testimonies emerging from those twentieth-century great migrations, for it illuminates some of the southern horrors and other challenges that propelled thousands of African Americans from the South to the North, the West, and the Midwest. For individual accounts, contemporary readers can look back to highly acclaimed African American literary works about the mid-century migrations—including novels such as *Invisible Man*, by Ralph Ellison, and memoirs such as *Black Boy*, by Richard Wright (notably, two titles that underscore the authors' phallocentrism), but far fewer texts document black women's experiences of interstate/inter-regional migration.

In its particular gendered complexity, *A Nickel and a Prayer* complicates what Joanne M. Braxton, in "Symbolic Geography and Psychic Landscapes," has argued is a "deep and abiding" anger "inevitably" characteristic of black women's autobiography.[1] Braxton bases this claim on African American women's experiences of multifold marginality in the United States. As one of relatively few black women's life narratives to appear in the middle of the twentieth century, *A Nickel and a Prayer* enables us to evaluate the validity of Braxton's contention about black women's psychological and ideological states. For in arguing that anger forms an integral element of black women's autobiography, Braxton observes that a black woman writes an autobiography only when she "develops enough awareness of self and self-esteem to believe that her life is worth writing about." Braxton contends, too, that the anger of the black woman autobiographer is "often masked." Thomas's edition of Hunter's autobiography not only offers a long overdue opportunity to examine a range of emotions manifest in black women's autobiographies, and evoked by them, but as importantly, it explores Hunter's deft masking and the other tropes of black vernacular expressivity Hunter deploys in *A Nickel and a Prayer*.

Augmented by Thomas's fluent and thorough annotation, this edition of Hunter's autobiography stands to inspire more scholarship on African American women's autobiographies produced in this fertile yet untilled landscape. At the same time, Thomas achieves a reconfiguration and expansion of existing canons of African American literature by enriching the multicultural US literary corpus with this reprint of the second edition of Hunter's life story. Thomas's research in fact unearthed *three* extant versions of *A Nickel and a Prayer*: the original edition in 1940, a second printing in 1941, then in 1984 a reissuing of the first edition by the Jane E. Hunter Scholarship Committee. Her own scrupulously annotated volume provides the contexts needed to comprehend Hunter as an accomplished—and yes, sometimes maddeningly conservative—author who skillfully balances her own roles as national leader and public servant with a depiction of black women as capable citizens worthy of civil and human rights. Rhondda Robinson Thomas enables our deeper engagement with Hunter and her life story; her own ardent attention to *A Nickel and a Prayer* has yielded this thoughtful, impressive perspective on Hunter and, in the process, Thomas offers the scrutiny and admiration that both author and autobiography merit.

Joycelyn K. Moody
Sue E. Denman Distinguished Chair in American Literature
University of Texas at San Antonio

Spring 2010

ACKNOWLEDGMENTS

When I arrived at Clemson University in the summer of 2007, I began looking for a book by a South Carolina writer for my African American literature students. A volunteer at the Pendleton Historic Foundation recommended Pendleton native Jane Edna Hunter's autobiography *A Nickel and a Prayer*. I was unfamiliar with Hunter but welcomed the opportunity to introduce my students to a local writer. My initial search for the book was challenging. Clemson's librarians informed me that their only copy, tucked away in Special Collections, was too fragile for circulation, so they created an electronic copy for my class. I was fortunate to find a signed copy on the internet to purchase for myself.

As my students and I neared the end of our enlightening discussions of Hunter's narrative, I asked them to share their reactions to the final chapter, "Fireside Musings." They looked puzzled, even after I offered hints to nudge their memories. We soon realized we were reading different editions of the text; my edition contained "Fireside Musings," and my students' edition did not. I was so intrigued by our discovery that I submitted a proposal to Clemson's Creative Inquiry program, which enabled me to give a team of undergraduates the opportunity to help conduct archival research for this annotated edition of *A Nickel and a Prayer*.

I am grateful to West Virginia University Press for its commitment to the recovery of African American literary history and its support of scholarly collaborations. Carrie Mullen has given enormous support to this project, as well as my editors, Joycelyn Moody and John Ernest, who have carefully and thoughtfully read and responded to my work. I would also like to thank the librarians at the Western Reserve Historical Society Library, Avery Center for the Study of African American Life and Culture, South Carolina Historical Society, Pendleton Historic Foundation, Ohio Historical Society, Clemson University Cooper Library, Cleveland Public Library, and the Manuscript Division of the Library of Congress for their assistance in enabling me to access a variety of important documents and details. I am especially indebted to Mandy Mastrovita, Digital Production Librarian at Clemson, and her students for creating an electronic version of the text, and to Barbara Abernethy, Ellen Harrison, and Betsy Johnson who assisted me in locating Anderson County property records.

Additionally, I am grateful for the contributions of many others to this project. My colleagues Susanna Ashton, Cameron Bushnell, Jonathan Field, Michael LeMahieu, Brian McGrath, Michelle Martin, Kimberly Manganelli, Lee Morrissey, Angela Naimou, Barbara Ramirez, Elisa Sparks, Timothy Drake, and members of my Race Theory and Rhetoric Reading Group supported my research and responded to my drafts. Clemson's Department of English, College of Architecture, Arts, and Humanities, particularly Chip Egan, the Humanities Foundation, and the Women's Studies Program funded research trips to Cleveland and Charleston. My Creative Inquiry Team— Philip Benvenuto, Chelcee Coffman, Hattie Duplechain, Tristan Endsley, Virginia Kerr, Julie Levans, Margaret Nicholson, Elizabeth Peaks, Devin Slipke, Lindsay McCullough, Michael Cameron Whiteside, and especially Camille Nelson who continued to assist me even after she graduated—completed a variety of research projects. Students in my African-American Literature class—Neil Barrett, Amy Chandler, Antwaun Dennis, Scott Dunlap, Colleen Gleeson, Romare Hodges, Candace Wiley, and Sawsan Zainal— initially read and discussed the book with me.

I am also appreciative of many family members and friends who have continually expressed enthusiasm for the project. Most of all, I am thankful for my beloved husband and best friend William L. Thomas Jr., who supports my academic pursuits and enriches my life.

INTRODUCTION

I n June of 1914, Jane Edna Hunter sought Booker T. Washington's endorsement of the Phillis Wheatley Association (PWA or the Phillis Wheatley) of Cleveland, Ohio, to catapult the organization onto the national stage. Just three years earlier, she had relied on a nickel and a prayer in founding the PWA to ease young African American female migrants' transitions into urban life. Hunter assured Washington that Cleveland's Chamber of Commerce and many of the city's respected citizens backed the PWA, and that she had written him on the advice of Mr. Powell, who she asserted would vouch for the effectiveness of the Association.[1] Securing the support of an African American activist of Washington's stature would help the PWA attract new patrons, offer more services, and position itself as the model institution for the racial uplift of African American women in the early twentieth century.

Rather than contact Mr. Powell regarding the propriety of accepting Hunter's invitation, however, Washington solicited confidential counsel from George A. Myers, a successful African American barbershop owner and Republican Party operative in Cleveland. Myers advised Washington not to endorse the PWA:

> The institution is hers, fostered by a few misguided whites endeavoring to relieve their conscience of the discrimination by the Y.W.C.A. against our women. The young woman at the head of this Institute . . . has no

standing among our better class of women. . . . It is my private opinion that the lady in question conceived the idea herself, in order to further her own aggrandizement and profit by the prestige of your approval and endorsement, holding the meeting in some one of the colored Churches and charging an admission thereto.[2]

Myers draws a distinction between himself, a member of Cleveland's established black middle-class elite, and Hunter, the southern outsider whom he did not deem worthy of identification by name. He perceived any organization that advocated segregation as a threat to racial progress and seemed confident that he could thwart Hunter's plans and implement his own integrationist strategy for black Clevelanders. About two months after receiving Hunter's invitation, Washington politely declined due to his busy schedule.[3]

Despite Washington's refusal to endorse the PWA, Hunter incorporated his philosophy into the development of its programs. In the mid-1930s, as she drafted the manuscript for her autobiography *A Nickel and a Prayer*, Hunter cited Washington's emphasis on vocational education as the inspiration for her achievements: "His philosophy of the dignity of labor, of doing a common job in an uncommon way, attracted not only the attention of Northern friends, but brought the white South to realize the value of the Negro as a useful and productive laborer . . . it has been my chief concern to emphasize the teachings of Booker T. Washington for the great masses of my race. To seek constantly to raise the standards of working girls, through proper and adequate training."[4] That training stressed domestic service, but the PWA also offered young black women opportunities to prepare for careers in the legal, business, medical, industrial, and social services fields. This approach transformed many of her most ardent critics—including Myers—into supporters. About ten years after he thwarted her plans to secure Washington's endorsement, Myers sent Hunter a $50 donation to assist PWA clients[5] and later offered "moral and financial" support[6] during the capital campaign.

Hunter's activism was also influenced by strategies she developed during her formative years in the South: building personal and professional networks, seeking educational and employment opportunities, taking risks and responsibilities, and exercising Christian faith and fortitude. Born in 1882 to Edward and Harriet Milliner Harris, descendants of slaves, on Woodburn Farm in Pendleton, South Carolina, Jane Edna Harris grew up during the post-Reconstruction era, a time informed by the legacy of slavery and the broken promise of a New South. Nurtured by a supportive extended family, a tight-knit African American community, and sympathetic whites, Jane developed into a young woman who desired a life that Pendleton could not offer. After completing her education at Ferguson and Williams College, a boarding school for African American children in Abbeville, South Carolina, where black Presbyterian missionaries Rev. Emory and Mrs. Ella Williams emphasized middle-class American social graces complemented by instruction in reading, mathematics, science, and history, she was no longer content with the hardscrabble existence that blacks experienced in her hometown. Jane soon realized her options were limited to the domestic sphere: she could become a housekeeper or a housewife.

At her mother's insistence, Hunter opted for matrimony, a decision she quickly regretted. Forbidden to accept the job she had secured in Abbeville or to wed the young man whom she loved in Pendleton, seventeen-year-old Jane soon found herself married to fifty-seven-year-old Edward Hunter, a wealthy man her mother may have hoped would provide financial security for both herself and her daughter. Within fifteen months, however, Jane devised a means to escape her loveless marriage and enjoy the independence she had always desired. She left her husband and drew on her network of family and friends to secure work in Charleston, South Carolina, where she also obtained nursing training and settled into a comfortable urban lifestyle. Charleston, with its large black population and opportunities for employment in an array of professions ranging from medicine to hair care, was a long way from Pendleton, and moving to the city was a major turning point in Hunter's life.

In 1905, Hunter became an accidental migrant when family friends she was visiting in Richmond, Virginia convinced her to drop her plans to move to Florida, where she had found a job after completing more nursing training at Hampton Institute, and join them on their journey to Cleveland, where she faced the challenges of finding a good job, safe housing, and suitable recreation. Six years later, inspired by a desire to honor her mother's memory and help other single black women avoid the pitfalls of urban life, Hunter convinced seven female friends to save a nickel each week and say a prayer with the goal of establishing the Working Girl's Home Association, which she soon renamed the PWA. In 1927, with contributions from white philanthropists and a variety of donors, Hunter built a new nine-story facility with two underground levels that ultimately functioned as a community center where blacks and whites in segregated Cleveland could enjoy cultural events, educational programs, and social activities.

During the years preceding the publication of her autobiography, Hunter adopted programs from the settlement house, Young Women's Christian Association (YWCA), and black club women's movements to develop an array of activities for an increasingly diverse clientele. In *The Open Door*, the PWA's newsletter, annual reports, and various Cleveland newspapers, she published descriptions of courses, advertisements for music lessons and concerts, and announcements for training programs that were available to PWA residents. Hunter also publicized the activities of different clubs, such as the Girl Reserves, Mother's Club, Business Girls Club, and Girl Scouts, as well as accounts of play performances, lectures, poetry readings, bazaars, concerts, holiday parties, teas, banquets, fashion shows, and sporting events, including swimming, basketball, and archery. Furthermore, Hunter distributed reports of the PWA's expansion of services through the establishment of PWA-sponsored neighborhood playgrounds, a beauty shop, daycare center, and summer camp.

Hunter's work earned her recognition from a variety of organizations and activists. W. E. B. DuBois invited her to write an entry about herself and the Phillis Wheatley for *The Encyclopedia of the Negro,*[7] a comprehensive record of African Americans achievements that he planned to publish, and the *Crisis* magazine that he edited lauded the Phillis Wheatley as "the best developed piece of social work for colored girls and women in the United States."[8] In 1926, the editors of the *Journal of the National Medical Association* praised Hunter as "one of the truly outstanding members of her race. She is literally giving her life for the saving and uplift of Negro girls and women, in which endeavor, she has truly accomplished wonders."[9] Through the years, she received honorary degrees from Allen University, Central State University, Fisk University, Tuskegee Institute, and Wilberforce University, and honorary membership in Alpha Kappa Alpha, an African American sorority.[10] From her humble beginnings as a farm hand in the cotton fields of Woodburn Farm, Hunter had become one of the most influential race women of the early twentieth century.

OVERCOMING BLACK CLEVELANDERS' RESISTANCE TO A "JIM CROW YWCA"

Hunter confronted numerous obstacles during her rise to a nationally recognized social activist. One of her greatest challenges came from members of Cleveland's black elite like Myers who had maintained a fragile alliance with the white community until thousands of African Americans began arriving in the city during the great migration. When Hunter introduced her idea of an association for black women to black Clevelanders, she encountered resistance from the community whose endorsement was critical for her success. The well-established older generation of middle-class African Americans withheld their support because they preferred the integration of facilities such as the Young Men's Christian Association (YMCA), YWCA, settlement houses, and other social service organizations that catered to white clients. One critic even described Hunter and the PWA as "Jessie Hunter and her Jim Crow Y.W.C.A."[11] Yet part of Hunter's motivation for founding the Association stemmed from the discrimination she experienced in Cleveland, where she "had been denied the privileges of entering the white social agencies for women and . . . turned away from the different departments."[12] When the Interdenominational Ministerial Alliance discovered that the YWCA severely limited the enrollment of black women in its programs out of fear that white clients and donors would not patronize an integrated facility, however, they endorsed Hunter's plans and convinced many skeptical black Clevelanders to back the project.

Hunter further solidified her support in the African American community by developing close ties to prominent blacks in Cleveland and throughout the nation. Well-respected author, activist, and attorney Charles W. Chesnutt served on the PWA board of trustees, extolled the Phillis Wheatley in his writings,[13] and made financial contributions to the institution. After Chesnutt contributed $100 to the building fund, Hunter gratefully acknowledged his gift: "I could not express my appreciation in more endearing terms than to say, I have always felt you were the dearest man in the world and I appreciate both your support and the support of the Misses Chesnutt. I shall endeavor to prove myself worthy of so much confidence placed in me."[14] Hunter nurtured a friendship with Robert R. Moton, the principal of Tuskegee Institute, and invited him to give the main lecture at the dedication service for the new PWA facility.[15] She also reached out to Harlem Renaissance writer Alice Dunbar-Nelson and author, historian, and publisher Carter G. Woodson. Dunbar-Nelson accepted Hunter's offer to participate in a PWA lecture series, offering the talk entitled "The Girl of the Race: A Problem or an Asset?,"[16] and Woodson taught a course titled "The Negro in Our History—What the Negro has contributed to the World and to Africa, and why the Negro should teach their history to their children."[17] By affiliating herself with some of the most prominent African American writer-activists of her time, Hunter widened her circle of influence and positioned the PWA as a patron of black arts, in addition to being a stellar social service agency for the black community.

THE ECONOMICS OF SOCIAL WELFARE:
WHITE PATRONS AND THE PWA

Hunter's relationships with white patrons complicated her efforts to win the endorsement of black Clevelanders, however. While soliciting support for the PWA, she approached Elizabeth Scofield, a white civic leader and president of the Cleveland YWCA, who eventually agreed to talk with Hunter and was elected as the first president of the PWA board at the insistence of white benefactors. By working with both women's organizations, Scofield sought to show an interest in meeting the needs of a city experiencing an unparalleled influx of black and white migrants and European immigrants. As long as the work of the PWA and YWCA remained separate, she could help ensure that the services and facilities were equal for black and white women. White female civic leaders would serve as president of the board of trustees throughout Hunter's thirty-seven-year tenure at the PWA.

White civic leaders like Scofield offered critical assistance that facilitated the growth of the PWA in its early years. They helped Hunter obtain contributions from white philanthropists, donations from white churchwomen's groups, and invitations to speak at white churches to garner more aid for the services the PWA made available for black working women.[18] Occasionally, white supporters' racial anxieties regarding the "Negro problem" surfaced, however. During the campaign to raise $600,000 for the new Phillis Wheatley building, committee chair Robert H. Bishop Jr., a prominent white Cleveland physician, distributed a fundraising letter in which he described black Clevelanders as a "great group [that] presents what is probably Cleveland's greatest immediate sociological problem. Improved conditions in housing, education and recreation must be provided or disease, moral laxity and crime will increase. The situation is full of danger to the community and to the colored people themselves."[19] Despite the persistence of such views, Hunter continued to rely on white patrons to advance the work of the PWA, a decision that caused some black Clevelanders to characterize her as an accomodationist in the vein of her role model Booker T. Washington. Nevertheless, Hunter risked losing African American support by establishing professional networks with white philanthropists such as Henry Sherwin, the president of Sherwin-Williams Paint Company, who paid the first year's rent for the PWA, and John D. Rockefeller Jr., who contributed $100,000 for the capital campaign. She needed wealthy white Clevelanders' financial contributions and business connections to finance her work as much as she needed black Clevelanders' donations and support to attract black female clients.

FROM FOES TO FRIENDS: HUNTER AND THE
FORMIDABLE BLACK CLUB WOMEN

Club women, a group of influential black Clevelanders, initially withheld their endorsement of the PWA. These civic activists, many of whom were affiliated with the Ohio State Federation of Colored Women's Clubs (OFCW), an auxiliary of the National Association of Colored Women (NACW), contested Hunter's initiative, because they considered the NACW to be "national in its scope . . . and circumscribed by neither creed or color, location or condition."[20] Thus, they perceived Hunter's actions as an attempt to force Southern segregationist practices on a progressive Northern populace.

As the Cleveland community and the nation slowly acknowledged Hunter's accomplishments in addressing the needs of black working women, however, black club women became some of her most loyal supporters. One of the most significant signs of their affirmation came when Hunter served as state president and national vice president of the NACW and later as president of the OFCW from 1942 to 1946.[21] Additionally, Hunter worked closely with NACW presidents Mary F. Waring and Jennie Booth Moton to widen the PWA's influence and became National Chairman of the Phillis Wheatley Department of the NACW in 1930. Hunter developed a network of ten Phillis Wheatley organizations in Connecticut, Illinois, Ohio, Minnesota, North Carolina, and South Carolina. The facilities offered preschool, health, recreation, education, cultural, and job training programs, as well as various services designed to help black women and girls become good citizens.[22]

Hunter's increased involvement with black club women enabled her to cultivate close friendships and working relationships with several prominent African American activists. Her interactions with Mary McLeod Bethune, the president of both the National Federation of Colored Women's Clubs and the Daytona Collegiate Institute for Girls (later known as Bethune-Cookman College), and Nannie Helen Burroughs, the founder and president of the National Training School for Women and Girls in Washington, DC, are particularly notable for both the closeness and longevity of their relationships. *The Open Door* includes reports of these women lecturing at the PWA, as well as Hunter collaborating with them on various projects, including the Phillis Wheatley Foundation and two trips to the White House with Bethune to meet with Eleanor Roosevelt and discuss women's issues.[23] They also worked together in civic organizations, supported each other's efforts in Republican Party politics, and promoted each other's work in their respective publications and organizations.

Personal correspondence provides a more intimate look into how the women nurtured each other in the difficult and often lonely world of race work. These letters give us a glimpse of Hunter's private sphere, a side to her life that few of her contemporaries may have known, for she chose not to include details of these friendships in her autobiography. In a letter to Burroughs, Hunter writes, "It was so nice to see you and know your real sweet self. Surely we will continue to cultivate a lasting friendship. I want to be your devoted sister in kindred thought and love. You are so deserving and so capable. Your work is unique and remarkable; to me it fulfills a need that is not ever attempted by other educators. I shall not be happy until I have made a definite contribution in a tangible way to your school."[24] They also confided their fears and concerns to each other, sharing secrets they dared not voice to anyone else. During the Christmas season in 1937, Hunter confided to Burroughs that she was "positively blue" and hoped her friend would surprise her with a visit because she "had so much buried within that the valves are about to burst. I suppose this is the price we pay for leadership. Somehow, those who dream alike must dwell so far apart in the physical world."[25] Later in her career as she wondered whether her efforts to convince the US Postal Service to issue a Phillis Wheatley stamp would be fruitful, Hunter received a few words of encouragement from Burroughs: "I urge you to be of good cheer and deepest gratitude to God because He has permitted you to accomplish miracles in the field of Social Science and Human Welfare. Whether you get the stamp is not important. You have built a colossal monument that will stand as long as America stands."[26]

Hunter, Burroughs, and Bethune not only wrote to each other, but they also took time to visit each other. Hunter often opened her home to her friends. For example, in a letter dated January 3, 1934, Hunter tells Bethune, "My little home is complete and your room is ready. I am looking forward to your coming anytime, now or later. Nothing under the heavens would do me more good than to welcome you to this little home of mine."[27] Such visits in the quiet, peaceful, restful privacy of home offered the women much needed time and space to candidly discuss their racial uplift efforts, rejuvenate themselves, and deepen their friendships.

IN THE TRADITION: HUNTER'S NARRATIVE AND BLACK FEMALE AUTOBIOGRAPHY AS ACTIVISM

Hunter's reluctance to share details about her closest friendships may have originated in her desire to write "a simple story of service" rather than an intimate memoir.[28] During the early twentieth century, she joined a growing number of African American female activists and authors who published autobiographies. In *Black Women Writing Autobiography: a Tradition within a Tradition*, Joanne M. Braxton examines the challenges these women faced in sharing their life stories. She asserts that autobiography by African American women is "an attempt to define a life work retrospectively and is a form of symbolic memory that evokes the black woman's deepest consciousness. Black women's autobiography is also an occasion for viewing the individual in relation to others with whom she shares emotional, philosophical, and spiritual affinities, as well as political realities."[29] In "Part III, Claiming the Afra-American Self," Braxton focuses on Jane

Edna Hunter's *A Nickel and a Prayer* (1940) and five other women's autobiographies, published during the 1940s: Mary Church Terrell's *A Colored Woman in a White World* (1940), Laura Adams's *Dark Symphony* (1942), Zora Neale Hurston's *Dust Tracks on the Road* (1942), Syble Ethel Byrd Everett's *Adventures with Life: An Autobiography of a Distinguished Negro Citizen* (1945), and Era Belle Thompson's *American Daughter* (1946). Braxton argues that these "motherless daughters" examine their "quest for place" in their narratives, positioning themselves as "resilient and self-sufficient individuals rather than as victims of their culture."[30] In 1910, while experiencing depression and considering suicide following the unexpected death of her mother, Hunter reexamined her "quest for place" in Cleveland where she had found lucrative employment as a private duty nurse. As she contemplated her life, she reconsidered her vocation and acknowledged a calling to racial uplift work for African American women.

Of the six autobiographies that Braxton mentions, Hunter's is perhaps the least familiar and the most misunderstood. Scholars in the fields of women's studies, social science, race theory, and African American studies have analyzed Hunter's life and work and produced four particularly insightful investigations. In *Jane Edna Hunter: A Case Study of Black Leadership, 1910–1950*, Adrienne Lash Jones presents an illuminating portrait of Hunter's life and work. For example, she offers details about many people, places, and events that would have been familiar to Hunter's audience but are foreign to contemporary readers.[31] Virginia Boyton's "Contested Terrain: The Struggle over Gender Norms for Black Working-Class Women in Cleveland's Phillis Wheatley Association, 1920-1950" contributes important insights into PWA residents' resistance to the rules and regulations designed by middle-class women that governed life for black working-class women who lived in the facility.[32] Hazel Carby's "Policing the Black Woman's Body in an Urban Context" provides critical analysis of the impact of urbanization on the "cultural representation of black women," particularly the practice of labeling them as "sexually degenerate, and, therefore morally dangerous."[33] She argues that Hunter sees black female migrants as helpless victims and situates herself as a matriarch who must eavesdrop on PWA residents' phone calls and interfere with the young women's dating choices to keep them morally safe.[34] Daphne Spain's "Safe Havens for Cleveland's Virtuous Women, 1868-1928" addresses significant issues that emerge when the PWA and YWCA are identified as "faith-based" organizations that built residential urban facilities in specific geographical spaces in Cleveland to facilitate their objective of protecting women's reputations while addressing their needs for housing, employment, and recreation.[35] While these works enhance our perceptions of Hunter, they do not fully address the significance of her role as a racial uplift activist for African American women in the early twentieth century.

Scholars have criticized Hunter for curtailing black women's independence; however, in identifying with PWA residents and clients, Hunter, a motherless daughter, offered the kind of assistance she had received from her mentors, particularly Aunt Caroline Milliner and Mrs. Ella Williams. For example, Carby's compelling commentary on Hunter's matriarchal view of Cleveland's young African American female migrants does not acknowledge several key incidents that I suggest shaped Hunter's identification with the black women she served and of herself as a social activist. In *A Nickel and a Prayer*, Hunter recalls that her mother allows her to work as a chambermaid in a men's boarding house at Clemson College despite reports of young female employees being assaulted there. She resists repeated sexual advances by guests and the proprietor before her Aunt Caroline comes to her aid, insisting that she work at Woodburn Farm under the protective eye of other family members. A few years later, Hunter's mother permits her daughter to attend Ferguson and Williams college, where Hunter encounters Ella Williams, who takes on a motherly role in nurturing Hunter's academic skills, supervising her social life, and boosting her self-confidence. Perhaps the most significant incident occurs when she nearly encounters "Starlight" in Cleveland. Shortly after migrating north, Hunter unwittingly accepts an invitation to a party where African American hustler Albert "Starlight" Boyd is recruiting black women for his prostitution ring. A young man informs Hunter of her perilous position and later introduces her to his mother and sister, who befriend and advise Hunter. These incidents reveal a vulnerability that Hunter repeatedly faced as a motherless daughter. They likely nurtured her desire to create a "safe haven" in Cleveland where young working women like herself could access an array of programs and services to ease their transition into urban life.

Instead of identifying this pattern of experiences as the impetus for her embrace of activism, however, Hunter characterizes the work of the PWA as a calling to aid black females who migrated to Cleveland in the early twentieth century in their transitions to urban life. In her autobiograpy and other biographical writings, she crafts a complex rationale for her uplift approach that echoes the rhetorical strategies many nineteenth-century black women writers relied on when describing and defending their approaches to helping black females escape the perils of urban life. As Hunter recounts her transformation from an accidental migrant to a black working woman's advocate, she posits her journey as a spiritual quest. In doing so, Hunter fashions her life story as a type of spiritual autobiography similar to those penned by motherless daughters like Maria W. Stewart and Harriet Jacobs, as well as other black women writers who drew on biblical rhetoric to empower themselves to implement social reform within their communities. She asserts that her Christian faith authorizes her to identify, confront, and remove any evil that besets her people, particularly women. Through her reliance on biblical imagery and allusions to represent her racial uplift work as a battle between the forces of good and evil, Hunter places herself firmly within the tradition of spiritual autobiography.

Hunter's evocation of *Pilgrim's Progress* (1678) to characterize individuals and systems that exploit black women as dreadful, powerful creatures that black Clevelanders can conquer epitomizes her rhetorical strategy. In Chapter 11, entitled "Starlight," of her autobiography, she places Cleveland's black community on a spiritual journey where they encounter "commercialized vice," a modern Apollyon[36] embodied in Albert "Starlight" Boyd, the "'Great Mogul' of organized vice." Hunter believes "commercialized vice" prohibits young women from cultivating the Christian character that would enable them to defeat their foe. In doing so, Hunter chooses the same type of imagery that Jacobs appropriates in *Incidents in the Life of a*

Slave Girl (1861) to describe slavery as a "demon" and "monster" that is too strong for her to resist. Jacobs identifies her master Dr. Flint as a "vile monster" who fills her mind with "unclean images" during his repeated attempts to force her to become his sex-slave.[37] Yet she exercises agency in defeating her monster by choosing her own lover to attain freedom.

Although Hunter relied on techniques that can be considered highly invasive and overly protective—such as eavesdropping on PWA residents' phone calls—she emphasized innovative educational, employment, and cultural programs as the best means to empower African American females to resist the lure of Starlight's world and to become self-sufficient citizens. Hunter, a conservative social activist, implemented a multifaceted political, economic, and religious strategy informed by personal experiences, Southern traditions, and early twentieth-century social reform movements to elevate black womanhood. After retiring from the PWA, Hunter continued demanding equal rights and greater oppurtunities for African Americans and supporting various inititatives to elevate her people, and she founded the Phillis Wheatley Foundation to provide college scholarships to assist women from Ohio and South Carolina in achieving their career goals.

NICKEL AND A PRAYER: THE TRIALS AND TRIUMPHS OF PUBLISHING A "SIMPLE STORY OF SERVICE"

Black activists joined Hunter in recognizing the importance of documenting her life story and providing a record of her work before she began writing *A Nickel and a Prayer*. In 1931, Sadie Iola Daniel featured Hunter as one of the seven[38] *Women Builders* she profiled in her collection of sketches about African American race women. Daniel traces Hunter's life from her birth on Woodburn Farm to her establishment of the Phillis Wheatley and subsequent accomplishments in Cleveland. She intersperses what appear to be direct quotes from Hunter throughout the narrative, giving readers the impression that they are listening to Hunter recount details surrounding significant events in her life; for example, her father's death, her migration to Cleveland, her difficult transition into Northern urban life, and her establishment of the PWA.[39] Daniel does not include citations in her work, however, so it is unclear how or when she obtained the quotations. Hunter's inclusion in *Women Builders*, produced by noted African American writer and historian Carter G. Woodson's Associated Publishers, helped establish her as one of the most influential race women in the African American community. While Daniel provided an overview of Hunter's life and work, Hunter documented the second part of her life story in a twenty-five-part series in *The Open Door* in 1927. She began with her arrival in Cleveland in 1905 and ended with her successful capital campaign for a new PWA building in 1926. PWA members, supporters, and potential donors learned the history of the Association at a pivotal moment when it needed increased assistance to sustain a new level of service.

By the time she published *A Nickel and a Prayer* in November of 1940, Hunter had gained national recognition as a social activist, lecturer, club woman, fundraiser, and interracial cooperation advocate. Yet her personal correspondence reveals that she did not consider herself capable of writing an autobiography. She sought advice from her friend Dr. G. Lake Imes, an African American educator and activist who had worked with Booker T. Washington at Tuskegee Institute, and Dr. Robert R. Moton, the former principal of Tuskegee who was widely known for his literary expertise. Moton was unable to assist Hunter due to illness, but Imes corresponded with her regularly from 1934 to 1937 concerning the editing of her manuscript and the philosophy of her story. These letters confirm Hunter's reliance on some of Imes's advice on how to organize her narrative. She confides to him that "more and more I feel I need an experienced person, who can read the matter, see if I have repeated myself and made necessary corrections on the philosophy of my story."[40] Imes responds with an offer to spend two weeks with Hunter, "thrash[ing] out those chapters which you think are particularly hard" during the day and giving lectures titled "The Negro: What Shall We Do About Him?" in the Cleveland area during the evenings.[41] It is not known whether Hunter and Imes followed through with this plan.

After receiving some editorial assistance from Imes, Hunter completed her manuscript sometime in 1938 and began submitting it to publishers. While waiting for their responses, she wrote Augustine Thomas Smythe III, seeking assistance in locating his brother-in-law, the writer, editor, and cartoonist John Bennett, whom she had met while living and working at Woodburn Farm.[42] At that time, Bennett was courting his future wife, Susan Smythe, Augustine III's sister, and documenting African American folklore and music. Hunter initiated her correspondence with Bennett by simply requesting permission to include his name in her recollection of his visit to Woodburn when he had asked her to sing while he made notations for his collection of Negro Spirituals.[43] By April of 1939, she wrote Bennett again to apprise him of her difficulties in finding a publisher. Harcourt, Brace & Company had informed Hunter that her text "did not come within the scope of their publications."[44] They suggested that she submit it to William Morrow and Company, who advised her that "what your story needs, is not so much an expansion but a readjustment of detail so that the more colorful and personal aspects of your life are dwelt on at greater length, and the building of your career, (which of course is important, but can be monotonous) might be summarized more briefly" and requested that she rewrite the manuscript.[45] She also notified Bennett that she had submitted the manuscript to Farrar & Rinehart, but she did not detail the response she had received from this publisher.

Despite repeated rejection from several editors, Hunter persisted in her quest to publish her story. In writing her narrative, she explains to Bennett, "May I be frank with you in saying that I have not attempted to produce a literary work, but have tried to tell a simple story of service, since so many people throughout the nation have asked for information about my work here. I have had three objectives in writing the story: (1) to inspire underprivileged Negro girls, (2) to win more white friends to my race, and (3) if by any chance the book produces a revenue, to place some in an endowment fund which the institution so much needs."[46] She then asked the Bennetts to review her manuscript, which she had revised using the editorial advice she received from William & Morrow.

The Bennetts agreed to assist Hunter and offered extensive editorial commentary for her manuscript. They insisted that she find a "real publisher" that could advertise and promote her book. They also encouraged her to write a more detailed account of her early life at Woodburn, particularly the relationship between blacks and whites who had lived and worked there and the day-to-day operations of the farm, and to provide more insights into her experiences in Charleston. The Bennetts were particularly critical of Hunter's recollections of her work in Cleveland, describing the second half of her manuscript as "far too much like a secretary-treasurers-managers' report of the details of your affairs than a story of the steady, difficult, and successful growth of the Phillis Wheatley Association."[47] They recommended that Hunter include information about the lives of the women she worked with and her personal responses to the challenges she faced.[48]

In the final version of her manuscript, Hunter adopted an engaging style in recalling her formative years in the South in the first half of the text, and then employed a more businesslike tone in detailing the establishment of the PWA and her outlook for African Americans in the second part of her narrative. She clearly perceived the book as not only her story, but also as a greater commentary about the PWA and race work. These competing publication objectives caused Hunter to oscillate between narrative styles. Sometimes the book is a call to action; at other times it constitutes an extended series of acknowledgements; at still other times it resembles a sentimental memoir. Despite the Bennetts's advice to write her narrative "from [her] point of view," Hunter does not seem willing to allow readers into her personal space.

The lack of intimate details in Hunter's narrative may explain why she likely self-published her narrative. One of the mysteries regarding her autobiography is the identity of her publisher, Elli Kani. Although no other texts affiliated with the publisher have been discovered, scholars who have studied Hunter's narrative, notably her biographer Adrienne Lash Jones in *Jane Edna Hunter: A Case Study of Black Leadership, 1910–1950*, have not questioned its identity. In the first edition of *A Nickel and a Prayer*, Hunter lists her publisher as Elli Kani Publishing Company in Cleveland, but she presents a slightly different publication history for her book's copyright registration. She did not submit details for the "Place, Publisher, Date" space on the copyright but instead listed Elli Kani with the PWA's address, 4450 Cedar Avenue, as the copyright's claimant and Parthenon Press, a printing division of the Methodist Publishing House in Nashville, Tennessee, as her printer.[49]

Hunter cited her publisher's name on several other occasions, however. When she planned a housewarming party after completing her private home in 1934 next door to the Phillis Wheatley, she informed guests that she had named her home "'Elle-Kani,' which in African tribal language means 'the house of faith.'"[50] When she was president of the Ohio State Federation of Colored Women's Clubs, Hunter hosted a reception in the garden of "Elli Kani," her home.[51] Additionally, she directed readers of *The Open Door* to order copies of her autobiography from Elli Kani at the address 4411 Cedar Avenue, which was located approximately one block from the PWA, but neither the company's name nor the address appear in Cleveland's 1939, 1940, or 1941 city directories. Nevertheless, in the preface of her autobiography, Hunter informs her readers that her "publisher" had insisted that she exclude her supporters' names and accomplishments. This advice echoes the recommendations she received from the publishers who rejected her manuscript, as well as the feedback from the Bennetts.

This evidence suggests that Hunter self-published her autobiography and hired Parthenon Press as her printer. In adopting this strategy, Hunter followed the lead of other African American activists who self-published their narratives, including her friend Hallie Quinn Brown, an African American educator, elocutionist, and club woman who identified the publisher of her family memoir *Tales My Father Told* (1926) as "Homewood Cottage," the name of her childhood home in Pittsburgh.[52] After two major publishing companies rejected her original manuscript, Hunter likely concluded that she should publish her "simple story of service" with editorial assistance from trusted friends.

Book reviews that associates and activists and Hunter wrote for a variety of publications encouraged interest in *A Nickel and a Prayer*. Shortly after the release of the autobiography in November of 1940, Charleston's *News and Courier* published John Bennett's favorable review, which was reprinted in Columbia's *The State*, giving the text publicity in two of the largest and most influential newspapers in South Carolina. In describing Hunter's "up from slavery" narrative, Bennett emphasizes and embellishes the more "colorful" aspects of Hunter's experiences, a technique he had encouraged her to adopt in revising her manuscript to appeal to readers and convince a publisher of the marketability of her story.[53] Hunter's autobiography received more attention in January 1941 when Woodson published a complimentary review in the highly respected *Journal of Negro History*. Woodson describes Hunter's success in establishing the PWA as "the most important achievement of the Negro race in Ohio since the Civil War."[54] He positions Hunter as a race woman, educated in African American schools in South Carolina and Virginia, who arrived in Cleveland with "both vision and unfaltering courage" to overcome the challenges mounted by "older citizens of color" to meet the needs of young African American working women.[55] Burroughs printed an announcement for the book in her monthly newsletter *The Worker* and arranged for Hunter to purchase a full-page advertisement in the publication.[56] Two influential magazines for African Americans also publicized the book: the *Crisis* in its annual compilation, "Books by Negro Authors, 1940,"[57] and *Phylon* in its "Mere Mention" column published in January, February, and March of 1941."[58]

Eugene F. Gleason describes Hunter as a "cultured, gracious woman" whose purpose through the PWA is to "discover, protect, cherish, and perpetuate the power and beauty of Negro womanhood"[59] in a positive review published in the *Cleveland Plain Dealer*. Rhoda McCulloch, editor-in-chief of the YWCA's *The Woman's Press* magazine who had given Hunter feedback for her manuscript, included a glowing write-up of the narrative in her publication, describing it as "a chapter in the long record of the way in which God fulfills his purpose through the life of one person."[60] Edna Kay Wooley wrote a favorable piece for the *Cleveland News* highlighting Hunter's formative years in South Carolina and inviting readers to purchase the book to learn the rest of the story of the woman who was "once ashamed of her blood, but is now proud of it."[61] In *The American Journal of Sociology*, noted sociologist Everett C. Hughes of the University of Chicago lauds Hunter for telling a simple, generous story of her rise from plantation life to the director of the Phillis Wheatley. He recommends the autobiography to readers interested in employment opportunities for African Americans and black institutions supported by white philanthropy.[62] Additionally, Hunter advertised her autobiography in the PWA's monthly newsletter *The Open Door* and boosted sales by making autographed copies available to subscribers.

As the demand for Hunter's autobiography increased, she revised her manuscript for a second printing. Hunter contacted John Bennett again, seeking his editorial assistance. Bennett asked his sister-in-law Hannah Smythe Wright to read the narrative, and Wright developed a list of minor editing changes and typographical errors for Hunter's review. Wright's suggestions included mentioning the Native American heritage of Hunter's maternal grandmother Polly Milliner and describing Hunter's parents as "regular wage-earners" rather than sharecroppers. Hunter incorporated most of the recommendations into the second printing of 1,000 copies that she ordered from Parthenon Press in November of 1941. The copyright notation for Elli Kani Publishing Company still appeared in the autobiography.[63] *A Nickel and a Prayer* remained out of print until 1984 when the Jane E. Hunter Scholarship Committee republished the first edition.

Of the three extant versions of Hunter's autobiography, the 1941 edition is the most compelling, because it includes not only Wright's recommended editorial changes but also a new final chapter entitled "Fireside Musings" that is not listed in the table of contents of any of the texts. In this chapter, Hunter relies on a colloquial approach to reinforce her life philosophy and belief in the value of her work. Indeed, the personal tone buttresses the sense of community that informed her work as an activist. Through the memory-saturated musings of the new chapter, Hunter takes her audience back to the beginning of her life story. This return gives the book a strong sense of coherence, particularly when one notes that Chapter 1 is entitled "*Old Times Are Not Forgotten.*" By beginning and ending her autobiography in the South Carolina Upstate where she grew up, Hunter acknowledges the South's importance to her success. She conveys her affection for her community through constant references to the consolation she drew from singing Negro spirituals and hymns, attending church, and enjoying the creature-comforts of a southern home. In using the new final chapter to restate the importance of home and heart, Hunter validates her mission and that of the black club women and activists who created community for black women struggling and triumphing in the face of adversity and oppression during the great migration.

Hunter's autobiography, with its interdisciplinary and historical appeal, will be of interest to a broad audience. Scholars and students can explore many different thematic concepts, including feminism, racism, migration, autobiography, women's work, philanthropy, politics, and culture. Indeed, her autobiography paints a multifaceted picture of the legacy of slavery, the impact of Reconstruction, the history of racism, the effectiveness of racial uplift, the diversity of African American culture, and the experience of the great migration. Hunter's writings also illuminate the struggles of women, the development of the nursing profession, the dynamics of the US economy and job market, and contrasts between the North and the South. Students of African American autobiography can examine the challenges that early twentieth-century leaders encountered in writing their stories while preserving their legacy for the race. Those interested in Women's Studies or African American Studies can explore the emergence of female race leaders after the Civil War. In this new edition of *A Nickel and a Prayer*, scholars, students, and general readers will find an illumination of racial, social, and political issues in turn-of-the-twentieth century America that will provoke thoughtful reflection and a reexamination of Hunter's life and legacy.

LIFE AFTER THE PWA: FROM ACTIVIST TO PHILANTHROPIST

In 1947, six years after publishing the second printing of her autobiography, sixty-five-year-old Hunter was forced to resign as general secretary of the PWA because she had reached the mandatory retirement age for the pension she would receive from the Cleveland Welfare Federation. She left reluctantly, regretful that she had not fulfilled three goals: "(1) the securing of a well trained woman to assist Miss Storey, (2) the building of the swimming pool at Camp Mueller, and (3) the sale of rental properties" to fund the expansion of the PWA building.[64] Hunter's departure from the PWA was also difficult because of increasing tensions between her and new, often younger staff who were seeking to move the Phillis Wheatley away from Hunter's accomodationist approach to a more aggressive integrationist strategy that demanded better employment and housing opportunities for black women. Despite these challenges, Hunter vowed to continue supporting the PWA.

Earlier that year, however, Hunter had begun directing her energies into other initiatives, including the development of the Phillis Wheatley Foundation that would become the focus of her efforts during retirement and the largest recipient of her assets after her death. The Foundation awarded college scholarships to women from South Carolina and Ohio initially to study social work. Chapters were set up around the nation to raise money for the scholarship fund and to sponsor programs and services for local women. Hunter also made political and motivational speeches throughout the country, published newspaper columns, and resolved some lingering resentments regarding her Southern upbringing. In 1955, as she reflected on her lifework in an interview published in the *Cleveland News*, she confessed, "I always hated the southern whites because I thought they deprived me of many things and made my life so hard as a child. . . . Of course I never told anyone how I carried this hate around for 60 years. Then during my meditation [at the International Convention on Moral Rearmament[65] in Switzerland], it dawned on me they were all dead and times have changed and opportunities are fresh."[66] Hunter forgave her childhood adversaries but may have had a more difficult time forgetting her painful parting from the PWA. When she drew up her Last Will and Testament in 1957, she invoked God's blessing on the Association that she looked fondly upon with a mother's pride and conveyed her desire "to leave my assets for a separate and other purpose," namely to provide scholarships for women through the Phillis Wheatley Foundation.[67] In 1971, Hunter died in Cleveland and was buried in Lake View Cemetery next to her brother Winston. Seven years later, the Ohio Department of Job and Family Services honored her as one of its first inductees into the Ohio Women's Hall of Fame.

Matriarch. Activist. Policewoman. Brown Jane Addams. Trailblazer. Republican. Godmother to America's Brown Daughters. Club Woman. Social Worker. Nurse. Motherless Daughter. Investor. Handkerchief Head. Fundraiser. Attorney. Scholars and admirers have employed all of these terms to describe Jane Edna Harris Hunter, one of the most prominent black activists to promote respectability and racial uplift for African American women in the early 1900s. Hunter's *A Nickel and a Prayer* reveals her responses to the complexities and contradictions of that time. Her "simple story of service" enriches our understanding of the challenges and triumphs that post-Reconstruction, first-generation free blacks experienced as they came of age and continued the fight for civil rights.

A Nickel and a Prayer

Introduction   27

Preface   29

1. "Old Times Are Not Forgotten"   31

2. Family Life Ends   43

3. College Days   49

4. I Feel Like a Motherless Child   54

5. A Career   59

6. Early Days in Cleveland   68

7. The Death of My Mother   76

8. A Nickel and a Prayer   80

9. Walk Together, Children   87

10. Our New Home   100

11. "Starlight"   104

12. Types of Girls Given a Chance   114

13. Training for Homemaking and Domestic Service   123

14. Friends Along the Way   133

15. Harvest of the Years   141

16. Looking Ahead   145

17. "Fireside Musings"[1]   155

BIRTHPLACE OF JANE EDNA HARRIS HUNTER. During the early part of her formative years, Jane Edna Harris Hunter lived with her parents and siblings in this two-room cabin that had once housed enslaved African Americans on Woodburn Farm in Pendleton, South Carolina (n.d). Phillis Wheatley Association Papers, Phillis Wheatley Association, Cleveland. Used with permission.

INTRODUCTION

The story of Jane Hunter is the story of the Phillis Wheatley Association.[1] Undaunted by discouragements and misunderstandings, Miss Hunter has kept before her the precepts of a religious life, faith in the ultimate accomplishments of her ideals and faith in God.

Jane Hunter is a realist who saw the tragedy of a young colored girl's coming to a city alone, struggling to meet the economic problem of livelihood, beset by all the dangers of an urban community where poverty and vice are found side by side, where rooming houses are frequently disguised houses of questionable character. She knew the discriminations, the injustices, and the lack of educational opportunities which make it difficult for a young colored girl to gain employment and a decent place to live. This story, simply, honestly, and fearlessly told, is the story of a Negro woman who has pledged her life to remove some of the hazards and to guide and protect the Negro girl in her search for decency and livelihood. The Phillis Wheatley Association was formed through her efforts and her spirit of consecration.

Step by step Miss Hunter has tried to right a wrong in the social fabric. By patient understanding she has fearlessly and undauntedly kept true to her ideal. With the same fortitude which characterized Jane Addams[2] and Dr. Graham Taylor[3] and other pioneers in the settlement movement, she has held to her purpose through the trials and vicissitudes of a changing world.

Cleveland responded to her call with a conscientious Board of Trustees, and fairly substantial financial aid. Finally her dream came true. This is the story of a struggle beautifully told—no self-pity, no rancor is left in her soul by poverty and social injustice—but there is a keen analysis of the intertwining influences brought about by mixture of bloods. Miss Hunter recognizes the two schools of thought[4] dedicated to the improvement of the condition of the Negro race, which are so often challenged by her own people.

The story is one of who is humble in the face of struggle and consecrated to a great social cause. She has pride in her race. Cleveland owes her a debt of gratitude for her achievement in interracial co-operation.

—George A. Bellamy[5]

PREFACE

I **have told** the simple story of one who felt herself called upon to undertake and perform an apparently neglected, but greatly needed task. There have been many inquiries as to the origin of the Phillis Wheatley Association, how it was started, its work, its growth, and its future. In these pages an attempt is made to answer these queries. If the recital of my humble efforts to be of service to Negro girls and women encourages in another a like spirit, in the field of social service or in other fields, no more fitting reward can come to me.

It has been difficult, in these pages, to restrain myself from making this volume the story of the many loyal friends who have done so much to forward the work of the Phillis Wheatley Association. To them is due in large measure the success of this work so dear to my heart. Without them, the results accomplished would be meager indeed.

But as the publisher[2] has insisted that this is my autobiography, and that I must not fill this volume with the names and beneficences of these noble men and women who have worked with me and made possible our present accomplishment, I feel obliged to give, in this preface, some small degree of credit to them for their loyalty.

Especially to Mrs. Robert H. Bishop, Jr.,[3] my debt of gratitude is due for her unselfish devotion to high ideals; her social influence in our behalf; her far-sighted vision for service to my race; and her understanding of my aspirations and efforts.

To Mr. and Mrs. D. W. Frackelton[4] my affectionate thanks for their faith and the long years of devoted service; for their sympathy in the problems which I confronted in my efforts to unite the races in a common cause.

I am appreciative to other friends for permission to use personal letters in their possession; and especially am I indebted to Mr. W. S. Richardson[5] for the use of material relative to the early interest of Mrs. Levi T. Scofield[6] in the Phillis Wheatley Association.

My thanks to Miss Zuleime Garrett[7] and others who gave kindly criticism and helpful suggestions in the preparation of this, my life story; and to Mr. John Bennett[8] and Miss Rhoda E. McCullough[9] for their gracious commendation of "A Nickel and a Prayer." Particularly do I appreciate the sympathetic understanding that the Board of Trustees evinced in my endeavors.

To my mother, and all these friends I dedicate this volume.

CHAPTER I

"Old Times Are Not Forgotten"[1]

My parents and my maternal grandparents were share-croppers except for the time they spent on the Woodburn farm[2] where they worked for wages. Nowadays, an exhausted soil and absentee landlords have made the lot of the Southern share-cropper one of abject destitution. In the years following the Civil War, the lot of the Negro was hard enough, it is true; still the majority of them I knew in my childhood lived somewhat happily on plantations their forbears had worked as slaves, the friendly interdependence of the earlier relationship of slave and master continuing to link tenant and landlord with ties that were personal and human.

That is the picture of conditions as I knew them on Woodburn Farm in South Carolina where I spent my childhood. At least, the faces I knew and loved were untouched by the melancholy and despair that are written in the faces that have been brought to notice by Erskine Caldwell[3] and Margaret Bourke-White.[4]

My father, Edward Harris,[5] the son of an English plantation overseer[6] and a full-blooded Negro woman,[7] was born in slavery. In complexion and features he was Anglo-Saxon, and his English blood ruled his thoughts and actions. He was devoted to his family, and determined that his children should receive every educational advantage which was procurable in the poor church schools of the period. From sunrise to sunset he labored in the field, cultivating corn, sugar cane, cotton, and wheat to support his wife and four children, Winston, Jane, Rosa, and Rebecca.[8] While he was a good father, industrious, self-sacrificing, thrifty, he had a violent temper[9] which, coupled with a jealous disposition, made our home a place of strife.

Like every child, I abhorred conflict; and also like every child, I had a bottomless fund of loyalty. Confronted with a task of choosing which was beyond me I inevitably became Father's ally in his differences with Mother.[10] It is often stated that such situations exert a lasting influence upon later life; and I have never doubted that my life was shaped by this initial pattern of conflict with Mother and unswerving loyalty to Father. As I grew older, with an increasing understanding of Mother's lack of understanding, I came to feel a deep remorse for my aversion to her. To atone for this bitterness, I undertook the work to which I have devoted my life.

My mother was born the day Abraham Lincoln signed the Emancipation Proclamation, thus escaping slavery by the narrowest of margins. Her first, and possibly lasting love, was much like herself, a mixed-blooded Negro, Tom Henderson. During one of his absences from the region, however, Father met, courted, and won her. As a half-white, he was accounted a much better match by Grandfather Milliner,[11] a native-born African, who was so delighted by the marriage that he provided an elaborate wedding supper with turkeys, pigs, and chickens.

The newly married pair went to live on the Hanckel Place,[12] where their first child, Winston,[13] was born; but they soon found it profitable to return to Woodburn Farm where they had first met. It was here I was born, December 13, 1882, and named for Father's English grandmother, Jane McCrary.[14]

The house in which we lived was a two-room, frame dwelling which stood at the edge of a sloping field not far from the red clay road which led to grandmother's house. There was an old well, an apple orchard, and an abandoned sawmill. In the garden patch Mother tended the tomatoes, okra, onions, mustard, and turnip plants; in the fields below, Father drove his plow through long rows of corn, cotton, and molasses cane. Flower seeds were too extravagant for the family's means, but Mother, who loved flowers, had our cabin surrounded by "house leaks"[15] which she had dug up in the woods and placed where the roof-drip kept their leaves fresh and succulent. This plant was believed to avert fever. Four o'clocks[16] bordered the yard, dreamily fragrant in the late afternoon, and between the house and the barn was a row of sunflowers.

There was not much work to be done in a house so small; but we children swept the yard, drew water from the well, went for milk, scrubbed the floors of the cabin, not forgetting to wash between the chinks of the boards, for Mother was a scrupulous housekeeper and trained us early in habits of neatness and cleanliness.

I can still remember the day Old Bill, the mule, took it into his head to run away while Father was ploughing. A storm had come up suddenly, and one flash of lightning was followed by a thunderclap so shattering that the mule broke from the plow-traces in his terror, and, plunging across the field in the direction of the sawmill, turned a complete somersault. Then he got up and walked calmly to the stable. By that time Father had reached the barn, and the anger which he vented on Old Bill terrified me almost as much as had my earlier fears for Father's safety.

It was about this time that I witnessed a similar outburst of his temper in which Mother was the target. I became aware of the growing differences between them. A Sunday camp meeting[17] had been announced across the Three and Twenty River; Mother, who loved outings, insisted on our going. Baskets were packed with fried chicken, sweet potato pies, biscuits, and blackberry jam—enough for the minister and his family, as well as for ourselves. The outing proved a huge success, except for Father; he seemed morose and moody. After the sermon and the shouting were over, some of the rougher element, who had been drinking, started a fight. All the women scurried for their children like frightened hens for their chicks, and I remember how closely Mother held me. For us, of course, this happening was only an added item in a day of glorious adventure; but when we returned home, the revel ended and its glamour died, as I observed the unwonted silence of my parents.

In the morning there were bitter words. From then on these quarrels were frequent. Gradually, by eavesdropping on conversations not intended for childish ears, I plumbed the reason for this discord. Tom Henderson, Mother's first love, had been present at the camp meeting and had addressed Mother. The interchange had been the most innocent; but it had inspired in Father a wild, unreasoning jealousy. That Edward and Harriet were having serious trouble soon became the common gossip, and the majority of the talkers appeared to side with Harriet. Turning it all over in my mind, I became the silent, unyielding champion of my father.

Looking back, I wonder how much of my sympathy with Father was due to paternal reasons, how much to cultural reasons. Of all the children, I most resembled him. My complexion was light, features fine, hair soft and wavy like his. I remember how forcibly this particular point of resemblance impressed me, as I sat on his lap and ran my fingers through his hair, tumbling it and smoothing it affectionately. Mother, too, must have been conscious of Father's predominant traits in me; and perhaps it was one of the causes of alienation between us.

When things became too unpleasant at home, there was always Grandma Milliner's home as refuge. Grandma Milliner was part Cherokee Indian[18] and in her work as a midwife she used many Indian remedies for sterilization. Many a time my little bare legs, trotting briskly down the red clay road bordered by beautiful trees, were quickened by thoughts of Grandma's blackberry jam and biscuits, or hickory nuts from the big tree behind the kitchen, or fresh milk provided by Reddy, the cow with the crumpled horn. For Reddy herself I had a respect born of knowledge. She was a good milker, but being underfed, she was restive and irritable; and in one of her peevish moments she had dashed at one of my cousins and gashed her lips with her horns. So I had learned through this experience to keep my distance.

My maternal grandparents owned the land they worked. They had paid two hundred and fifty dollars for its sixteen acres, their home being the first in the region to be owned by former slaves. Even as a child, I derived an enormous pride from the reflected glory of their distinction; and it remains a source of pleasure to me that the homestead still belongs to the family. Their log cabin had touches of beauty and comforts unknown to my parents. Daffodils grew along the drive that led from the house to the foot of the pine grove; in the yard there were snowballs,[19] roses, lilacs, and morning glories[20] climbing from the ground to the eaves of the porch. In the spring the tall cedar beside the house dripped with purple wisteria; and in front of the house stood a holly tree whose bright berries were a fine touch for our Christmas presents when everyone scampered about shouting, "Christmas gift" to friends, and taking trophies, as well as paying the forfeit, in true Southern fashion.

Grandma, a refined and cultured mulatto,[21] was the busiest woman in the community. She had nineteen children to look after; performed all the duties of a farmer's wife; and wherever a child was scheduled to arrive in any neighboring home, was always on hand to act as midwife. She had been trained as a practical nurse by the young master, Dr. Thomas Pickens.[22] When things became a little too much for Grandma and her heart was heavy, she would go out in the garden and chop weeds. I have often heard her praying aloud as she worked, lifting her voice in the plaintive strains of "I wonder where my mother has gone," with the refrain, "Oh, you must have that pure religion."[23] I am confident that Grandma had all of the attributes of pure religion, for she lived a life of usefulness and service.

Over the kitchen ruled Great-grandmother Cumber,[24] a hardy soul, who reached the age of a hundred and eleven years. My admiration for her was only surpassed by the fear excited by the switches which she kept tied to her waist and brought into action whenever any chore was slighted. The moment she heard my footsteps approaching the cabin, she would hand me a cedar bucket, a gourd, and send me down the long, steep hill for spring water. Often I met there the green snake and sometimes the water moccasin. As I trudged back up the slope, spent and breathless from excitement and exertion, I often thought that the wages for this labor were not worth the drudgery—a cup of fresh buttermilk and a hunk of hot corn pone[25] from which Granny had wiped the ashes. In the summer time there was the added delicacy of watermelon rind from which I was allowed to suck the juice, after Granny had eaten out the red heart. She was cunning in her selfishness. When the hickory nuts fell, she had me gather them into baskets and bring them to her bedroom. There she would open a cedar chest, scoop out a handful of stale nuts left from last year's harvest; these were my pay. Of the fresh juicy ones for which my mouth watered, I received not a one. But I was cunning, too. After dinner, as Granny sat on the porch and dozed, I used to tiptoe into her room or out under the big tree and fill my pockets with the trophies that had been denied me.

To one possessed of strength, my labors must have seemed slight enough. I have often seen Granny carrying three pails of water up a steep grade—one pail in each hand, the third balanced on her head. During the fall season previous to her death, she picked a hundred pounds of cotton in a single day.

I shall never forget the last time I looked on her wrinkled face, as she lay quite ill on a pallet on the floor of Grandma's front room. One of her great-grandsons asked how she felt.

"Great-granmudder libbin' here on summun udder's time. Oughta been gone long time 'go," she replied.

My cousin was thunderstruck by this. "If Great-granmudder is living on my time," he remarked to Grandma Milliner, "I wish she'd go." And from then on, he was deeply troubled by the thought that his aged ancestress was cheating him of his allotted time. Oddly enough, he survived her by only a few years.

Even though the quarrels of my parents cast shadows on my childhood, I had plenty of fun on Woodburn Farm. Our favorite pastime was hunting frogs along a meadow stream on Sunday, when Mother and Father had driven off to church in their hug-me-tight buggy.[26] After we had killed the frogs, we made a fire and roasted the hind legs. This delicacy, supplemented with odd bits from Mother's kitchen shelves, made a feast which my brother and sisters and I shared with neighbor children who were poorer than we were. A frequent climax to this celebration was a fight with a water moccasin curled up on the river bank sunning himself, and ready to strike. Disregarding the lofty warnings of the boys that this was no sport for a girl, I gathered sticks and stones and joined in the pelting of the unfortunate reptile. It was great fun waiting for the tail to die. This, by sacred tradition, occurred only at sunset, and it was good luck for the killers to watch the last wiggle. Not infrequently, however, it proved to be bad luck; for when the grown-ups came back to find the chores still undone, my fate was a licking administered by Mother.

Once again a religious meeting fanned the embers of Father's jealousy.

A revival[27] was being held at the Methodist Church,[28] and shortly before its ending, someone told Father that Uncle Tom, as we called Mother's earlier suitor, was planning to join the mercy bench[29] where Father was leader. This drove Father wild. Taking down his double-barreled shotgun from the wall the next day, he swore that if either Mother or Uncle Tom came to the mercy seat that night, he would shoot them both. Mother fled at once to Grandmother's house. Not even the fear of sudden death, however, could keep her from the meeting, and high fears were felt by friends and relatives. Tom, as it happened, stayed away; and this gesture must have touched Father, for he and Mother came home that night happy as larks. As long as Tom kept out of sight, this peace lasted.

An old man, known as Uncle Dave, made a living by driving his ox cart along the road, exchanging commodities from town for whatever farm products he could secure from his women customers. Mother knew nothing of the value of raw cotton, and she had an inordinate fondness for cheese and crackers. Accordingly, when Father was out in the field, his raw cotton would go town-wards in Uncle Dave's ox cart to be replaced later by cheese and crackers and stick candy for us children at rates of exchange which netted Father a heavy loss. Following these inroads on his stores, Father, noting the state of his cribs, would call me out to pick up chips while he cut firewood. "'Sing,'[30] who was here today? Who took cotton from the cribs?" And thereupon I would divulge the entire transaction.

Mother would divine that I was the talebearer; and when Father was in the field, would invent some pretext for punishing me. And so it went. Mother and I grew farther and farther apart, neither quite aware of our emotions. The gap between us widened, and the tie with Father grew stronger.

Here again the cultural motive wove the pattern of my father and mother's relation to each other and to me. In the happier circumstances of slavery,[31] there had been a trustful dependence on the part of the Negro, and affectionate protection on the part of the Master. But there was always the possibility of cruelty in the domination of the owner, and beneath the trust and dependence of the slave smouldered resentment that might readily kindle into flame.

Wherever the blood of the white man flowed in the veins of the Negro, there was a conflict which conditioned his reaction to the people of his own race as well as those of the white race. I know now that it was this conflict that aroused Father's jealousy and drove him to mistreat Mother; and it was the resentment bred of slavery that made Mother seek to thwart Father's will.

To Mother, I was the living expression of this difference which made happy family life impossible. She disliked and feared the characteristics of the white race in me, and she disliked and feared them in Father; but with no power to explain or rationalize her feelings.

Of course, my naughtiness often merited correction. I remember when Mother and Father were both in the field, I lighted a pine torch and set fire to the scalloped paper which adorned the mantel. Then, frightened by the blaze, I screamed loudly for my parents. They arrived in time to check the conflagration; but the punishment I received from Mother seemed far more severe than the occasion warranted.

When Father gathered and sold his crops in the fall, it was his practice to bring back a new piece of furniture. Seeing his wagon coming, I would run to meet him, avid to glimpse the new treasure. "'Sing,'" he would say, "I brought this for you." Sometimes it was a dresser, a bed, a chair; and once, unforgettably, it was a "New Home" sewing machine. "My" new possessions remained "mine" only as long as peace ruled the household. In his periodic rages at Mother, he was in the habit of taking an axe to the furniture.

In spite of these scenes, there were times when we were a happy and united household. Seated around the fire, we told riddles; and the person who told the best one received, as a prize, the largest piece of cake or pie. Once I brought the biggest laugh with a riddle about Humpty Dumpty which I had learned from a member of old Uncle's family. It so delighted Mother that she forthwith dubbed Rebecca, the baby of the family, "Umpty." Unfortunately, a moment later she discovered that I had not done my night work, and this discovery netted me my most dreaded punishment. I was sent out into the pitch dark where toads abounded to poison with huge warts the hands of little girls; and Jack O'Lanterns gleamed terrifyingly through the trees, while in the distance could be heard the howls of wildcats. Having once glimpsed the last named of these monsters on Woodburn Farm, when I crept forlornly out into the night, every hair on my head sprang to erect attention. No danger I ever faced in later life equaled the horror of those wildcats.

After Christmas of 1889 Father decided that he wanted to live near a school, so that his children could attend. He disposed of his farm equipment, the mule, and the other live stock, and moved into the town of Pendleton.[32] For a while he dug ditches on nearby farms for seventy-five cents a rod.[33] Some days he would dig one and a half rods, and thus the new work was more profitable than farming. In order that we might attend the school,[34] which was conducted by the Silver Spring Baptist Church,[35] Father moved his letter from the Methodist Episcopal Church which he had previously attended, and submitted to baptism by immersion at Silver Spring.

At this time, Mother, to help support the family, became a cook in the home of a Mr. Richardson.[36] There I was noticed by Miss Ruby Sands,[37] Mr. Richardson's sister-in-law. She was the housekeeper and cared for the Richardson children. The first time to my remembrance that I entered the home of a white family was at the time Mother cooked for the Richardson family.

Miss Sands took a fancy to me and persuaded Mother to let her have me. I became a part of the Richardson household, under the special care of "Miss Ruby." This made Father furious. Compelling Mother to give up her job, he came in person to the Richardson house to demand my instant surrender. Miss Sands refused to give me up, telling Father he would be shot if he did not leave the premises. At this, Father betook himself to the nearest justice of the peace and returned armed with papers commanding my surrender. "Miss Ruby," thinking it was something I had said that had prompted Father to have recourse to this procedure, gave me a spanking that night. I believe, though, she was genuinely fond of me; for the next day when Father came to claim me, her eyes filled with tears. I was delightfully happy with Miss Sands and the Richardson children, for I was a member of the family and was treated as such. I can remember no difference in the care given us children.

It was not long after this that we moved again, this time to the old Werner Place,[38] across a red clay road from Woodburn Farm and near Grandma Milliner's. Here we encountered hard times. Day after day, all we had to eat was the cornbread and milk which came from Grandma's house.

In these days we were close enough to destitution. Still I realized how far removed were the cleanliness and decency of our home from the filth and squalor in which many of the Negroes lived. As we had no stove, Mother cooked what there was over an open fire. Inasmuch as there were not enough chairs, we sat on the floor to eat our cornbread and milk out of tin cups; but the scrubbed planks were as clean as a dining table in the finest home. Mother knew that cleanliness was next to godliness.

As a child I realized Father's stern regard for morality, and his staunch guardianship of our family life. While he lived, we remained together; he even opposed Mother's going out to work, yielding only when want made it necessary.

In the fall, we picked cotton on the old Fant plantation.[39] Afternoons, when backs ached and spirits drooped, someone would start up the old song, "Oh, Lawd, Won't You Hear Me Pray?"[40] Others would join in, and soon from the rich chords came a resurgence of spirits; and, our pains forgotten, we were ready to start all over again. For years after I left the farm, I could hear in memory the rich voices of the cotton pickers, singing "Swing Low, Sweet Chariot,"[41] and other spirituals. My favorite was "Walk Together, Children, Don't Get Weary."[42]

Before sundown, Mr. Fant's son would come out into the field to weigh the cotton and pay off the hands with thirty cents for every hundred pounds of cotton. Aunt Neat,[43] the fastest picker, often earned as much as ninety cents. She picked so rapidly, no one could keep up with her. Often when she reached the end of the row, I could hear her singing, "We are climbing Jacob's ladder; We are climbing Jacob's ladder. Every round goes higher and higher; I'm a soldier of the cross."[44] I was the slowest cotton picker. Mother had offered brother and me twenty-five cents a week if we averaged fifty pounds a day, but I always fell short of my quota. Often young Fant took pity on me and tipped the scales in my favor; but I am sure he made up the difference on poor Aunt Neat.

The spirituals were my work-songs and chief emotional outlet in the fields; but, when I wanted to shock "proper folk" and be abysmally wicked, I sang reels,[45] "Georgia Gal, My Heart Aches to See Your Soul and Body

Shake," "Swanee River," and "Old Black Joe." However the big moment of these years was when we walked many miles through the woods to produce the play we gave at St. John's Baptist Church[46] near the old Fant Plantation. It was ridiculously childish. "Nigger John" was struck dead while stealing from his master; then the corpse, as his friends set about laying him out, underwent a thrashing about of arms and legs, which never failed to bring roars of laughter from the audience. Of course to me it was as glamorous as any professional play; and knowing that I had made a hit with the audience in my pretty white dress, blue stockings, and black slippers, I longed to become an actress.

Our affairs had taken a turn for the better. Father had found a job as hod-carrier[47] with the firm that was building Clemson College;[48] Mother was taking in washings from the professor's families; we had moved to the Carey Farm[49] across the road from Grandma. Our new place had three rooms; and for the first time, therefore, we children slept separately. No longer was it necessary, when we awoke in the morning, to push our trundle bed with its yellow home-spun tick,[50] filled with wheat straw, under our parents' bed. The Carey Farm adjoined Major Smythe's Plantation on the east and Grandma's on the south-east. Our house was located on the edge of beautifully wooded land, near a spring with water clear as crystal. Down at the spring Mother did the professor's washings, as well as our own family's laundry. My brother and I walked five miles every morning to the Silver Spring School. Though his trousers were cut from Father's jeans, and my aprons were made from worn-out sheets, and though in the winter time we wore brass tipped brogan shoes,[51] neither of us thought of ourselves as other than well-dressed. We were clean and happy. Brother was an apter pupil. He could spell every word from the "Blue Back Speller," while I missed on an average of five a day, and drew a whack for every miss. I shone, however, in recounting the story of "The Little Red Hen," and other choice bits from the "First Reader."[52]

In 1892 our little run of luck came to an end. Father had been seriously ill with jaundice for several weeks. Dr. Pickens had come to see him for the last time. With sadness in his face he scratched his head, a symbol of great danger, and told Mother the worst for Father would soon come. It was the last day of the year. A heavy snow had fallen, and by nightfall it was piled knee-high in drifts. When the doctor had gone that afternoon, Rosa and I were packed off to Grandma's house. As we sat at dawn before the great logs of the fireplace, I heard the voice of Brother coming from the pine woods half a mile away. Barefoot through the snow we ran, I outstripping Rosa, and arriving just in time to say farewell to Father. I wept convulsively at the "setting-up,"[53] while neighbors sang "I'm Going Home to Die No More,"[54] Father's favorite hymn, which has always stirred my deepest emotions. Riding to the graveyard in the wagon which bore Father's body, I told myself that my truest friend was gone.

CHAPTER II

───── ◆ ─────

Family Life Ends

After Father's funeral, sister Rebecca and I went to stay with Aunt Flora,[1] while Winston and Rosa were parceled out to other relatives. Mother gave away our household effects, and shutting up the house, went to Clemson to cook for the Calhoun family.[2]

Family life was ended; childhood was over. There followed the unhappiest period of my life. A month after the death of Father, Mother sent me to Anderson[3] to earn my room and board in the James Wilson[4] family. I was ten years old, and cooked, cleaned, washed, and ironed for a family of six; in addition, I looked after two younger children. Mrs. Wilson, a sister of Miss Ruby Sands who had been so good to me earlier, in no way resembled "Miss Ruby." There were times when the white and colored people in the neighborhood were moved to protest my mistreatment at the hands of my employer. The only happy times I had that year were when the oldest of the Wilson girls came into the kitchen and taught me how to write my name and to read nursery rhymes. My schooling at Silver Spring had not gone beyond the "First Reader."

From a child I learned that "Miss Ruby" was coming back from Europe, where she had gone to study art, and that she would arrive the following day. To make sure of seeing her the moment she arrived, I crawled into her bed; and I was awakened by the tears that fell from her kind eyes on my dirty face. Kissing me and taking me into her arms, she whispered that if she had known her sister would so mistreat me, she would never have permitted me to enter the household. For a while, at least, all my hurts were healed. "Miss Ruby," I told myself, had come all the way from Europe to defend me.

She bought clothes for me; found an old colored woman to rid my hair of vermin; and, I think, spoke her mind to her sister. At any rate, from then on my tasks were lighter. Never shall I forget what this love and sympathy meant to me in my wretchedness and loneliness. It was my first experience of true graciousness and nobility, and it aroused in me an ardent wish to emulate it.

Not long after "Miss Ruby" went back to her studies, Mother wired me from Clemson that she was ill and I should come at once. Mrs. Wilson gave me the train fare to Cherry's Crossing; from there to Clemson was a three-mile walk, unless I were lucky enough to ride with the mailman. My big concern was the little paper box trunk filled with gingham and homespun dresses given me by "Miss Ruby." How to get it to the station? Finally, a toy wagon was provided by Mrs. Wilson; and with much teetering of its burden, and great amusement for the bystanders, I effected the transport, hurried home with the toy wagon, and returned to the station in time to join my baggage.

Mother had remarried,[5] meanwhile, and thoughts of the scolding letter I had sent her upon learning of her marriage filled me with apprehension of what lay before me. Her broken ankle, however, put corporal punishment out of the question; for this, I was not sorry. After caring for her and running the household for a year, I left for Charleston at the invitation of Aunt Anna[6] to care for her little daughter Ersie.

Aunt Anna lived on the premises in Franklin Avenue where she earned good wages as a domestic. She dressed her daughter like a little princess; and, as I pushed the child's perambulator[7] along beautiful King Street[8] in historic Charleston, we presented a ridiculous contrast: I, a mulatto, barefooted, in rags; my charge, a full-blooded Negro, dressed in pink silk with streamers of ribbons. Ersie liked it better than I; and after nine months of humiliation, I was glad to go back to Clemson.

For a short while I took care of a professor's child, and earned the small sum of fifty cents[9] a week. I was clothed accordingly by Mother, until some impertinence to my employer cut short this glory and won me a licking from Mother.

I was undisciplined and inefficient; yet to no one did it occur that this was not my fault, or that my employer, young and newly married, was to blame. The least bit of understanding and sympathy would have saved the day. That was forty-three years ago. Since then we have made vast progress in the relationship between mistress and maid, although the old ways are still too common.

The next effort at earning my living had hazards of a more serious order than the whims of inexperienced women. I went to work as waitress and chambermaid in a hotel patronized by the men who worked on the campus and traveling salesmen. It meant constant battle against unwanted advances, a studied ignoring of impudent glances, insulting questions. Whenever I entered a room to clean it, I pushed the door wide open and looked into every nook and corner to make sure no one was lurking there. Frequently, I had to bolt my door, for the proprietor was as shameless in his pursuit of pretty mulatto girls as were any of his patrons.

When Aunt Caroline[10] heard where I was working, she came the distance from Pendleton to Clemson to tell Mother the stories she had learned of young colored girls who had met disgrace in such establishments. When Aunt returned to dear old Woodburn Farm, I accompanied her. Now that I was older and safe under the wings of the folk on the farm, I had a childlike sense of security and a feeling that happy days were ahead for me.

Woodburn Farm was a family estate owned by Captain Joseph Ellison Adger,[11] who during the Civil War lost all of his wealth, including the farm and his slaves. In order to preserve the plantation to the family, Major Augustine T. Smythe,[12] nephew of Captain Adger, purchased the magnificent twelve hundred acres. Woodburn was surrounded by several other rich estates, but it was considered the most beautiful and productive of them all. Its excellent reputation over the surrounding plantations was due to the unique pioneering in farm production by its owner. Instead of the usual cotton farming, Major Smythe introduced grain growing and the raising of high grade cattle. Here I learned the dairy business, working with the overseer's[13] daughter. Hundreds of head of Jersey cows produced many thousand pounds of butter which was marketed chiefly in Charleston, the winter home of the Smythe family. Before the cream separator was invented, Miss Orpha[14] had me skim with a spoon the cream from the top of the milk—cream so rich and thick I could cut it with a knife. The "blue John" or creamless milk was fed to the Berkshire hogs and the young calves on the plantation. In the springtime, before the Smythe family arrived from Charleston, brother would give their riding horses exercise on the race track where the country fair was held annually. My brother's nickname on the farm was "Dang," derived, I think, from the fact that he was a good buck-dancer,[15] a dance akin to the famous Charleston.[16] On my way to the fields to work, I used to watch my brother, a mere boy, as he galloped the horses. How much fun he seemed to have, as he lay flat on the back and neck of the fastest thoroughbreds. He never permitted me to mount one of those horses; the only fun I would have was when Uncle rode the donkey home for dinner. In my attempt to ride this mean little fellow, he threw me flat to the ground and gave me a back kick which barely missed my shoulder. I finally learned to ride horseback very well on Uncle's buggy mare.

Uncle Abe[17] was an interesting and thrifty man. While working as foreman under the overseer, he purchased from Major Smythe one hundred and five acres of the old Woodburn Farm. Here and on the Woodburn plantation I toiled in the field alongside Uncle's children; knocking cotton stalks, dropping corn behind the two-mule plow from sunup to sundown, cutting corn for the silo, hoeing, and picking cotton. The hardest job was that of stripping fodder.[18] It stung my neck and hands unmercifully.

Early mornings often found Major Smythe, the Misses "Susy" and "Hannah," and the Major's two sons on their horses,[19] galloping across the farm to observe the farm hands at work. Once I overheard the Major remark that Jane was a good worker; and I said to myself, "If he only knew how I dreaded the touch of the corn blades, he would give me a different job to do."

When not out in the field, I helped Aunt Caroline do laundry work for the Smythe family. This brought me in closer contact with the daughters of the household, and I valued this privilege highly. "Miss Susie," the youngest daughter, married Mr. John Bennett, a handsome, kindhearted gentleman who, we heard, was a Yankee. Mr. Bennett, who I thought was much like the Major, was venturing into the work of writing Negro spirituals. He often invited me along with other young people to sing for him, while he reproduced the music for his book. For my services he paid me twenty-five cents. This sum for a few minutes' pleasure was as much as I earned for cutting a load of wood on Uncle's place. Mr. Bennett's kind attitude toward the servants of "The Big House" made him an accepted friend on Woodburn Farm.

There were seldom more than three white families on the farm, including the overseer and his assistant. While I worked there I noticed but little race friction. Uncle Abe served as race horse breeder; and when he was not traveling with a full-blooded stallion, he was foreman of the field workers. On one occasion, one of the white men came to work quite intoxicated. He had a jealous disposition, and over a minor disagreement called Uncle a bad name. This so roused the latter's ire that in his anger he threw a stone at the drunkard. Within a short time, all the poor whites from adjoining farms assembled to incite a lynching party against Abe. The overseer wired Major Smythe for advice. Before the lynchers could effect their organization, Major sent orders to rush Uncle Abe out of the state until the white man could be dismissed. Within a few months, Uncle returned to his work. This was the only conflict between the races I could find recorded at Woodburn Farm, a fact which bespoke the splendid attitude of the Major's family toward Negroes.

While living with Aunt Caroline, I took out my second membership in the church. This time I joined King's Chapel of the African Methodist denomination. I had been baptized while I worked at Clemson. Prayers had always been a regular part of our family life, Father always maintaining the family altar by conducting prayers each Sunday. Uncle Abe sent his family to church every time the church doors opened. In spite of all this tradition in the family, I doubt very much that I had any particular religious belief. I was merely a summer time revival "jiner"[20] without any personal convictions. Like other young people, I went to dances and played cards in the winter. I often asked myself if the minister would turn me out of church when he found that I had been disobeying the church's rule. Then when the revival service came along, I joined in and shouted with the others. But the time was not far distant when the example of a friend and teacher would direct this emotional fervor into the performance of Christian duty.

CHAPTER III

College Days

I **was now fourteen** years old; but, except for the few months at the
Silver Spring School and three years at Pendleton County School,[1] I
had no schooling. At last opportunity came my way. Two Presbyterian
missionaries, the Rev. Mr. E. W. Williams and wife,[2] who visited for a brief
while at my Uncle's home, were so favorably impressed by my earnestness
and desire to please that they suggested a plan whereby I might earn board
and tuition at their school in Abbeville, South Carolina. Aunt Caroline prevailed upon Mother to give her consent to this plan; and by working for the
overseer of the Smythe Plantation for two dollars a month, I contrived to
earn enough to buy a few clothes and a railroad ticket to Abbeville. Thus,
in the fall of 1896, I entered Ferguson and Williams College,[3] where upon
examination I was assigned to the senior class in the high school connected
with the college.

English, reading, and spelling were difficult for me; however, in mental
arithmetic and history I excelled. But the periods of the day which afforded
me the most enjoyment were those given over to music and public speaking. To chant the familiar old spirituals took me back to the happy days of
my childhood; and it was fascinating to have our voices recorded, then to
hear them coming back to us from phonograph records. Naturally enough
I made many amusing blunders. "What do you sing?" asked the instructor,
trying to place my voice, when I entered her class. My answer, "Bringing

in the Sheaves,"[4] brought a burst of laughter from my classmates. None the less, my fluency of speech enabled me to shine in her class; and with very little training, I carried off the oratorical honors.

Even more valuable than the academic training I received was the practical experience and sense of responsibility which I developed, as head of the students' dining room. It devolved upon me to see that the food was properly served, the dishes cleared away, washed, counted, and placed in order on the shelves. No liveried butler[5] ever handled the finest silver with more care and devotion than that I lavished upon our black-handled knives and forks and tin spoons. There is always joy in the humblest household task for the worker who is proud of her position, and who possesses a lively sense of appreciation of the contribution she is making to the total happiness of those around her. Given this, she ceases to be a rebellious drudge and becomes a cheerful co-operator in human service.

On Monday, the school holiday, I did the washing for the Williams family, a trying task in the winter time, when the clothes almost froze to my hands. The ironing was finished up between classes during the rest of the week.

During the vacation which followed my first year at school, I earned only enough money to buy the barest necessities, with nothing left over for railroad fare. But a friend promised to pay this, and my heart was lightened. The day I left to return to school, about twenty of our neighbors came to the station to see the other students and me off. I looked around me. The friend who had promised to pay my fare was not in sight, and already I could hear the train whistling in the distance. When it drew up at the siding, I burst into tears; I was sure I would be left behind. But heads were put together, and one sympathetic soul, known as the "grave digger," rushed hastily about and took up a collection; and in no time I had the despaired-of ticket, as well as a half dollar. "Jane," the "grave digger" whispered to me, "who was that no 'count who promised to buy your ticket?" I refrained from saying.

The margin had been a narrow one, though; and had it turned out otherwise, it would have brought me my first knowledge of real bitterness. As it was, in my happiness, I determined that I would some day do for some others what these warm-hearted souls had done for me.

This year I had my first experience in social service. Our rooms were without stoves. "Why not give a party for the town boys, charge a small admission fee, and use the proceeds for stoves?" was my query. Mrs. Williams agreed. The invitations were posted; and under the vigilant regulations laid down by her, the great event was staged. No dancing was permitted, and we were allowed to talk with any one boy no longer than five minutes! In the grand march, of course, if one were lucky, one might have a coveted partner; and we contrived somehow to exchange winks and smiles, despite the hawk-like surveillance over our behavior. But before much could be made of these activities, the Dean was on deck with new diversions, such as "Little Sally Walker, Sitting in the Saucer, Crying for Some Young Man to Come,"[6] or "London Bridge is Falling Down."

The proceeds of the affair came to the neat sum of thirty-five dollars, with which we purchased thirty-five tin constructed stoves, enough to equip a few of the boys' rooms also. We had great fun that winter, as we raced each other to the wood pile to get the largest chips left from the cutting of the firewood for the kitchen. Saturday night baths had become a pleasure, and we no longer crept into bed with cold feet.

Now I learned my first lesson in cheerful and regular giving. From her hard-earned wages, Grandma Milliner had sent me two dollars. The money was a godsend, for the soles of my shoes had worn through, and it was difficult to keep the uppers on my feet. The Dean had received the letter containing the money order. She insisted that it was my duty to give God ten per cent of this windfall. "How can I," I protested, "when I need all for myself?" But, when I departed from her office, I left twenty cents behind me for the mission; for although my desire had been to exhibit my generosity before the entire congregation, Mrs. Williams persuaded me to see that I would derive more happiness by giving secretly. It was one of the best of the many lessons I owe to her teachings.

My responsibilities were becoming greater. I carried the keys to the store room, notified the buyer when the grits and meal were low, and began to feel myself a person of importance. The problem of feeding sixty boarding students was a serious one. Often tears coursed down Mrs. Williams' cheeks, as she led the morning prayers and besought God to help her husband, who was in the North trying to raise funds to keep the school going.

I am afraid that my youthful levity made it impossible for me to sympathize as I should have with the Dean's anxieties. One night supper consisted of grits and beef-lights.[7] By mere thoughtlessness, when the blessing had been invoked, every student sat motionless, neither speaking nor raising a fork. At length the head monitor dismissed us, and the rejected food was sent back to the kitchen. It fell to my lot to open the literary meeting that evening with a verse from the Bible. To point the silent protest with a verbal one, I read the words, "Blessed are those who hunger and thirst, for they shall be fed."[8] Matters were not better when one girl after another took up the words and repeated them with accents of disgust and irony. The monitor excused us; and, as the presumed ring leader, I was called to the office and awarded a two-day suspension for misconduct. In the belief that I had been unjustly punished, I unwisely wrote my mother the whole story; and within a few days my stepfather came to the school to take me home. The Dean sent for me. Generously admitting that she might have been mistaken, she erased the black mark from my record. I realized then how foolish I had been in giving Mother an excuse to cut short my schooling, and I returned to the dining room work with fresh seriousness.

A hot temper, however, remained a problem for me. Once when a jealous classmate tried to burn my report card which carried prized evidence of proficiency in my studies, I fell upon her and she landed on the floor. It was not the first outburst of the kind; and only the fact that in this fourth year I had made obvious efforts to improve my scholarship and conduct saved me from severe punishment.

A punishment for stubbornness blighted my first love affair. I had been sent to the blackboard by the English teacher to write fifty times, "I am as stubborn as a mule." I had hoped that the boy across the aisle would feel sorry for me and write me a consolatory note. Instead, he laughed with the others, and my nascent sentiment died a speedy death.

Commencement, at last! Would I be given a part in the exercises? Remembering my wayward acts, I dared not hope so. How delighted I was when Mrs. Williams told me I was to recite Tennyson's "Queen of the May;"[9] and be crowned queen on the first night of the festivities. What to do for a frock? I was the only girl in the school who had not a white commencement dress tucked away for weeks. Fortunately for me, a barrel of clothes, sent by some Presbyterian ladies in the North,[10] arrived at the school a few weeks before commencement; and in it there was the identical dress of which I had dreamed—a white organdy with beautiful puffed sleeves.

On the second night of commencement week, as we sat waiting for our diplomas, the President delivered an address and in it spoke of Jane, the little orphan girl[11] he had brought from Pendleton four years ago, and how pleased he was with the fine dependable woman she had grown to be. My heart almost burst with pride. The last evening at school it was my assignment to conduct the industrial dialogue with all the boarding girls exhibiting their work. This exhibit made a deep impression on the audience.

For the opportunity given me and the influence of Mrs. Williams I owe a debt I can never repay. I can recall her earnestness and simplicity as she talked to us of Jesus, leaving with me impressions which I have never lost. What would have become of me, if this noble woman and her husband had not interested themselves in me, I do not like to think.

CHAPTER IV

—————•—————

I Feel Like a Motherless Child [1]

With school days behind me, I entered upon a disagreeable transition period in which I was perplexed, troubled, and saddened. Aunt Caroline's home, where I had gone on leaving Ferguson, was filled to overflowing with other homeless children. I had to sleep on a pallet. After having had a brief taste of the decencies and amenities of existence, I found the old ways insufferable, and felt a strong, if unguided, desire to better my lot and station.

Some consolation for my sorrow in this period must have come from the natural beauty of the Southland—a beauty which I hope always to remember, and which calls to me insistently in these later years.

Most intimately associated with my childhood experiences are the streams and the trees of my native state. There was the little water stream on Woodburn Farm that I crossed every day on my way to work, stopping and falling on my knees to cool a dry and thirsty tongue; to watch the cartwhips,[2] and to gaze at the snake doctors[3] as they hummed and skimmed over the surface with their beautiful iridescent wings. Water moccasins made their homes near streams, and I needed to be a little wary. Once as I tripped along with a basket of clothes on my head, I felt a queer soft something under my foot and, looking down, saw one of those dangerous reptiles crawling toward the stream. A lucky escape, I thought.

I loved the maples and oaks for the shelter they gave me, when a sudden shower drove me from the cotton field. In the branches of the poplar I used to risk my life to get the sugar-coated blossom with its delicious juice. The coffins of the Negroes and the poor whites were made of the wood of this tree, Negroes believing that since the fibres of the poplar disintegrated rapidly, the bodies of the dead would sooner return to dust, thus speedily fulfilling the biblical injunction.[4]

The Negro of those days used to betake himself to the woods when his overwrought soul felt the need of more than usually fervent prayer. My father, when he most earnestly sought divine assistance, went to kneel among the trees. Once he told me of a strange vision that had been vouchsafed him as he prayed there. This practice of praying under the trees was something more than a mere belief of the colored folk. It was their intuitive knowledge of the healing strength that comes from growing things, and of the quiet of the woods where they could hear the "still small voice."[5] In later years when I returned home to visit, I found strength and peace in the woods, just as Father had.

Against the background of the forest I like to remember the dogwood in the Spring, the wild cherry, peach, and apple blossoms. Most of all, I loved the fields of cotton—in July and August, hundreds of acres of pink, blue, yellow, and rose blossoms nodding on green stalks. By the middle of September the bolls opened their sticky pods, and in a fortnight the uplands were like a field of snow.

Then the cotton pickers, thirty and more in a group, with sacks across their backs, stretched for miles across the country, picking while they sang:

When the mist is rolled away and the morning comes,
We shall understand it better by and by.[6]

At noon, when the bell rang and the sawmill whistle blew, the pickers, their heads bent low and sometimes even crawling on their knees, dropped their bags and left the field, chanting:

I'm almost home, I'm almost home,
Come along, my sister, come along.
The time is drawing near;
The angels say we'se nothing to do,
But to ring them chiming bells.[7]

When the long day was over, weary, but with unfailing spirits, my people would troop out of the fields singing:

Walk together, children,
Don't you get weary.[8]

Tired women, after a day's work, bidding each other good night, trucked out into deserted barren land to gather broom-straw which they cleaned and bound together to use in sweeping the rough planks of their cabin floors. Dreamily now I hear them, as I used to hear them, when I snuggled into the bush-mattress of my trundle bed—the mellow, plaintive sounds coming up from the river:

Weep no more, my lady,
Weep no more today.[9]

The voices of my people! Theirs is the music to which my life is attuned! The joys which they chanted are mine; and their sorrows. Their sorrows! How much of the beauty of their music was wrung from anguished hearts?

At that time, I, too, sang with anguished and homesick heart. It seemed unbearable to reflect that I and my mother's children were as homeless as rabbits!

One day at noontime after chopping cotton all morning, sister Rebecca lay sound asleep upon the floor; I sat resting on the porch of Grandma's house. Memories of the days when we had all been together gripped me, as I looked at Rebecca's recumbent figure. I was seized with a desperate and uncontrollable longing for family and home. A wild idea flashed into my mind. "Dear Mamma," I wrote, "please come home at once. 'Umpty' is very low. If she gets any lower she will go through."

Mother was living in Georgia; but in less than a week a messenger came from Grandma's house to say that Mother was there and waiting for me. Through the woods, across the creek, up the red clay road, I ran like a streak, my heart pounding. Mingled with my longing to see her again was the fear of her punishments. Halfway up the hill, I got on my knees and begged God to pardon the lie I had told, and save me from Mother's ire.

Mother was sitting on the porch, five hickory switches beside her. "Gal, why did you write this note?" I fell beside her and sobbed, "Oh, Mamma, I wanted you to come home. We have no place to stay."

Her reply was not reassuring. "Gal, if I ever get a hold of you, you'll pay for your lying." Her heart must have been touched, though, for she refrained from whipping me.

I was still a motherless child. That August, Uncle John[10] took me to Florida to live with him and help in the boarding house which he ran for Negroes and Cubans. The Cubans were insistent suitors. "I teachee you Spanish," one said to me, "you teachee me English." After three lessons, Domingo suggested that we get married. "For sixee mont' me havee you for wife and gone to Cuber." That ended the lessons. Life in the boarding house was neither pleasant nor safe; Uncle's work as foreman of Pullman car cleaning[11] kept him away most of the time. At length I prevailed upon him to send me back to South Carolina.

I was homesick and weary of being tossed about; my hope of further education had gone glimmering. The boy I really loved and with whom Mother had forbidden me to keep company had made a loveless marriage with an older woman; and when some time later Mother urged it on me, I capitulated to her urgings and was given in marriage[12] to a man who was forty years my senior, Edward Hunter.[13]

He was kind and fatherly, but I could not be happy in such a union. I am sure that it was wrong to live in wedlock without mutual affection. After some fifteen months of mental anguish, I decided to leave. He was only too glad, for economic reasons, to acquiesce in my proposal to go to Charleston to work for a few months. A great weight rolled from my mind as I left him, determined to find and keep the freedom which I so ardently desired.

Here again appeared the pattern woven in childhood by the dark and mysterious forces of the blood. Side by side with sympathy for Mother and my Mother's people, there grew up a desire to escape racial heritage as a Negro. The escape motive was unconscious—I would have denied it indignantly had anyone formulated it for me—but in the years to come it was to carry me far away from my native environment into new and strange ways of life. There, struggle and determination were to bring me the joy of success and the satisfaction of making my small will prevail in some measure against the buffets of chance. Then the miracle! Having escaped, as I thought, the curse of being a Negro—poverty, contempt, subjection, the badge of sufferance which my people had worn for many years—I was to be overwhelmed by the realization that I was, above and beyond all, my mother's child—a Negro; that I was proud of the blood of my black ancestors; that my life henceforth was to be a solemn dedication to the people of my mother's race!

CHAPTER V

A Career

Fortune favored me. As a nurse maid for the three lovely children of Major and Mrs. Benjamin Rutledge[1] in Charleston, I had employment in surroundings of a far more attractive type than any I had yet known. The Rutledge home stood on South Battery, overlooking the Atlantic Ocean; and except for the Smythe mansion, it was the most beautiful house I had ever seen. The Rutledges were a noble family. Mrs. Rutledge took a personal interest in my welfare, watched over the company I kept, and required me to be in every night by nine o'clock. I grew very fond of the family, and they were not ashamed to show their fondness for me.

The entire atmosphere was diametrically different from the one I had known years earlier in the employ of Mrs. Wilson at Anderson. In this new position I was patiently shown how to perform each of my duties, and treated as an intelligent human being, not a useful robot. Years later in my present work, when it became my duty to supervise the training of young women for domestic service, I looked back to the days in the Rutledge household and felt grateful for that experience.

It was while in the Rutledge household that it occurred to me that only the select lived hidden in the evergreens, amid beautiful gardens of flowers. I began to understand how wonderfully Nature had endowed the earth, and how a skilled landscape artist could assist Nature so to charm the human eye by a touch of cultivation. In the parks with the children I saw great oaks, the graceful elms draped in moss; the palm tree from which the palmetto fan is derived, and from which South Carolina takes its name, "The Palmetto State." How wonderfully fragrant were the magnolia trees with their white blossoms, the harbinger to the Southerner that springtime has come.

Like Paul the apostle[2] I considered myself fortunate, indeed, to be in the "Big House" on the front, sharing these bounties with the family. As I grew older, the thought often ran through my mind whether the other servants downstairs in the rear of the mansion saw and appreciated these scenes of beauty, and enjoyed the peace of the God-made trees, as I was privileged to enjoy them.

The Rutledges paid me better wages, which helped to send Rebecca and Rosa to Ferguson and Williams College. Rosa was given the job I once had at the school; and now that my sisters were under the influence of the Williamses, I could go ahead with my own ambitions. Mrs. Ella Hunt,[3] an influential Negro woman, took an interest in me. With her suggestions I applied for admission to the Cannon Street Hospital and Training School for Nurses.[4] There were eighty applicants on the list ahead of me; but because of Mrs. Hunt's interest in me, I was accepted for training within a month after filing my application.

Students in any well conducted hospital of the present day would be amazed at the strenuous manual labor exacted from the nurses at the Cannon Street Hospital. There were few servants. We nurses did most of the cooking and cleaning for the entire establishment. In time we became expert barbers; haircutting and shaving of the men patients devolved upon us in the absence of orderlies.

There was no attempt to induct the young woman gradually into the more distasteful and repellent aspects of hospital work. My first afternoon in the hospital was spent in observing an appendectomy—a distressing and hopeless case, since the appendix had ruptured and gangrene had set in. At eleven o'clock that night I was called out of bed to prepare the dead man for burial. Together with three other nurses, I carried the corpse, swung in a sheet, down the stairs to the morgue. But I had my mother's exuberant vitality and love of life; no experience, however gruesome, could discourage me.

The methods of instruction were as direct and practical as those of the Squeers School.[5] I had a thorough lesson in anatomy at an autopsy on the body of a Negro worker who had broken his neck in the phosphate mines. In autopsies the nurses assisted, using the scalpel and saw as frequently as did the lecturing surgeon. We examined every organ and part of the human anatomy, which knowledge proved a source of great help to me. I learned the composition of the blood, as I carried it fresh from the slaughter house and whipped it, as I went along, to separate the fibrin from the serum.[6] Crude though the methods of instruction may seem, they must have been effective. Before I had finished my course at Cannon Street, I was entrusted with treatments and manipulations which usually demanded the skilled hands of the surgeon.

There were other circumstances that might have disheartened one who had less vigor and determined spirits. Favoritism, rivalry, and jealousy kept the training school in a state of feverish agitation. Here, as elsewhere in the South, the caste system based upon color[7] prevailed. I witnessed an interesting instance of this species of discrimination when I attended a Negro church and found the congregation grouped chromatically—"high yellows" to the right, "chocolate browns" to the left, and genuine "ebony blacks" in the middle section!

However scornfully I may have regarded such snobbery, I found myself profiting by it during my first year at the hospital. I was lighter in complexion than any of the other students, and this difference of pigmentation won favors and privileges for me. When at the end of a year, a student whose skin was a shade lighter than mine entered, I was displaced. All that really concerned me, however, was my profession; hard and disagreeable work, jealousy, unjust discrimination could not deter me from giving the best in me to the doctors and patients whom I served.

Progressing rapidly, after only six months' training, I was recalled to the Rutledge home as nurse for one of the children who was ill with scarlet fever. I was "Nurse Hunter," now, and I worked hard to justify my new dignity and save my little patient, to whom I was devoted. It was my first case away from the hospital, and I felt my whole future might turn on how I handled it.

Our hospital was staffed by colored doctors; but most of the major operations were performed by white surgeons, chief of whom was Dr. T. Grange Simons,[8] the leading surgeon in Charleston. He was said to dislike Negroes; however that may have been, he liked my work as surgical nurse, and gave instructions that I should be assigned to duty for all of his cases. Recognition from a source so important gave me enormous confidence. Only a short time since I had been a field hand, a cotton picker, a laundress; I was now on my way to an accepted place in a trained profession. I studied indefatigably, mastering the names of a hundred instruments, keeping eyes and ears alert at all times to the needs of the operating surgeon, and leaving no stone unturned to master the details of nursing.

When I was ready to graduate, Dr. McClellan[9] offered me the position of head nurse. But my deep admiration of Dr. Simons and my success in serving him had made me decide to ask him for work in private practice. With plenty of nurses of his own race eager to work for the head of surgery at the Charleston City Hospital,[10] would he employ me? That was the question. One night, like Nicodemus,[11] I mustered up courage and stole to his office. The reception room was in a state of disorder, books and papers scattered all about. Stooping quickly, as he emerged from his private office, I recovered a book which lay face down on the floor, leaves crumpled; and handing the book to him, I remarked that it deserved better treatment. The incident undoubtedly served to remind him of my carefulness in the operating room. When I told him the object of my visit, he took my name and address and promised that I would hear from him.

The call came a day later. It was Dr. Simons himself, who came to employ me, my lack of phone service preventing his reaching me more directly. So marked a courtesy from this gruff, kindly dean of his profession placed me under double obligation. I gave to the typhoid patient every ounce of my skill and devotion.

My decision to serve Dr. Simons was justified, and my courage rewarded. The opportunity for a larger life came when my mind was most receptive to the new and broader education which awaited me.

My first call to nurse in Summerville, South Carolina, the little town of

Pine Hurst Inn and a winter resort for the wealthy people from the North, came one hot day in July. I had learned from the physician that the patient was suffering from nervous exhaustion. On the train en route to Summerville I wondered how I could satisfy a Northern lady, when I had never seen one before, to my knowledge. I had heard that Yankees were impatient and difficult to please. However, the scenery and the sign boards between Charleston and Summerville arrested my attention and saved me from becoming nervous over the new case. The patient was an expectant mother, suffering from nervous exhaustion, as the physician had informed me. I applied gentle Swedish massage,[12] which served as a sedative to the patient. No medicine was to be ordered, so my only recourse in saving my reputation built up in Charleston was to give frequent baths and continued Swedish treatments, except, of course, when the patient was asleep.

That was my first hard case. I remained with the patient for six weeks. Then she returned to New York for the birth of the baby. I received an excellent recommendation from her, which helped to place me in another family.

This new patient was a member of the Wagner family, which owned the Wagner Sleeping Car Company[13] before the Pullman Service invaded the South. The patient's first baby was born in New York under a great obstetrician, and at the cost of several thousand dollars, I was told. The interesting feature to the family in the case of the second birth was that it was a more beautiful and healthy baby.

Throughout the many years, I have held the names of these first babies sacred. One need only scan the social registry of the South to find their names listed among active and useful citizens.

As I traveled from Charleston to Summerville, it became known abroad that I was an efficient nurse and a hard worker. Dr. Charles U. Shepard, the owner of the Shepard Tea Farm[14] in Summerville, sent for me to nurse a case of typhoid fever—a young Negro girl whose parents he employed. I took charge of the case and gave the best my skilled profession had to offer. Dr. Shepard and the attending physician called each day to see the patient, until the danger stage had passed. When the child recovered, Dr. Shepard offered me the position of Head Nurse in his

Negro Hospital. Here, unaware, I had won another influential friend, a man who had contributed much to the municipal growth of Summerville and its citizenry. I declined this kind offer to serve the hospital. He continued to be helpful, however, and introduced me to an eminent physician whose practice was far-reaching, and caused me to receive numerous and regular calls to Summerville.

In spare moments, I visited with my own people. From both races I learned of the cordial relationship of the Negroes and whites. The educated Negro was held in high esteem among those of both races.

The Negro servant who gave loyalty to his employer in his long years of service was contented and happy. The employer, in most cases considerate and kind-hearted, exercised a continual paternal interest in the welfare and advancement of his Negro employees. He was interested even to the point of giving free legal service in the courts when there seemed to be imposition upon the Negro.

Because of his trustworthiness and loyalty to his employer, great responsibility was often put upon him. The training the Negro received, through his contact as an individual with the white man in the South, laid the foundation stone for his rapid progress. Especially does the Negro in business need to remember the days when such contacts and training enabled him to make the shoes and clothes worn by the white population, when machinery was less in vogue, and competition not so keen as it is today. In a measure, the Negro's early vision for his future was enlarged by these opportunities.

In 1933 I returned to Summerville to find it more beautiful than ever. In passing through the town, I paused to inquire about the families there I had once served. Dr. Shepard had passed away, but on the main street I spied on the second floor of a building the name, "Legare Walker, Attorney-at-Law."[15] I said to myself, "Why, that is the name of the man into whose home I helped bring the most beautiful baby I have ever seen." I stopped the car and climbed the stairs in that building—to find here, not the father, but a handsome son. He had not yet been born when I left Summerville twenty-nine years past; but he said his mother had often told him and his sister about me, their nurse. It was good to know that I was remembered for the service I had rendered.

You may be sure that in the early years of my nursing career I worked more zealously, and for longer hours than many a white nurse. Racial prejudice was an obstacle that could be overcome only by unusual devotion to duty and outstanding success. My prayer was not to lose a single case. I have said I was fortunate in my professional contacts to have had work with cultured people. This was no snobbish feeling, but a realization that my success in these situations would give me a prestige valuable to my career. Then, too, I was able to acquire some of the gentler ways which my earlier underprivileged years had denied me.

Work in the horrible slums of historic Charleston[16] was no less a privilege than the experience in the homes of the well-to-do. In the Negro quarters of the city I saw conditions that were much worse than any I had known. They quickened my sympathies and renewed my purpose to do something to help the people of my race.

Much of my work was in the obstetrical field. I remember the case of one wretched Negro woman whose common-law husband had deserted her and her five children ranging in age from one to six years. Another baby was expected within an hour. The doctor called me at twilight on Sunday and told me where to go and what to do. I felt sure that he would follow shortly.

When I entered the one-room apartment, I was amazed to see the mother sitting on a filthy ash-strewn floor, and huddled about her the five children, crying from terror and pangs of hunger. There was one stick of wood, but not a lump of coal in the house. How could I effect the necessary sterilization? While one of the neighbors rushed for the doctor, only to find him out, another hurried to the head nurse of the hospital, who sent me a lantern filled with kerosene and a bundle of newspapers. Cramming the latter into the open fireplace and striking a match, I contrived to raise a fire and heat some water. Then covering the filthy mattress with newspapers, I ordered my patient to get into bed.

"Ah no get into bed. I nebber libbers on de bed. I always libbers on de floor."

"Well, Auntie, you aren't going to 'libber' on 'de' floor this time," I replied.

But as it happened I was mistaken; for before I could get her onto the mattress where I felt only a miracle could prevent infection, a twelve-pound baby boy, black as ebony, bounced into the world to set up a wail as lusty as that of any year-old infant. Fortunately the delivery was normal. Bathing and applying antiseptic precaution and sterilized dressings to the mother, I proceeded to bathe the newcomer and wrap him in one of my underskirts, the only layette I could put my hands on. Then I cleaned the floor and put the wretched room into a semblance of order. When I took my departure, the mother was on the floor, reclining contentedly on an old coat.

The nurses at the hospital were so touched by this story that they made up an outfit for the baby and a flannelet gown for the mother, which I took with me the following day. The doctor came in during my visit; and upon examining the baby's eyes and navel cord, praised my work. He was sorry to have left me in the lurch, he explained, but Sundays were the only days he had with his family!

For several weeks my sympathy for the woman and her family kept me in touch with this case. I was curious to discover whether the baby's extraordinary inkiness would diminish. It didn't. If ever a full-blooded African was born in America, that child seemed to be the one.

The time had come when I felt the need for more advanced training. At Dr. Simons's advice, I entered Dixie Hospital and Training School for Nurses[17] at Hampton Institute,[18] Virginia. The training I received here was excellent, but was attended with trials and tribulations. For three months I was a probationer, washing walls, scrubbing floors and a long corridor, helping in the kitchen and dining room. A kindly matron, Miss Mollie Williamson,[19] assisted me in passing many ordeals until I was assigned to a ward and allowed to demonstrate my efficiency in nursing. Patients began to ask for "Nurse Hunter," and the Superintendent showed her approval of my work by assigning me to the operating room, where I attracted the attention of the senior surgeon and was kept busy handling his cases.

The consciousness of greater success and new power in my profession made me very happy. My social life, too, had become fuller and more enjoyable. On Sunday in the Hampton Institute Chapel, I loved to listen to the students singing spirituals, again reviving the happiest memories of childhood. On Saturdays the Hampton boys were permitted to call on the Dixie nurses. While I enjoyed the friendship of a number of fine young men, among them a splendid machinist, I never permitted myself to become seriously interested. My marriage had been a failure; I must be careful not to encourage any of these young men.

How good it was to be in Dixie!

There was a cloud on the horizon, however, that I had been too busy and too happy to see. One morning when I had been at Dixie for one year, the Superintendent sent for me and said that my services were no longer required. My pride was severely hurt, but my conscience was clear. Although I was well aware, through petty persecutions, of the head nurse's dislike and jealousy of my popularity with the student body, I was innocent of any infraction of rules or dereliction of duty. I made up my mind, then and there, that if I ever became superintendent of an institution, I would never dismiss a student without first satisfying myself that there was a cause for the dismissal, and without explaining it to the student.

Bitterly as I resented this injustice, I have never held Hampton Institute responsible for the wrong.

Dismissed and disgraced, but with undaunted courage and full confidence in myself, I turned my thoughts toward Florida, where I intended to practice my profession.

En route I stopped at Richmond, Virginia, to visit with Mr. and Mrs. William Coleman,[20] friends of Uncle Parris. They were at church when I arrived; so I sat on the doorstep to await their return. After these good friends had greeted me, Mrs. Coleman said, "Our bags are packed to go to Cleveland, Jane. We are going to take you with us."

I was swept off my feet by the cheerful determination of the Colemans. My trunk, not yet removed from the station, was rechecked to Cleveland.

CHAPTER VI

Early Days in Cleveland

T he train which bore me to Cleveland on May 10, in the year 1905, was forced to wait near Delaware, Ohio, until a severe storm—rain, hail, and high wind—had subsided. The storm, while it did not frighten me, to my imaginative spirit, standing on the threshold of a new adventure, suggested the turbulence and inclemency which I might encounter there. When the storm ceased, it was good to find a hopeful sign in the blue skies ahead.

Thus the Colemans and I were on our way to that city where, in a few years, I was to conceive the plan of a home for colored women, and to awaken the charitable impulses of thousands of citizens in behalf of Negro girls, as poor and homeless as I.

Faith in God and hope for the future were the only assets I had when we arrived in Cleveland. My first quest found me knocking unknowingly at the door of a house of prostitution. The owner saw that my appearance was different from that of the usual applicant; and, besides, the Colemans were with me. Had I been alone, I might have walked into a dangerous situation. The accommodations which we finally found on Central Avenue[1] certainly were not to my liking; but, tired of walking, we accepted them. After I had paid one dollar and twenty-five cents for a week's lodging in a rooming house and twenty-five cents for a stewed beef dinner, there was only a quarter left in my purse. I must find work soon. My self-respect would not let me depend upon the generous Colemans, whose resources were almost as meager as my own.

Meanwhile, my search for lodgings gave me a keen insight into the conditions which confront the Negro girl, who, friendless and alone, looks for a decent place to live in Cleveland.

I remained on Central Avenue for only a few months. Answers which were received to my advertisements by which I hoped to secure patients and build up a practice in hydrotherapy and massage opened my eyes to the dubious and unsavory implications of my address in this district. A strong intimation of the evil influence of this rooming house came when I observed the pink silk undergarments of the landlady's daughter, who went out regularly every afternoon and returned home quite late at night, and more often, in the early morning.

"Where does Velma go every afternoon, dressed so beautifully?" I asked. "Oh," explained her mother, "she shops for wealthy women. They give her those lovely silk hose she wears when she goes away." It was not long until I discovered that Velma's "shopping" took her to the dives of Hamilton Avenue, a district from which, in a few years, the stream of vice would pour into other parts of Cleveland.

Soon enough I found that it was necessary to be on guard against the friendliness of Velma and her family. Sometimes, coming into the kitchen suddenly, I was aware of the hasty pushing of bottles under a table or into a cupboard. Constantly I was urged to drink beer because, being thin, I was thought to be in need of a tonic. However, the few months on Central Avenue made me sharply aware of the great temptations that beset a young woman in a large city. At home on the plantation, I knew that some girls had been seduced. Their families had felt the disgrace keenly—the fallen ones had been wept and prayed over. In Charleston I was sent by the hospital to give emergency treatments to prostitutes, but they were white women. Until my arrival in Cleveland I was ignorant of the wholesale organized traffic in black flesh.

One evening loneliness and desire for a little fun—I had had no recreation since coming to Cleveland—led me to accept an invitation to go to Woodluff Hall.[2] There would be dancing and good music, I was told.

True enough, the music was good. But there was not a little in the conduct and appearance of the guests to cause me uneasiness—women with heavily painted faces and indecently short skirts; men slightly intoxicated and somewhat noisy. I learned later that there was a saloon on the first floor, but full enlightenment came only by a happy chance. A neatly dressed young man introduced himself and asked me to dance. After the dance he tarried for a few minutes' conversation. I gave him my name, my profession, and told him how I was earning and hoped to continue to earn a living in Cleveland. "Little girl," he said, looking seriously at me and speaking somewhat severely, "you're in the wrong church and the wrong pew. This is not the place for nice girls like you. I want you to meet my mother and sister." Here, an evening which might have had unfortunate consequences for me, marked the beginning of a lasting friendship with a fine family.

Woodluff Hall, I discovered, was the resort of bad women, coming largely from the Hamilton Avenue district. It was also a recruiting station for the notorious "Starlight"[3]—procurer for wild, wealthy men; later, master of the underworld; and, finally, manipulator of the Negro vote for unprincipled politicians. "Starlight" at that time was scarcely more to me than the ogre of the fairy tale. The time would come when he would be a real monster, standing in the path of my life's greatest endeavor. Annoyed and somewhat alarmed, although I regretted to leave the Colemans, I moved to Arthur Avenue, located in a quieter and safer neighborhood, and took up abode with another family far superior in character to my first contacts in a rooming house.

Only less serious than the moral aspect of the lodging problem for the homeless girl, I decided, was the economic aspect. Indeed it was a strong contributing factor to the situation which too often ended in the moral degradation of the girl. In the average rooming house of that period—and the same conditions prevail today—the Negro girl had to pay one dollar and a quarter a week for a small, low-roofed, poorly furnished room. She was charged extra for the use of the laundry and gas. If she wished to invite a caller, she was frequently required to clean the whole house in payment for the privilege. The use of the bath tub, when there was one, was discouraged.

I remember one landlady in whose home there was an enamel tub; she permitted the use of a single tea kettle of hot water for a bath.

These observations gave me a first-hand knowledge of the dangers and hardships that beset the Negro woman who is a stranger in a large city, together with an overwhelming sympathy for her defenseless condition. I did not at that time realize that, when the moment of my inspiration should come, the reaction between my sympathy and this knowledge would produce the interesting work of my life.

But these things were stored up in my heart as I tramped the streets and looked for work. How often I met rebuffs which seemed much more severe than those encountered in my upward struggle in Charleston. One physician, who was approached by me for work, told me to go back south—that white doctors did not employ "nigger" nurses. These words I had not heard before, for in the South Negro nurses were favored by white people. My indignation was stronger than my wounded feelings. "I am not a 'nigger,'" was my reply, "and if there are other nurses practicing in Cleveland, I have enough faith to believe that I, too, can succeed."

The physicians to whom I applied in those first days, with one exception, offered me no encouragement. Dr. Christian LaTrobe Mottley,[4] a West Indian of good standing in his profession, brought me employment through introductions to many of his white colleagues.

But even unprejudiced physicians were not immediately responsive. Meanwhile a cousin who had learned that I was in Cleveland looked me up, offered a loan of ten dollars, and arranged several cleaning jobs for me in the building in which he worked on Prospect Avenue and East Twenty-second Street.

His assistance tided me over until it was my good luck to wander into the office of Dr. L. E. Sieglestein,[5] who gave me my first professional engagement in Cleveland. When I presented my diploma, he said, "That piece of paper cannot do my work. If you can deliver the goods, I will employ you."

Upon Dr. Sieglestein's recommendation, Mrs. John T. Kepke,[6] the wife of his assistant, employed me to give her a course of massage treatments; other engagements followed. Now I could enjoy two good meals a day, pay my room rent in advance, and return the loan of my cousin. While employment lasted I earned fifteen dollars a week; but there were slack times when I was glad to go to my cousin for cleaning jobs or to take odd laundry jobs for women who had more laundering than they could do.

Living in the east end of Cleveland, I was near Bolton Presbyterian Church.[7] On my appearance there I was welcomed and soon invited to the Young Women's Bible Class. Mrs. Cornelia F. Nickens[8] and her son were the only colored members of the church. Although they and many of the white members were kind and helpful in many ways, I was homesick and longed to be in a church of my own people. Accordingly, I became a member of St. John's A. M. E. Church,[9] where I met the office secretary of Dr. H. F. Biggar, Sr.,[10] a physician to the late John D. Rockefeller.[11] Through this contact Dr. Biggar placed me in the best nursing position I had yet received. I spent five months as a nurse in a home on Euclid Avenue in the exclusive millionaire row. This employment saved me from starvation, and the prestige and favor won through working for Dr. Biggar sent my stock in the profession bouncing upward. To Mrs. Marie Taylor Gates,[12] whose influence made this possible, I owe a debt of affectionate gratitude.

Later I nursed in the home of Mrs. W. S. Gilkey[13] on Amesbury Avenue, another exclusive residential section, with beautiful lawns and flowers. This was only the first of many periods of employment in this home. As long as I was active in the profession, Mrs. Gilkey would have no other nurse. In her home it was my good fortune to meet Dr. Harlan Pomeroy,[14] at one time dean of the nurses' training school of Huron Road Hospital, and his son, Dr. Lawrence A. Pomeroy,[15] fresh from the Yale Medical School. With admiration I watched the skill of the young surgeon, whose methods and technique, so lately learned, were new and marvelous to me. My meeting with the Doctors Pomeroy was the beginning of my success as a nurse. These physicians were free of prejudice. They not only recommended me frequently, but were prompt to defend me against the discourtesy and prejudice of others.

Dr. Lawrence A. Pomeroy invited me to Huron Road Hospital[16] to sit through an operation on a Negro girl in whom I was interested. Upon my appearance at the door of the sterilizing room, I was made to feel the resentment of one of the nurses, who treated me as an interloper. Dr. Pomeroy politely asked her to place an apron and cap on me. When she pretended not to hear, he repeated the request again with politeness, but with a peremptory note that brought compliance. Never again was I embarrassed at Huron Road Hospital. I was always on the alert to do my best and appear well groomed in my profession, as I was keenly aware of the prejudices which were hurled against a Negro nurse. In trials such as the one encountered here it was helpful to remember the good advice given me by the late Dr. James H. Dillard,[17] who on many occasions related the difficulties he had experienced in trying to win to the cause of education for the Negro, men whose minds were prejudiced because of a lack of knowledge and proper understanding on their part.

Since coming to Cleveland I have met many distinguished men and women in every walk of life—both local and national characters; many of them have been my loyal friends. I would not exchange any one of them for all the wealth I have seen. I have enjoyed distinctions and honors because of their friendship and help. But the honor that I cherish most highly was the privilege of having nursed Dr. Harlan Pomeroy in his last illness; for it was his sympathy and friendship along the way that assisted me out of poverty and want to a place of useful service and recognition.

Slowly winning my way to success, the problem of daily bread was becoming less insistent. There were days, however, before success came, when my daily diet was one raw egg, a plate of hot rice, and a glass of milk. Often I walked five miles from Arthur Avenue to the old Sheriff Street Market to buy seventy-five cents worth of food. Car fare, of course, did not come within the budget. I did not mind the hardships—all I desired was a chance to serve.

Once, when asked by a patient if I saved my money, my reply was, "Yes, I save every dollar that I can." "Save the pennies, and the dollars will take care of themselves," she advised. Her smugness both nettled and amused me; but I wisely forbore to tell her the story of my self-denial and careful scrimping to keep body and soul together. I knew that the less I cried "poor," the more respect my friends would have for me.

The time came when I was fairly well known among my own people. My life, crowded to the brim with important duties, had left me little time for social pleasures. A careful limit had to be placed upon my indulgence in those matters. In this respect my devoted friend, Dr. Beatrice Gaines Adams,[18] suggested the kind of affairs I should attend and those from which it was best to stand aloof.

Living as I was forced to do in one rooming house and then another, moving sometimes twice a year, was discouraging. I went to live with a very kind and gentle woman who took an interest in looking after my calls when I was away. She seemed to appreciate the distinction of having a professional woman in her home. I maintained two unbreakable rules while living in the homes of others; the first, to leave with my landlady explicit information as to my whereabouts when I was not at home; and, second, never to remain out of the home after midnight when I was not professionally engaged. These two rules inspired faith and confidence; my landlady never questioned my integrity. Today many of these women come to me for advice in their domestic relations.

Another incident occurred when the mistress of the home in which I lived gave a party to have me meet some of her friends. Among the invited guests was a woman whom I had met and who took much interest in securing work for me. I had great respect for her. But at this party I was lucky and unlucky in winning first prize in progressive whist.[19] My friend was so enraged that she left the house. I met her often at other parties in the homes of friends, but she never again was as interested in me, although I persistently made overtures to her. The remorse which I suffered on losing this friend cut so deeply into my heart that I never again played a card game for prizes, nor did I touch a card or play a game for eighteen years after this incident occurred.

Eager for service, an altruistic feeling induced me to enter a Popular Lady Contest,[20] conducted for the benefit of The Home for Aged Colored People.[21] My circle of acquaintances was small, and my strongest opponent had arrived in Cleveland four years previous. But the contest, which was a friendly rivalry, ended in a tie, each of us having turned in more than a thousand dollars for the Home. The prize of ten dollars paid my rent in advance for two months. The greatest personal benefit I derived from the undertaking was the friendship which I gained in a splendid civic affair, and the loyalty of my strongest opponent. In years afterward she shared in the building of the great civic service of my life. In these experiences I am again and again reminded of the sustaining influence of the song as I used to sing as I traveled alone on the plantation in Pendleton—the comforting words in the hymn:

> "I need Thee every hour; stay Thou near by,
> Temptations lose their power, when Thou art nigh."[22]

A girl alone in a large city must needs know the dangers and pitfalls awaiting her. She must have abiding faith in God's love and care for His own. I was glad to have had a real Christian faith taught me; for in hours of distress and hunger He, like a shepherd, has led me on my way.

CHAPTER VII

The Death of My Mother

"Toiling, rejoicing, sorrowing."[1]

I had won a fair measure of success. The farm girl who had stripped the fodder in the fields, and fallen asleep at night on the plank floor, covered by quilts in her aunt's cabin, had become a useful woman in her profession, loved by many friends, respected and honored. Best of all, she had the wisdom that is born of suffering and a keen sympathy for the people of her race.

"Old, unhappy, far-off things"[2] were faint wraiths looked at from the sunny slopes on which I had set my feet; no premonition warned me that the moment was at hand when the most important person in my early life, my mother, was to be taken from me. My childish vindictiveness toward her, arising from her battles with Father, my later disgust when she married again six months after his death, rebellion against her punishments, the resentment of her opposition to my hunger for education, the bitterness at being coerced into a loveless marriage—all these had softened with the lapse of years and the coming of maturer understanding.

I had long since learned to see Mother against her background; to realize that both her faults and virtues were the product of that background. Throughout life she had remained a child—happy, fun-loving, but with the limitations of childhood. At hide-and-seek she was as carried away as any child; and when I visited her after I was grown, it was not unusual for her to romp with me as she had when I was a little girl.

From her father she had inherited slave-driving energies. Hard work she knew and practiced, and so should her children, aided by the stimulus of switches. That the Negro could possibly better his lot, she thought only by hard work. She had little sympathy with Father's desire to educate the children.

With these limitations she had energy and decisiveness of a positive character. Nothing could deflect her, once she had reached a decision. Her zest for life was insatiable; I can still see her dancing the Virginia Reel or the Quadrille[3] at "hot suppers,"[4] her cheeks glowing, her eyes twinkling; returning home, the festivities over, her apron full of sweet potato pies—favors bestowed upon her by admiring partners.

Her warm generosity exerted a compulsive power on all who knew her and made them love her. With what care she prepared my favorite dishes—rice cooked in chicken broth, okra purloe,[5] mallata rice[6] cooked with tomatoes and bacon fat—the most delicious and famous Southern dishes of today. If I failed to eat all that had been placed before me, she would go out in the yard and urge the balance upon the first pedestrian to come along. Mother loved to give; she would have given her head away if she thought it would help someone.

While in Charleston I thought up a plan whereby she and I might have an opportunity to know each other better and come to love each other as a mother and daughter should. I would bring her to Charleston for a visit; perhaps she would like it and decide to stay. The plan did not work. After three weeks, she became homesick for familiar scenes, and decided that the climate of Charleston was injuring her health. So, for the sake of peace and her health, I bought her a return ticket to Clemson.

My visits to Pendleton had been infrequent. I could not be happy in the crowded conditions of her two-room home; and while I felt a twinge of remorse for feeling so, the fact remained that I felt superior to the old surroundings.

In the summer of 1909 I bought an acre of ground in Pendleton—a stone's throw from where her favorite sister lived—planning to build a cottage in which she might spend her declining years in peace and comfort. But my gesture came too late for realization. In June of the year following word reached me of her sudden death. The news was unbelievable; for I had seen her a few short weeks earlier, and she had looked the picture of health, young and beautiful. Thinking that the wire must have referred to Grandmother, who was eighty-six and had been critically ill, I wired Uncle Tenus,[7] only to receive a confirmation of the original message.

The grief of the next thirteen months robbed me of all interest in my profession. I had waited too long to bring about the reconciliation I so greatly desired, and now it was forever beyond me. At moments of despair I contemplated suicide. But old grandma's loving words, "Trust the Lord, Jane; He will care for you," recurred to me and drew me back from despondency. It was in one of these moments that I prayed God to show me what use I could make of this agony of remorse and frustration.

The hardships of early years, the struggles to establish myself in my profession, and the emotional crisis resulting from Mother's death had impaired my health. I had to give up nursing and take a position as assistant in the offices of four of the physicians for whom I had nursed.

One afternoon in August, 1911, I turned over in my mind the problem that had been with me ever since the death of Mother—how could I best give to the world what I had failed to give to her? I thought first of the need for a hospital, staffed by Negro doctors and nurses. Professional interest made this a natural objective, but reflection showed me that this need already was met by existing hospitals. Moreover, such a project demanded large financial backing. Any project I started would have to begin in a very modest way.

"Miss Janie, Ah clah Ah don' know what Ah'm goin' to do." My musings broken in upon, I looked up at the speaker, a colored girl who with her illegitimate twin babies had come up from Alabama some six months earlier to get away from the opprobrium cast on her by her family and neighbors. Ruth had been having a hard time making ends meet. I had secured her work with a family for whom I had nursed; but the first day, in trying to light the gas, she had damaged the stove. She was a poor laundress, a wretched cook, helpless, useless; her only redeeming virtue being a savage devotion to her fatherless infants.

She told me she had come to the end of her resources; she had had no work for three weeks; the landlady had put her bags and babies out in the street and closed the door on her.

"How can ah feed my po' lambs? Oh, Miss Janie, don' you know some-one needs a good woman for washun'? Ah knows ah'm no good cookin,' an' ahnin' not so good nuther; but ah's a faih washuh. Oh, mah po' li'l babies." She fell in exhaustion at my feet, wailing bitterly.

I had no doubt whatever as to what was demanded in this matter. I had written her father a week earlier, telling him of her plight; and a letter which had reached me that morning assured me that there was forgiveness for the prodigal and a place at the family board for herself and her children. There remained the matter of railroad fare, but I knew a group of kindly women who would join me in providing that. I showed Ruth her father's letter and assured her of a place for herself and her babies to spend the night.

It was the old story, I thought, as I hurried to the street car after arranging for Ruth's lodging with a friend of mine; and how often the story was repeated. The young Negro girl pushed from the nest by economic pressure, alone and friendless in a northern city; reduced to squalor, starvation; helpless against temptation and degradation. It might easily have been my own story, had I been so poorly prepared to earn my living as was this girl. And how helpless, too, in such a situation would have been my mother—immature, impulsive mother. As I clung to the car strap and was jostled by other workers, black and white, I seemed to hear above the grinding of the car wheels the strains of the old spiritual, "Ah Feels Like a Motherless Child"; and it was borne in upon me that here was my work, my salvation; here was the supreme task for which God had designed me, the one which would take up the discords of my early life and resolve them in harmonious music.[8]

CHAPTER VIII

A Nickel and a Prayer

In setting about to establish a home for Negro working girls, I turned instinctively, not to the wealthy and influential friends I had made among white persons, but to the poor and lowly of my own people. In so doing I may have been unconsciously influenced by the example of Christ. It was not to the wealthy and powerful He had turned, but to fishermen and tax gatherers,[1] the obscure and lowly.

One September afternoon in 1911, a group of Negro working women, my closest friends, met in the tiny parlor of Hattie Harper's[2] home to discuss the rooming-house problem and find ways and means of ameliorating the hard lot of homeless girls. Hattie, our hostess, daughter of the presiding elder of the African Methodist Church in South Carolina, had come north some years earlier and by hard work—she washed and ironed every day, sometimes far into the night—had rented a small house which she occupied with her sister. She was thin and wiry, a bundle of energy, but sympathetic, warm-hearted. Not so aggressive, but quite as kindly, was Florence Evans,[3] who worked in a home on Amesbury Avenue. Ruth Strickland,[4] tall, with beautiful black hair, also worked as a maid; but she was ambitious to be a nurse, and later entered training at Lincoln Hospital.[5] Amy Cohen,[6] another trained nurse and a graduate of Dixie Hospital at Hampton, worked with me, side by side. There were Jeanette Tubbs,[7] a big, roly-poly woman, with an infectious laugh which saved many a difficult situation; pretty little

Rebecca Haynes,[8] who, it was whispered, had strayed a little onto the way-ward path and needed the influence of older and stronger heads; and Rose Harris,[9] who was quiet and retiring in manner but, nevertheless, an enthu-siastic follower.

Working women, all of us, we had known much the same trials in our early days in Cleveland, the despairing search for decent lodgings—up one dingy street and down another, ending with the acceptance of the least disreputable room we encountered. Negroes who could afford better houses were above taking roomers, and our chances were restricted to the unsightly, run-down sections of the city where houses rented for as little as fifteen dollars a month and the landlady who secured two roomers at one dollar and a quarter could realize two-thirds of her rent. It was after putting up with these surroundings for a number of years that Hattie had contrived to rent her own home; and I had also been so fortunate as to find a pleasant home with friends.

But the rest of our gathering, like the majority of their race, still had to return on their days off or during periods of unemployment to dark, little rooms under the eaves; lumpy straw mattresses; dim gas lights which had to be turned off at ten o'clock; surly landladies to whom women lodgers were nuisances to be put up with when no men lodgers could be had.

These were some of the conditions Negro women, coming to Cleveland to work, had to face. Even when employed, they still had to submit to them, in order to have storage space for their trunks, a house to which they might come in their off time, and a place where they might entertain callers. Most landladies even refused the hospitality of their kitchens to women roomers.

"How do you 'spose I felt last week, when Edgar Winfield came to take me out to Euclid Beach?"[10] asked Rose, eyes flashing. "What do you think that Mrs. Slocum did? Pushed right ahead of me, when I went to let Edgar in, and stood looking down at his feet. Wanted to see if they were clean enough for her floors. It's pretty hard, I tell you, for a girl to have the right kind of beau with that sort of treatment; and it's pretty hard for her to keep her self-respect."

Janet[11] chuckled sympathetically. "Remember the winter I walked miles when Joe was courting me? Idy Cox wouldn't let no beau step inside her house, clean shoes or not. It's funny I didn't walk myself to a shadow, but I didn't lose a pound."

"Well, I remember one place where company had to be brought right into the sitting room; and the whole family, from Grandma to little John, sat around the whole blessed evening. It was no matrimonial bureau, that place, certain." Florence's voice rose with indignation as she recalled the embarrassing moments.

"You certainly had good sense, Hattie, to save your money and rent a house; and you're just lucky, Jane, you and Amy, to be with friends."

"Of course, Jane's better off than most of us in most ways," Florence remarked wistfully but without envy.

At the time Miss Cohen and I were the only professional nurses of our race in Cleveland, and this fact gave us a recognized distinction.

"Never mind, Ruth," I remarked consolingly, "you're going to be a nurse some day yourself, and a good one."

"But seriously, girls, it's not so much what we have suffered, though that counts, too, since it has made us know and feel for others. And we aren't living in luxury now. But we are a lot better off than we were five years ago, all of us. And hundreds and hundreds of girls here in Cleveland[12] are living in the most squalid surroundings. Some of them are thrown out like Rebecca. Some are ruined for lack of clean, decent fun and a place to entertain company. And next year it will be the same story, and next year, and always. The city government isn't going to do anything about it. The white folks have their own Y.W.C.A.'s[13] and settlement houses[14] to look after. For the matter of that, how could they even know anything about the conditions which confront the Negro woman worker? Or knowing, don't most of them imagine that Negroes are satisfied with these surroundings and want nothing better?"

"Well, what's the answer, Jane?" asked the practical Janet. "Poor people like us can't do anything, surely. And just talking won't help a bit."

"The wrong kind won't," I answered, "foolish complaining talk. But the right kind of talking at the right time, to the right people—that, I think, will help. And, what's more, it's only poor people like you and me who can do anything. Some times I feel I've just been living my life for the moment when I can start things moving toward a home for poor Negro working girls in this city. It's what the Lord sent me here to do, but I didn't know it till that afternoon when Ruth walked into my office. We've all of us been poor motherless children, and the Lord is going to help us build a home for all the other poor motherless daughters of our race."

My auditors were quick to respond to this enthusiasm; they caught the vision.

"Then we must have a club and elect officers and have dues," remarked Hattie.

And then and there The Working Girls' Home Association, J. Edna Hunter, President, came into existence. Much difference of opinion developed as to the amount of dues. Some thought twenty-five cents[15] a week; I suggested a nickel. There were objections. "How can you ever build a home from sums that small?" asked Rose Harris. "It would take a hundred years." "I know it will be slow," I said, "but we want this to be the work of poor people, and almost everyone can give a nickel. In that way the club will grow. It is for us to let our light shine before men[16] and leave the rest to God."

The irrepressible Janet drew a coin from her purse and placed it with a flourish on Hattie's table. "If you are starting in that low, you're sure to skyrocket later, and I'm coming in on the ground floor."

"And we'll meet again next week?"

"Let's try to get at least ten members before next Tuesday."

"Why not get up a social and raise some money?"

In the light of the enthusiasm thus kindled, one motherless child felt nearer home than she had felt for many a year.

FACING ADVERSE CRITICISMS

"And all these other things will be added unto you."[17] When, twenty-nine years ago, I offered this assurance to those whom I gathered around me to help establish Phillis Wheatley Association, I spoke sincerely and with complete faith in Divine Goodness.

Yet, even then, I knew that we should have to make our own path uphill through thorny country; that rocks would sometimes block our way; that we might stand on the brink of a great chasm, over which only faith could build a bridge. Furthermore, there were those who, having begun the journey eagerly in the freshness of the morning, would grow faint under the heat and burden of the day, and walk no more with us. The faithless ones would shake their heads and declare that we had taken the wrong path. Worst of all, those who did not understand would lay snares for us, and severe criticism would rain upon us.

The first opposition to our undertaking made itself felt at the third meeting, to which we had invited the general public. And, strangely enough, the opposition came from Negroes—a small group of club women[18] who, blessed with prosperity, had risen from the servant class and now regarded themselves as the arbiters and guardians of colored society. Arriving at the meeting, they took complete charge of proceedings, threw a shadow, and attempted to inject discord into all that had been said or done in an effort to start a home.

The chief spokesman was dominating in spite of her wavering voice and her hand trembling with palsy. Segregation was the bogey which she held before our dismayed eyes. "We have never had segregation. Our girls must go to the Y.W.C.A., along with the white girls. Why should you," turning a reproachful glance upon me, "come up from the South and tell us what to do?" Here I kindly asked whether the group knew of the progress the Negroes had made in the South because they had worked together.

"We're club women, and we represent all the club women of Cleveland," declared one lieutenant, "and we will not permit you, a Southerner, to start segregation in this city."

"We call on the white people, and the white people call on us," remarked a woman suavely. "Now that the more intelligent of us have broken down the barriers between the races, you are trying to build them up again with your absurd Southern ideas for working girls. We shall never permit it. The Y.W.C.A. is for all, I tell you, for all."

"Yes," I replied; "but can you use it? Will our girls feel free to act and speak in that institution? Will they be welcomed by white girls?"

Such attacks as these dismayed some of my followers, who were so frightened that they withdrew from the organization. Sick at heart, I went to my room after the meeting and prayed that God would forgive those women, for they knew not what they were doing.[19] I asked for wisdom to make clear my plans; begged that my faith would not be weakened, that I would not be moved by biased and thoughtless folk.

Opposition of this kind, motivated by a fear of segregation, we have had to meet all along the way. It is of two kinds—the unintelligent and somewhat snobbish dislike of that which seems to isolate the life of the colored population from that of the white man; and the genuine and sincere distrust of all that seems to set apart the industrial and economic life of the Negro.

My belief, as I shall show in a later chapter, is that the Negro must develop race pride and enterprise, and continue to make his own contribution to the world—as a Negro. As for those who, from motives and prejudice, criticize my stand in this matter, I have found it wise simply to preserve silence—following in this the example of Booker T. Washington.[20] "I have made it a rule," he said, "never to answer my critics." Withdrawal, I, too, have found, is the best weapon against the attacks of prejudice.

So it was in the case of the militant club women. They failed to appear at the next club meeting; and, in a comparatively short time, our faith and courage had broken down their opposition. In later years many of them became staunch friends of the work. They were prototypes of others whom I have continued to meet in social work; but never have I deviated from my original policy—not to stoop to controversy.

Difference of opinion which comes, not from prejudice, but from heartfelt conviction, is another thing, and must be met in another way. At the outset I felt the necessity of securing the co-operation of the ministers of the Negro churches; yet, with the exception of one member, the Interdenominational Ministerial Alliance[21] refused to indorse my plan. That discrimination against our race could exist in Cleveland seemed unbelievable to them. They remained unconvinced even when I reminded them that discrimination had sent me, a stranger, to a questionable house instead of to a Christian institution, and that the same discrimination later had refused to admit me to certain clubs. Even a survey which I had made and which seemed to present sufficient proof that the existing social agencies would not accept Negro girls failed to remove their skepticism.

Finally a meeting was arranged between a committee of the Ministerial Alliance and the Board of Trustees of the Y.W.C.A. After the conference, the Rev. Mr. Charles Bundy,[22] one of those who had opposed our movement because he honestly felt it worked for segregation, came to my home, declared that he had been mistaken in his stand, and that he was entirely converted to the need of a home for our girls.

The Trustees of the Y.W.C.A. had told him and the members of his committee that when Negro girls came to the "Y" building in large numbers and were the majority in any activity, the white girls would withdraw. Negro girls, they said, should be cared for by the Negro race. These were the very words that Mrs. Levi T. Scofield, Chairman of the Board of Trustees, had used in speaking to me. In fact, they had been repeated by the heads of all departments to which I had applied for training. Now these same words had convinced the Ministerial Alliance and won our battle for us.

"I have watched every move you have made; and every step you have taken has been logical," said Mr. Bundy. "I have opposed you and your movement, but now I am with you. You can count on me." From this moment the minister became one of my most resourceful helpers, and worked hard to establish my work.

˙All ministers of good standing accepted membership on the Advisory Board, and consented to the use of their names on our letterheads. No sooner had we printed the first of these, then the one dissenting voice requested that his name be removed. What a predicament! The cost of printing the letterheads had practically emptied our treasury—there was no money for a fresh supply. Finally, I devised a way of erasing his name, and we used the stationery in its somewhat defaced condition.

This experiment was rather costly to my pride; but it taught me that in the future it was necessary first to be certain of the sincerity of those who gave their blessings. The most cruel and outspoken obstruction was the criticism of the editor of the *Cleveland Gazette*.[23]

CHAPTER IX

Walk Together Children[1]

Here in the city of Cleveland the most civic-minded and unselfish elements of two races have worked together for twenty-nine years to build and maintain an institution which, while it ministers primarily to Negroes, has improved the cultural and economic conditions of the whole city by eradicating evils which were preying upon both colored and whites, by nurturing mutual sympathy between the two races, and, above all, by demonstrating that the only efficient method of dealing with a submerged minority is not the paternalistic method of working for it, but the democratic spirit of working with it.

The first member of the white race to become a part of our undertaking was the woman whose memory we gratefully perpetuate in the Sarah C. Hills Training School.[2]

Mrs. Hills' active interest lasted as long as she lived. It was she who introduced me to the Women's Missionary Board of the Second Presbyterian Church.[3] To this group I described our projects and won the interest of its members. Then, again through her influence, I spoke before the Presbyterian Missionary Society of Cuyahoga County[4] and so stirred the sympathetic interest of the members that they undertook a broader interpretation of my work to many other groups of the white race. The women of Boulevard Presbyterian Church[5] pledged themselves to make all the curtains for our new home. Mrs. Hills became my early counselor, sponsor, and guide, introducing me to those whose interest I might win, restraining my enthusiasm when it seemed excessive and imprudent, urging me forward when I seemed to be moving in the right direction.

To her I owe my discipline and training in the handling of finances. When she became President of Phillis Wheatley, it was my habit to go over the accounts with her every month, checking and auditing the books. Once, I remember, there was a shortage of fifty cents; and the most careful search did not reveal the reason for the shortage. "Miss Hunter," said she, "that fifty cents will have to come out of your pocket." On another occasion, when we were unable to establish a balance because of a trifling sum on the credit side, and I would have added the small amount to the treasury, she was just as business-like. "No, Miss Hunter, that is not good bookkeeping. You will have to take the surplus." How much I owe to her rigorous training in accountancy!

At this time I was actively engaged in my profession. While on a case I drafted a letter which I hoped would prove satisfactory to all concerned. The following letter to prospective donors was my first attempt to make a public appeal:

WORKING GIRLS' HOME ASSOCIATION

Miss J. Edna Hunter, Pres., 2167 East 76th Street

Miss L. R. Bailey, secretary

J. S. Hall, Treasurer

cleveland

Dear Madam:

After six years of study and thorough investigation, I have gotten at the root of the domestic problem involving the working girls and their inefficiency of service in well-governed and systemized homes. I found that lack of interest, ambition, training, and association is due largely to this trouble, which, perhaps, you and thousands of women have had to endure.

It is apparent that the time has come when something must be done to eradicate this evil.

The persons whose names appear on this letterhead believe that the only solution of this condition would be a Home Association where these women might have pure and pleasant surroundings when out of employment; a place where they be taught the art of housekeeping, the technics of hygiene, the beauty in personal neatness, the importance of loyalty, etc. The object of this Board is to establish just such a place and to have the above mentioned subjects taught.

We are endeavoring to raise means by which we intend to lift the standards of working girls. It is earnestly hoped that you will co-operate with us in some way to help make this work a success.

My good friend felt that this letter as drafted, going directly to sympathetic people from me, would have a stronger appeal than any which she might compose.

Although there was delay in getting the organization started, the interest of my people grew stronger and stronger. Now it became my duty to harmonize these interests and unite these two dreams—the purposes and desires of my people and the policies of the white friends whose material support we sought.

Sometimes these forces seemed to coincide naturally and easily. At one of the public meetings, held at the Antioch Baptist Church[6] in July, 1912, Dr. A. B. Meldrum, minister of the Old Stone Church,[7] was the speaker. The eloquence and influence of this clergyman did much to make the public believe in our work. Our Trustees began to believe in the sincerity of our white friends, and the old fear of segregation diminished.

The next effort in the amalgamation of these interests came about less directly. It was the frank avowal of the Trustees of the Y.W.C.A., you will remember, that removed the hostility of the Negro ministers. It occurred to me that we should secure the counsel of the Young Women's Christian Association, which, though we would work independently and free from domination, hoped to serve the same Christian ends. With this in mind, I called upon Mrs. Levi T. Scofield, Chairman of the Board of Trustees of the Y.W.C.A. Although she expressed a desire to become a part of our movement, she did not give me the assurance I desired.

Through the kindness of Patrick Stephens,[8] I met Mr. Henry A. Sherwin,[9] President of the Sherwin-Williams Paint Company, who gave me very sound advice in the art of building a permanent organization. He also volunteered other support on condition that I secure a group of white women to advise and work with Negro women. Imbued and enlightened by his advice, I returned to Mrs. Scofield, who, pleased at Mr. Sherwin's valuable counsel, consented to serve on our Board of Trustees.

But again we faced a difficulty. There arose a tide of misunderstanding by misinterpretation of my relationship with white friends. All interviews with white donors had been open and above board. I had ever kept uppermost in mind to be always helpful to my people in every way possible; yet it seemed at times that the wave of unfair criticism would engulf me.

Very soon matters reached a crisis. Certain white friends whom I had invited to serve on our Board of Trustees refused places until they were granted the privilege of selecting those of my race with whom they were to be associated. A certain man, objected to for the reason that he was a newcomer to Cleveland with little to contribute to the movement, they felt should be eliminated. With justice enough, this man, who had been of service all along the way, refused to resign from the original Board and threatened to influence others not to withdraw. This created a delicate situation. I was faced with a choice between offending members of my race who had given far more than they could actually afford, and yielding to influences which could give our organization a sound financial basis. I was called upon to make a decision which gave to us the support we needed. It seemed necessary to sacrifice personal feelings for the sake of the cause.

When we sought to make our organization a legal entity, we encountered new difficulties. The Director of Public Welfare,[10] after investigation, had assured me that he would recommend our cause to the Secretary of State.[11] But on returning to his office he found there an application from a man asking for legal rights to establish an organization with almost the same purpose as ours and bearing the same name. For a while this gave me great concern. He and his wife[12] opened a home on Central Avenue.

However, when the Welfare Director again returned to Cleveland for further investigation, he was certain of the priority and validity of our claim; and, in due time, we received our document of incorporation.

Confusing though the situation was, it gave us an opportunity which now seems to have been divinely created—that of changing the name of the organization, "The Working Girls' Home Association," to "The Phillis Wheatley Association."

A better name could not have been chosen. Phillis Wheatley,[13] a Negro girl brought to America and sold in a Boston slave market, through native ability and the sympathetic assistance of Mrs. John Wheatley, mastered a new language and expressed in verse the upreachings of a free soul. It seemed appropriate to us that this African girl should serve as an everlasting inspiration to other Negro girls.

Since the founding of the Phillis Wheatley in Cleveland, the National Association of Colored Women[14] has established like-named institutions in nine cities of the United States; and has, by the action of its Executive Board, set up a Phillis Wheatley Department[15] of which I am the national chairman.

"Walk Together, Children," I used to sing when I picked cotton on the old Fant plantation. Then the friendly presence of other cotton pickers and their voices, as they blended with mine in the stirring rhythm of the old spiritual, quickened my spirit and gave me the energy to go on with the monotonous toiling. Now the old words had a larger significance. I thought of the large number of people of diversified stations and occupations who had united their charitable endeavors to make the Phillis Wheatley Home possible, and realized that our undertaking would some day be the most remarkable example of interracial co-operation in the field of social work in America.

In the work of drafting a constitution, which was necessary before we could become incorporated, I depended upon a friend who took quite some weeks to deliberate. I grew anxious. Never shall I forget the words with which this kind, wise attorney rebuked my impatience. "We must go slowly, Miss Hunter, and make this constitution proof against attacks. Just now you are the only one who cares deeply for the Phillis Wheatley work; the time will come when they will want to take it away from you."

When the constitution was ready to be presented and the new Trustees were to be elected, we approached another crisis—the issue of a mixed Board of Trustees. The home of Mrs. Elmer F. Boyd,[16] where we met, was crowded with both friends and foes. How acutely I felt the tenseness of the atmosphere; how heavy was my heart when I considered the strength of the opposition I was facing! I hoped I had convinced my followers that our objective would remain unchanged and that the inclusion of white members in the Board was necessary to acquire a larger range of influence and sufficient funds to carry on the work.

But our opponents were many; and their leader, the most intelligent layman in the group, had already announced that he was ready to offer vigorous opposition to a new constitution unless it included the policy of Negro domination in the affairs of the institution.

The work to which I had dedicated my life seemed doomed. After a night of communion with Divine Guidance, I arose to find new hope and fresh courage. Calling on one of our white friends, I suggested that if they would accept as a trustee the Negro whom they had rejected, we could get the constitution passed as originally submitted. But these friends were firm against compromise. The constitution, as written, would be adopted, or I could count them out of the picture.

In my perplexity I turned to a Negro minister.[17] With the wisdom of one experienced in the procedure of organization, he advised me to send notices to the members, announcing a meeting to be held in two weeks for the purpose of reconsidering certain sections of the constitution. Giving the recalcitrants time for consideration would forestall any accusation of unfairness on our part. At the same time, it would give time to gather my forces and provide them with courage and ammunition to meet the attack.

When the day for the meeting arrived, my followers were there a hundred strong; but not a single insurgent appeared. The victory was ours by default. The constitution was adopted; the mixed Board of Trustees elected.

At last we could walk together, Negroes and whites, toward our achievement and with harmony of purpose.

The next struggle was to raise the funds necessary to lease and equip a house.

"Miss Hunter, you do the work, and the money will come." This remark of a friend, offered at a time when I was lamenting the lack of material resources, I have never forgotten; and my experience of twenty-nine years in seeking financial support of our enterprise has proved that the friend was correct. In the hours of greatest need, Heaven has always sent a deliverer. The Phillis Wheatley came into being as the expression of the faith of a group of poor Negro women and their devotion to the poor and homeless of their own people; a nickel and a prayer started it. But it was only because we continued in the spirit of prayer and work, animated by faith in the Kingdom of God, that larger means were added to our small beginnings.

Between that evening of September, 1911, when the charter members of the Phillis Wheatley Association held their first meeting in the little parlor on East 108th Street, and December of the next year, I had gifts amounting to five hundred dollars. Now we were incorporated, had adopted a constitution, and in March of 1913 elected a mixed Board of Trustees; interracial co-operation was assured. Early opposition had been defeated and antagonistic elements had been reconciled. We were ready to carry the candlelight of service into larger circles.

At the meeting of the new Board, Mrs. Levi T. Scofield was elected President; Mrs. Adin T. Hills,[18] Vice-President; J. R. Wylie,[19] Treasurer; and Jane E. Hunter, Executive Secretary. The other members of the Board were Mrs. Laura S. Goodhue,[20] John P. Green,[21] and Robert E. Lewis.[22] The election of these persons marked the beginning of my addressing large groups. I was invited to tell the story of the Phillis Wheatley in a number of white and Negro churches; and because of the interest aroused in this way, contributions amounting to $1,500 were added to our treasury. Mr. Henry A. Sherwin, impressed by our success in carrying out his advice in securing a mixed Board, gave six hundred dollars with which to pay the rent for one year. In contributing this sum, Mr. Sherwin remarked to me that colored people often asked for fifty cents when they needed five dollars. This hint coming from this good friend taught me to decide upon what was needed for a given project, and then present the facts.

A nickel and a prayer started the Phillis Wheatley Association. These are the friends who enabled me to open the door of safety and protection to hundreds of girls, and made it possible for us to walk together in faith.

A DREAM COMES TRUE

The vision I had glimpsed on that August afternoon in 1911 when, remorseful and lonely, I had sought for some means of atonement to the mother whom in life I had not understood, found realization when the first door of the Phillis Wheatley Association for Negro working girls was opened. This home was a twenty-three-room house on East Fortieth Street.

By a wise provision of the Trustees, $1,500 was tucked away before the opening to take care of a year's expenses, such as heat, light, matron's salary, and other operating costs.

Then, with the lease in hand, came the sad realization that there were no funds to furnish the home—a plight, indeed. But as always in any emergency, good friends stood ready to help. Furniture (mostly used), rugs, curtains, and drapes were supplied generously.

Cleaning, scrubbing, painting, upholstering, absorbed the interest and time of Mrs. Elmer F. Boyd, Miss Amy Cohen, and myself for three weeks. Then we were ready to receive our guests; happy and proud, indeed of the home that we had been able to make so comfortable and so attractive for others.

Preparation had been made to care for ten girls, although many interested in our project doubted if the demand would be as great. From my own experience, I realized how many of our girls had no place to lay their heads. The rooms were applied for more rapidly than we were able to get them ready. In fact, weeks before the formal opening, fifteen young women had already taken up residence in the Phillis Wheatley Home.

It had been rumored that admission would be regulated by a caste system, based upon color. How I laughed at these stories; but when applicant after applicant appeared, all mulatto girls, I became worried. Then came Emma Henderson[23] of ebony hue. You may be sure that I felt relieved, and welcomed Emma with open arms and that I smiled triumphantly at my detractors.

At the formal opening we already were a going concern. Throughout the day hundreds of guests came in to inspect our home, and the evening throngs were so large that crowds of people were unable to get within a half block of the house.

We had won our cause. We had begun to balance the scales of social justice for Negro women; we had brought thanksgiving into the hearts of many lonely girls; we had laid the foundation for our social service program. My plan had been not only to furnish safe shelter for homeless girls, but to afford them special opportunities for recreational pleasures and religious training.

New needs kept appearing, new opportunities kept opening up. I knew our girls were in need of work, and that there were many housewives who desired efficient maids. This demand caused us to open an Employment Office, which sounds grander than it really was; for at first the only piece of office equipment was a telephone. The May Company,[24] hearing of our need, gave a desk, and Charles Blue[25] made a large table which served during the day as an employment desk and the evening as a library table around which the girls gathered for reading after their day's work was done.

The need of a dining room soon became apparent; for there was only a kitchen at first, where the girls prepared their evening meals, consisting mostly of crackers, tea, and canned beans. It was also apparent that these meals were neither adequate nor nutritious. Because of the new impetus placed on our needs, Dr. and Mrs. Paul F. Sutphen,[26] believers in education and champions of the cause of the low economic groups, already were our staunch and enthusiastic friends. Mrs. Sutphen was active on our cooperative Board, and was among the first persons to assist me in providing a decent place for us to assemble and eat together at the close of the day's work. By dint of continual persuasion on her part, and as a crowning argument, producing two hundred and seventy-six dollars that we had collected through entertainments and special gifts for the purpose, we were able to convince the Trustees of the need of a dining room. Two rooms in the basement were opened, where we served two meals a day to our girls at a weekly charge of two dollars and a quarter.

During this development, our cafeteria grew to be the finest restaurant for Negroes and whites in the midwestern States. The earnings of this venture, which netted from $1,500 to $2,000 yearly prior to the depression years, were used to provide further leadership in the group work service.

WAR YEARS

All social institutions and movements were, of necessity, greatly handicapped in the year 1914 and thereafter by the war. Hordes of Negro laborers poured in from the South to work in munition plants and other industries. The overcrowded condition consequent upon this influx, of course, greatly increased the number of Negro girls exposed to the evils of the cheap rooming houses.

The twenty-three-room home, that had been overcrowded from the beginning, proved totally inadequate in these times and under these new conditions. A larger building where we could take care of more girls was an imperative necessity. It was the spring of 1917, Congress and the President stood ready to make the decision that would plunge the United States into war. Already war hysteria had seized the minds of our citizens, almost to the exclusion of all else. Around the table in the main building of the Cleveland Trust Company[27] sat eighteen women and one Negro man,[28] deliberating on problems of Negro girls.

"Better go slowly—this is no time to ask for money—other matters must come first," warned conservative Trustees. But these remarks did not curb my enthusiasm. I would storm Heaven and earth to meet this urgent need.

"Phillis Wheatley must wait," some said. But I, aware of the urgency of the case as the Trustees could not be, made answer, "Phillis Wheatley cannot wait; the need is upon us, and we must meet it." And I continued to beleaguer the Board until it yielded. The great decision, so near to my heart, turned in my favor when Mrs. Stevenson Burke[29] offered the motion to test the interest of friends, on the very day on which President Woodrow Wilson issued the declaration of war against Germany.

So great was my ardor that within a week I had secured pledges of $13,000, which amazed the Trustees and gladdened their hearts as well as my own.

At this point now arose a new obstacle.

The Phillis Wheatley Association had grown so large that some members of the Board felt it should be reorganized as a branch of the Young Women's Christian Association. During my absence from the city, a few women met to discuss again affiliation of the two institutions. I am told that the motion was made and carried to the effect that the Phillis Wheatley Association become a subsidiary of the Young Women's Christian Association.

Upon my return, and at the earliest convenience of the Board, a meeting was called. With no rancor, but with a deep sense of the rightness of my belief that we could stand on our own feet, and that only as an independent organization could we win a full measure of justice for colored girls, I made my position clear.

"Here are the pledges," I said. "I have collected them in your name, and they are yours. However, if the present organization becomes a part of the Young Women's Christian Association, I shall organize another Phillis Wheatley Association." I withdrew from the meeting and went home, deeply perturbed. For several days I was in a quandary. Further discussion I felt was futile.

At the end of the week, I was informed that the Trustees had withdrawn their motion to place the Phillis Wheatley Association under the jurisdiction of the Young Women's Christian Association, and that I might continue soliciting funds for larger quarters. Within a few weeks the fund grew to $27,000.

Then, worn out as I was with the worry I had been through, my doctor ordered me home to South Carolina. There I enjoyed four months of sunshine amid the familiar scenes of my childhood, and the inspiration I had gleaned from reading Dr. Harry Emerson Fosdick's *Meaning of Prayer*.[30] Although I had been many times led to the Throne of Grace by Dr. Fosdick's simple stories of love, yet I had not before felt the deep, abiding truth as it touched me then. Each day I made an effort to live again by doing things I used to do as a child when I lived and worked on Woodburn Farm.

I would steal away to the meadow below Aunt Daisy's[31] home where stately oaks and a few pine trees grew; walk down the cowpath to a favorite tree, and there sit reading, singing, and looking up to Heaven. Under the deep blue Southern skies I communed sincerely with God. Grandma once told me that the juice from the pine needles would heal the lungs. Having faith in whatever she said, I chewed the green pine needles to gain their healing strength.

Before I left Cleveland, Mrs. Robert Bishop suggested that I cut wood, as it would give me exercise. At first my strength would not permit more than a half dozen swings of the axe. By persistent effort, and before returning to Cleveland, I felt the urge to hew the tallest tree in the woods. I thought how blessed I was to have friends, books, and a loving Father who cares for His own. It was the abiding faith in these influences which meant so much in the restoration of my health and made me a new creature and a stronger woman.

Old discouragements forgotten, I returned to Cleveland in the autumn to resume leadership of the Phillis Wheatley Association.

During my absence, a three-story apartment building on East Fortieth Street and Central Avenue,[32] with accommodations for seventy-five girls had been purchased by the Board. Nothing had been done to rehabilitate the place. It was dirty, unsanitary, and needed much done to make it habitable.

The pledges secured before my vacation had all been used in the purchase. Once again, therefore, I appealed to friends; and again I was met with generosity—securing donations sufficient to remodel and beautify the eighty-eight-room apartment.

Then we rolled up our sleeves and went to work with a will—scrubbing floors, washing windows, scraping twenty layers of paper from the walls.

We had bought and furnished a comfortable home for seventy-five girls and were prepared to serve our community in a diversity of ways.

We continued to expand, and in the spring of 1919 raised another sum of money with which we purchased a two-story building[33] adjacent to the Home, thus providing a large hall for the Girl Reserves[34] and rooms for other clubs and community activities.

The integrity and independence of the Phillis Wheatley Association had been preserved.

CHAPTER X

Our New Home[1]

Dr. Paul F. Sutphen described the work of the Phillis Wheatley as a great gas well, with forces stronger than the veins through which the gas is directed. This comparison in its full significance burst upon us in 1922. We had added a music department,[2] classes in handicraft, and dancing; had secured a gymnasium, and opened our doors to church and neighborhood clubs. In the full sense of the word, we had become a community center.

It was agreed that the time was ripe for us to have a new and adequate building. Repeatedly I had pointed out that it was quite time for Negroes to discontinue the custom of taking over secondhand buildings and trying to adjust them to their needs. I believed that our work would be higher in standard and of greater usefulness if it could be carried on in a building constructed to fit the needs of our program.

Never had we had a stronger, more influential Board; nor a wiser, more unselfish President than we had at this time in Mrs. D. W. Frackelton. With her help the Board of Trustees made the appeal to the public to help us raise $550,000. No social agency for Negro girls had ever sought so large a sum, and some of the Board members doubted the possibility of raising such an amount. But the President and I never wavered nor lost faith. We knew that if we asked we should receive.[3]

The Negroes themselves established a nucleus of $15,000. Mrs. Robert

H. Bishop, Jr., who headed the Preliminary Gift Committee, opened the way to the hearts of large donors. Mrs. Stevenson Burke, a civic-minded and wealthy woman, and a member of our Board, inspired the workers with a gift of $25,000. In the summer of 1924, Mrs. Bishop and I secured pledges for $90,000. With these gifts, the amount arose to $130,000.

Most encouraging to me were the gifts of the working men and women whose contributions meant a real sacrifice. The staff also gave from their small salaries. Even our cook, "Mother Rich,"[4] contributed one hundred dollars; while another cook, Ellen Jackson,[5] gave two hundred and fifty dollars, a part of her life's savings.

The committee decided to make an appeal for assistance to the Rockefeller Foundation.[6] Mrs. Bishop and Mrs. Edwin Burke[7] journeyed to New York and presented our need to the Laura Spelman Foundation.[8] As it happened, our case did not come within the scope of this Foundation, but so impressed were its members that they brought the matter to the attention of Mr. John D. Rockefeller, Jr.[9]

Mr. Rockefeller, influenced no doubt by the fact that his mother had always been much interested in the colored race, and, if living, undoubtedly would have been responsive to this need, made a pledge of $100,000. As was his custom in the giving of large gifts, Mr. Rockefeller made the following stipulations:

First: that $450,000 should be secured by the Association on or before February 1, 1928.

Second: that his pledge should become due and payable only pro rata with the amount received in cash from other contributors to the building fund.

Third: that if the balance of the sum pledged should not be paid on or before the above date, his pledge would lapse and all his obligations thereunder would terminate.

Great indeed was the jubilation over this very magnanimous gift which proved the spur to the success of the campaign when it opened in January, 1925. When enthusiasm was at its height, there arose a most unfortunate circumstance. The more one seeks Divine Guidance, the more Satan tries one's faith.

A Negro undertaker[10] and a white real estate broker,[11] with every earmark of ulterior motives, purchased a home in a fashionable residential district, moving a hearse into the yard and placing a large sign on the house. This act stirred the ire of the people of the Heights,[12] and so affected the campaign workers that the campaign committee was forced to purchase the property from the enterprisers at a much higher cost than the original price. A few friends made up a purse and repurchased the property from our committee. It took some time for the ill will engendered by this unfortunate circumstance to subside, and only by great faith and extreme tact were the campaign workers kept together. In this difficulty, I was reminded of the severe storm of the elements I faced en route to Cleveland in 1905. The swift storm of life is very often of spiritual value to one struggling for achievement. Thanks were due especially to Messrs. Charles Adams,[13] who employed Negroes in his factory, Charles K. Arter,[14] and A. D. Baldwin[15] for their successful efforts in helping to allay the bad feeling.

As children of the Heavenly King, we had walked together, under the leadership of Mrs. Arthur D. Baldwin,[16] who exercised divine patience and kept the faith, that His will might be done upon earth.[17]

On June 19, 1927, the cornerstone[18] of our new home was laid with sacred ceremony. At this momentous occasion, Dr. Sutphen and friends of great wealth were present. When the building was completed, only a small sum could be spared for furnishings. With careful planning and a generous gift from a friend, one entire floor was beautifully furnished and named for our late and noble friend, Mrs. Solon Severance.[19] The home was soon comfortably furnished and in readiness for its occupants.

A memorable day it was when on December 15, 1927, the keys were delivered to the Board of Trustees by Mr. David E. Green,[20] Chairman of the Construction Committee, and one hundred young women moved into the beautiful new home at Cedar Avenue and Forty-sixth Street. Nine stories above ground, two below, it stands a monument to interracial co-operation. Its strong and enduring walls, its great height, towering above all other buildings in the vicinity, are a symbol of the firmness of character that the people of Cleveland and their benefactor, Mr. John D. Rockefeller, Jr., desire to see in the lives of Negro women in this great city.

The dedication occurred on April 24, 1928, Dr. Robert R. Moton,[21] President Emeritus of Tuskegee Institute, delivering the address. Four hundred of the first citizens gathered for this service, and broke bread at another delightful interracial feast.

Paying interest on a mortgage of $86,500, reducing the principal, and developing a program for girls at the same time was a Herculean task. A small committee of Negro women and the staff raised a goodly sum each year. So pleased was Mr. Rockefeller with the brave effort made by the Negroes in the midst of the depression, that he forwarded the remainder of his pledge which had been withheld because of our failure to meet the conditions of his generous offer.

One of the most touching incidents during this period occurred when Frank Radke,[22] a small merchant tailor, put into my hands a purse containing five hundred dollars. He wanted Negro girls to have this gift in memory of his wife, Mrs. Kaney Radke,[23] who, through her life, had been interested in working for underprivileged folk.

Final liquidation came in 1936, the year of our Silver Anniversary. Men of the Cleveland Bar Association, the press, Parent-Teacher Associations, Post Office workers, city and county employees formed another interracial volunteer army with the single objective of freeing the Phillis Wheatley from debt. We bear in mind that the greatest wealth of the Phillis Wheatley Association lies not in its material possessions, but in the treasure of devoted friends who, for the last quarter of a century, have walked together and worked together, believing that "the whole world must be cleansed, or not a man or woman of us all can be clean."[24]

CHAPTER XI

———— ✦ ————

"Starlight"

A s a child on **Woodburn Plantation** I had often been thrown into teeth-chattering, blood-curdling panic by my terror of wild-cats. Now, as a guardian of a social enterprise, I found myself facing a much more dreadful monster—commercialized vice. Like Apolly-on who[1] bestrode the path of Christian, this creature spawned by greed and ignorance, was hideous to behold. "Out of its belly came fire and smoke, and its mouth was as the mouth of a lion."[2] The service it imposed upon the wretched of my race was hard, "and its wages were death."[3] It tried to win us by fair promises; it wrestled with us, and had almost pressed to death. But when we fell, we rose. "And although we must continue to wage bitter warfare with it, we know that we shall be more than conquerors through Him that loved us."[4]

The story of American history, and, indeed, of all Western history in the nineteenth century, is a record of unprecedented aggrandizement of ur-ban populations. In Cleveland this mushroom growth, as regards its Negro population, achieved in the decade between 1910 and 1920 the phenomenal acceleration of three hundred per cent.[5] Drawn from rural regions and vil-lages by the lure of better wages, the Negroes, like other underprivileged groups, offered a glaring mark for the rapacity of realtors and the dishon-esty of politicians. Where once they had been scattered throughout the city, their very numbers now confined them to definite sections, and these "black belts"[6] quickly underwent a degeneration, civic and fiscal, of a type known to virtually all American cities.

Here was a golden opportunity for unscrupulous politicians; and greedily they seized upon it to serve their purposes, playing upon the ignorance of the Negro voter to entrench themselves in office, and then delivering the Negro over to every force of greed and vice which stalked around him. My second insight into this unholy alliance of organized vice and corrupt politics came to me in the course of my professional labors. Dr. A——,[7] from whom I took cases, maintained two practices—one in the downtown section, one for Negroes on the edge of the underworld. It was while attending one of his patients, the madame of a house of prostitution, that I acquired first-hand experience with a resort of this character, and learned the ties which linked its evils with municipal politics. There were two children in this evil den—one a child of two, my patient's daughter; the other her niece, a girl of fourteen who acted as a porter, admitting patrons and collecting the two dollars charged them for their visits.

It was from the latter, Willie Mae, that I learned the set-up and acquired my knowledge of "Starlight," the unsavory creature who thrived upon the tolls which he exacted from this place and hundreds like it. His name, Willie Mae told me, came from the fact that he always wore a large, flashing diamond beneath his black bow tie. He was the "Great Mogul" of organized vice. Suave, impressive, impervious to shame, and gifted with the art of leadership, he was a born political henchman; and many a young colored girl, misled by hopes of an easy, glamorous existence, became the victim of his false promises and found herself, too late, a hopeless prisoner of shame and degradation.

Chance brought me in immediate contact with his first victim, a beautiful mulatto girl named Osie,[8] whom he waylaid as she was on her way home from high school and won over with promises of marriage and a life of luxury. When her parents found her days later, she was living in a house of prostitution[9] at Scovill Avenue and Fourteenth Street, where gambling and liquor offered a good time to libertines of both races, and dissolute white men sought a thrill with loose Negro girls. Osie's task was to keep the patrons drinking; and when business boomed, to seek fresh recruits for the trade. Pending the addition of these recruits, the greed of her husband frequently compelled his helpless victims to entertain as many as forty men in a single night. The time came, however, when this helpless first wife, Osie, was divorced by "Starlight" and abandoned by all her associates. She went from bad to worse; the police, acting under "Starlight's" orders, had denied her even the right to practice her unsavory profession to which he had dragged her; and at length, broken in health, sicken with pneumonia, she crawled back to her mother's home to die there, mourned only by her own mother. I stood at her bedside when her eyes closed in death, and heard her unhappy mother cry, "Thanks be to God, now my trouble is over." Once more it was borne in upon me that only but for the grace of God this fate might easily enough have been mine, and I felt a renewed determination to help the homeless and imperiled daughters of my people.

"Starlight," meanwhile, waxed wealthier and more powerful each year. New houses of prostitution were opening frequently with procurers hunting Negro girls at our very doorsteps, and the issue had reached point where it was no longer possible to ignore it.

What to do? Very early in the history of our social work for girls, tours of dance halls, which I made with Mrs. Mary Rathburn Judd,[10] General Secretary to the Young Women's Christian Association, had opened my eyes to the evil influence which the commercial dance hall was exerting upon the morals of the Negroes. Even then it was apparent that the only answer lay in supplying similar recreation under wholesome influences; and though this step involved the risk of alienating those of our supporters to whom dancing under any auspices was abhorrent, I now determined that the Phillis Wheatley should inaugurate a recreational hall. We rented a barn in the rear of our home for ten dollars a month, put in a new floor, plastered the walls, and announced our first party. Guests came only on invitation; no admission was charged at the parties which were held twice a month. The new addition to the Phillis Wheatley Association proved a huge success. Not only did we use the hall for dances, but we had it fitted up as a gymnasium. A Sunday school in the neighborhood held a bazaar, and from the proceeds bought dumb bells, Indian clubs,[11] and other paraphernalia.

Preventive measures, however, were not enough. We determined to carry the warfare into the enemy's camp and do battle with the political corruption, "Starlight's" chief mainstay, which had made of our neighborhood a region of brawling vice, known throughout the city as the "Roaring Third."[12]

At the moment, the Democratic and Republican parties were engaged in one of their periodic battles over the local railway system; the Democrats declaring for reduced fare, the Republicans aligning themselves with the stockholders of the Street Railway Company[13] for "good service" at the existing fare. Eventually the issue came before the electorate, and fearing the outcome, the Republicans determined to clinch it by organizing the Negro vote in their favor. The task was not difficult. By tradition then the Negro vote was still overwhelmingly Republican,[14] and all that was needed was to ensure that this vote should be delivered in bloc. The respectable Negro vote, the vote largely of the church people, was won by appeals to racial pride. The other, a numerically stronger vote, was in the pocket of "Starlight," placed there by the far-flung ramifications of his evil influence. If you care to investigate this chapter of Cleveland politics, you will discover how completely "Starlight" justified the confidence that was reposed in him by his masters, the politicians, and how intimate can be the relations between a general and public economic issue like that of a street railway franchise and the more private, but basically not less, economic issue of the prevalence of organized vice.

The Republicans won in 1910, and a part of "Starlight's" share in the victory was the privilege of naming a councilman to be elected by that body from our district. Great was the pride of the Negroes in this person, Tim Flagman,[15] a popular young lawyer, who took his seat in the Councilmanic Chamber.[16] Social leaders, especially those of us associated with the Phillis Wheatley, did not join in these plaudits, however, for well we knew what it foreboded; and when Tim was promptly slated for the all-important post of Chairman of the Fire and Police Committee, not the faintest doubt remained to us that evil days were upon us, and that henceforth vice would enjoy a free hand in the city. Our fears were not long in being realized. New dives and brothels opened all around us, all attempt at concealment was abandoned, the headway which the Negro had made toward the state of good citizenship at the time was tumbled gutterward, and faith in Negro leadership was turned to derision.

It was only this result, however, which could open the eyes of the gullible and misguided, and pave the way to a reaction. Now with evidence all around them of how shamefully they had been duped by "Starlight's" promises, the law-abiding citizens set to work to fight his baneful influence before and after municipal elections. Prominent in this movement were the members of St. John's A. M. E. Church, the Antioch Baptist Church, and other members of my group who had been "anti-Starlight" from the outset.

Our war cry was "Down with 'Starlight' and corruption," and we did not lack for campaign material; for scarcely a week went by that I was not summoned to police court to assume responsibility for some girl who had been arrested in a house of prostitution for which this monster was responsible. We had no campaign funds, but we did not lack enthusiasm. As the election drew near and our infectious zeal spread in every direction, our opponents began to feel a little worried. One ward-heeler[17] came to my office and asked what I was doing, what I wanted for my district—in short, where I was standing.

"Go back and tell your boys I'm not standing," I told him, "I'm on my knees."

"Hell, get up then," he blurted out rudely, "you've got the boys worried sick."

This was welcome news; and in the light of our enthusiasm, defeat now seemed impossible. Alas, for the simplicity of our illusions! Never once had it occurred to us that only the count determines an election, and that many a victory is won after the polls have closed. The returns were simply incredible! We were barely in the running. It was not until years later that I learned how we had been cheated out of a hard-earned victory.[18]

Politicians think their maneuvers irresistible. I was very much amused after this campaign by the various attempts which were made by "Starlight" and his crowd to tie the Phillis Wheatley to their chariot. "Starlight" went so far as to apply for membership in the Association; and when we respectfully returned the check he sent us for dues, he came back with an offer to furnish a living-room in the house. We informed him that we would not accept the offer, since his actions did not accord with the purposes and spirit of the Phillis Wheatley Association—a rebuff which he received with unruffled suavity.

His next move was covert and more successful. He sent to the Phillis Wheatley Home a light mulatto woman named Dora,[19] who was fairly well educated, had pleasant manners, and dressed like a Paris fashion plate. It was not generally known that Dora was a scout for the "Starlight-Tim" combination. As a free lancer, she sought to recruit new blood for their underworld practices, and became identified with numerous social, religious, and political groups. In this way she interested herself in the work of our Association. It happened that one of the girls living in the Phillis Wheatley was reported as keeping late hours, in violation of dormitory rules. Dora learned of this and came to me under the pretense of friendship for Inez, and requested that I permit her to admonish the girl. Very soon it was discovered that Dora's real purpose was to entice Inez, because of her attractiveness, away from the institution and lure her into the "Starlight-Tim" dives, for this is where I subsequently found Inez. This experience was sufficient to put me on guard against future activities of this woman in the affairs of the Phillis Wheatley Association.

In fact it was necessary at all times to guard our girls from evil surroundings. I kept a vigilant ear at the switchboard[20] in my office to catch conversations of a doubtful character, and to intercept assignations. No effort we made to restrict tenancy to girls of good character could exclude the ignorant, the foolish, and the weak, for these had to be protected as well. In the company of a policeman whom I could trust, I would sometimes follow couples to places of assignation, rescue the girl, and assist in the arrest of her would-be seducer.

Two years passed, and once more we were facing an election. This time our candidate was Howard E. Murrell,[21] a successful business man with marked talents for organizing and directing a campaign. The contest proved much more bitter than the first one. Feeling on election day reached the pitch of violence. One of our workers, more daring than prudent, became engaged in controversy with one of "Starlight's" crowd, and had her coat torn from her shoulders. While I had always sought to avoid controversy, I could not stand by and allow one of my followers to be treated in this fashion, and I hurried to her succor.

My arch enemy saw me and stopped me forty paces from our door. "Might as well give up, 'Miss Janey,'" he announced suavely; "you're wasting time and energy. Go home and take it easy. Do now." The quiet insolence of the man made my blood boil. Everything decent and right which my parents had implanted in me and stood for, was affronted by his presence. I shook my finger in his face. "Some day I'll get you, you rascal."

The events of the next few hours, however, were to corroborate "Starlight's" boasting. Hour after hour, I sat in my office waiting for the belated returns from our district. Shortly before midnight, the issue still not known, I heard the crash of drums and the screeching of horns. It was "Starlight" and his forces, two thousand strong, sweeping down the street past the Phillis Wheatley, throwing their searchlights into our windows, and shouting their derision. Out of defiance or a desire to show myself a good loser, I threw open the door on Central Avenue and stood there on the threshold. The unruly mob surged up the steps. One burly Negro rushed forward, his fist clenched to strike me. But someone in the crowd roared, "Don't you touch her," and he fell back. The mob rejoined the procession; and as they moved out on Central Avenue, I heard someone say, "Ain't Miss Hunter brave?" It was a pleasing tribute, doubly so in defeat; but the cold fact remained that we were in for two more years of "Starlight" and that our efforts had gone for nothing.

Then, abruptly, one month from the day I faced and denounced him, word of his death flashed through the district. He had contracted pneumonia; and, weakened by over-exertion and exposure during the election, had been unable to fight it. It seemed too good to be true. It was only when I stood watching the funeral procession that bore him to the church for burial that I felt sure that "Enemy No. 1" of Cleveland had at long last been vanquished. What a mockery it seemed—that procession, the masses of flowers, the stately music, the marching societies in gleaming regalia, the religious ceremony—all to honor a man who had destroyed virtue and spread ruin.

With the passing of "Starlight" in 1921, better days dawned for the Third District. Politicians had come to feel a certain respect for my influence, and the Phillis Wheatley Association continued to afford a safe refuge for the unprotected. From this time on I took no further active part in politics, except to keep our followers informed of the caliber of the men on the municipal and county tickets. Since direct campaigning seemed futile, the moral seemed to be that our best hope lay in our work of education and protection; and so we went on supplying recreation and beauty to the young, counsel and correction to the wayward, and a home to the homeless. Sweeping changes in social conditions we felt would have to await a more enlightened and responsible electorate.

But I am sorry to admit that the death of "Starlight" dealt no serious blow to open and protected prostitution. The evil was too deep-rooted for that; the foundations which he laid for an underworld of gambling, prostitution, and vice generally remained to menace unborn generations.

Dance halls have multiplied, and their unsavory atmosphere is a growing cause of concern to parents. Under a former city administration, measures were taken to supervise these places. A dance hall inspector was appointed, and the establishments that met certain standards were licensed for operation. This reform, however, has been largely nullified by political pressure exerted by unionized orchestras who dislike the peril to their livelihood presented by effective regulation and consequent reduction of attendance. Slot machines and the policy racket have also operated to set up lower dance hall standards. Few, indeed, are the commercialized amusements which have escaped exploitation and control by gangsters.

A survey made in 1939 of conditions in my neighborhood shows that the old evils still flourish in most places of amusement. The dice roll, strong liquor flows; lewd men and wretched women crowd about gambling tables in basements, often wagering as high as forty dollars, to emerge with a dime. They stagger out in the early morning, the men sometimes waiting to catch some innocent girl, as she rushes off to work or hurries home from a night job. Dives, run by Greeks and Italians in my district, flourish beside schools, and are frequented regularly by children of both the senior and junior high schools. At my instigation and with my assistance, a Negro policeman succeeded in having the license of one of these places revoked.

These are the ancient evils. But my last tour of inspection brought me in touch with something more anomalous; vice as a spectacle not for the ignorant or the unfortunate, but for patrons from society's leading families. It is located, this night club of which I am speaking, in the heart of a newly created Negro slum district, and its appointments are elaborate and costly. Here, to the tune of St. Louis voodoo blues,[22] half-naked Negro girls dance shameless dances with men in Spanish costumes, while daughters from highly respectable families, attended by escorts, clap their dainty, white hands and shout their approval. The whole atmosphere is one of unrestrained animality, the jungle faintly veneered with civilized trappings.

When one of the entertainers discovered my presence and announced in a loud voice that Miss Jane Hunter was present, the applause which greeted his announcement filled me with the deepest confusion. As unobtrusively as possible, I took my departure, saddened and disgusted.

Decent and self-respecting members of my race, I told myself, are not allowed to live in respectable white neighborhoods; yet a white aristocracy penetrates Negro slums to enjoy, patronize, and encourage the worst that my race has to offer. Interracial co-operation built the Phillis Wheatley Association and is carrying on its work; a co-operation of Negroes and whites for worthy purposes; which can gauge the spiritual contribution the Negro has made to American life, since his arrival in America. But in the meeting of blacks and whites in night clubs of the type I had encountered, there is to be found only cause for regret and head-hanging by both races. On the one side an exhibition of unbridled animality, on the other a blasé quest for novel sensations, a vicarious gratification of the dark and violent desires of man's nature, a voluntary return to the jungle.

And behind it all, the hideous god of greed; greedy landlords avowed to reap enhanced returns at the moral cost of the community; racketeers and gangsters frightening the honest but cowardly into the service of evil; and dishonest politicians using public office to undermine the decency and morality of society. Yet at the bottom, the responsibility rests with the citizens of our community. Given what is lacking, unselfishness, imagination, courage, they could easily enough rout the forces of vice which they have supinely allowed to flourish.

It was these virtues that made possible the building of the Phillis Wheatley. Out of the prayers and nickels—the interested benevolence of a few Negro working women—has grown a movement which has erected buildings for the welfare of hundreds of homeless women, and radiated the influences of fellowship throughout an entire country. We have proved that white and black can co-operate unselfishly for the common social good.

CHAPTER XII

Types of Girls Given a Chance

How many girls of good intentions, before the days of the Phillis Wheatley, had to give up the struggle to rise above the circumstances of their unhappy environment? What other organization, for instance, could have saved "Mamie," whose ignorant stepmother and indifferent father withdrew her from school and turned her out on the streets to find work?

"Mamie" wandered into the office of a Cleveland Editor who directed her to the Phillis Wheatley Home. This editor had once declared that our Association was a subservient force, encouraging segregation of the colored population for Cleveland. At last he had come to recognize that it was a real haven for the Negro girl. With some assistance from our Trustees, "Mamie" returned to school, was graduated from Central High[1] and from the School of Education at Western Reserve University[2] and taught in the Cleveland public schools. She married a splendid young man, has three children, and is now a successful homemaker.

From the day our doors were opened, we knew that if we were to be an agency of service, we must offer more than a lodging place to the girls who came to us. In all of the activities our aim has been to offer to Negro women an opportunity to live happy and useful lives, thus unfolding the beauty within them to make the lives of others more beautiful.

Mabel Parks, a pretty brown-skinned girl, joined our clubs while she was in elementary school. Her father being an invalid, the burden of support was thrown upon Mabel's mother. Mabel herself was able to earn a little money by working after school, until she entered high school. Longer assignments and more difficult subjects of study made it practically impossible for her to continue to be a student and a wage earner. Impressed by her intelligence and earnestness, the Greater Cleveland Federation of Women[3] contributed a sum that made it possible for Mabel to continue her education and be graduated.

Mabel was ambitious to become a nurse; I encouraged her to apply for admission to Harlem Hospital.[4] She was admitted, and in a few years finished the course at that institution. In competitive examination she won an appointment as a public health nurse in New York.

Later, she was called back to Cleveland by the death of her mother, and it made me glad to observe the intelligence with which Mabel directed the affairs of her mother's household. In New York, Mabel was making a contribution as a nurse to the health of her people; before returning to her work, she volunteered to send a girl each year to Camp Merriman,[5] in memory of her mother.

The Phillis Wheatley serves as a laboratory for the discovery of talent and ability in colored young women. One evening about four years ago, I noticed with unusual interest the careful and dignified manner with which one of the waitresses in the cafeteria arranged the silver and linen, and the courtesy with which she inquired what I wished for dinner. This girl's duties in the cafeteria were a part of her practice work as a student in the training school.

"Louise," I asked her, "what are you doing out of school?"

"I have finished," she answered.

"As most girls do—with just enough credits to graduate, I suppose?"

"No," she said, courteously, but with assurance, "I did very well."

"Then go to the dean and ask her to send me a transcript of your grades."

Louise appeared in my office the next morning bearing a letter from Miss Edna M. Studebaker,[6] at that time Dean of Girls at Central High School. Louise had graduated with very high grades, said Miss Studebaker, and had qualities of mind and character that merited further academic training.

Aided by the Cleveland Foundation,[7] our Board of Trustees, and a few personal friends, Louise entered the School of Education of Western Reserve University. In 1938, she received her diploma. The years she spent in college were a hard struggle, to be sure, against prejudice and poverty—her mother was widowed with four younger children. In the fall, Louise received her appointment as a teacher in the Cleveland schools. Now she is able to raise the standards of living in her home, and is serving girls, as a member of our Junior Board.

Not all the girls we serve have the intelligence of Louise and Mabel. Some of them, coming from the deep South, are amazingly backward, and their reactions are conditioned by the feeling of inferiority which tradition and a lack of education have bred in them. To these defenseless souls, the Phillis Wheatley owes protection and love quite as much as to those whose greater intelligence may bring greater returns.

One of the most interesting of such cases was Charlotte, who came to Cleveland from Mississippi. She was brought to our door by a minister who had met her on the train. Plain-faced and awkward, Charlotte had a forthrightness of manner that was amusing. She waited not for an introduction from the minister, but demanded at once—

"Whar is de sup'intenden' of dis hyar place?"

"I am the superintendent," I replied, "and what may I do for you?"

"Ah wan's a place to stay; how much is it?"

The matter of lodging being arranged, Charlotte registered with our employment bureau. She was asked for her former address.

"Ah'm from Atlanta, Georgia. Ah lib on Peachtree Street."

This amused me, for I knew that Peachtree Street was in one of the aristocratic neighborhoods of Atlanta. "Why, Charlotte," I asked, "what were you doing on Peachtree Street?"

"Ah, war cookin' dar. What you think ah doin' dar? Now, ah wants to put an ad in de papuhs fuh wuk. Say in dar ah'se fust-class cook, an ah wants twelve dollars a week; an ah wants to lib on de lot."

It was difficult to make Charlotte understand that in the North, servants did not "live on the lot," but usually occupied a room in the house of their employer. She shook her head and looked incredulous.

Next day, returning from a walk, she burst into my office, breathless and triumphant.

"Miss Huntah, yuh kin bu'n me fur a fool, but yuh won't git no ashes. Ah wuz down Prospect Street, and ah seed way back in de yahds, houses wid big doahs an cuhtains at de windows; an dat's whar de serbens lib, on de lot, same ez ah done say!"

We explained that she had seen garages over which the chauffeurs often lived, but that women servants lived in the house. Charlotte remained unconvinced until, having found employment, she discovered for herself the whereabouts of her living quarters.

Charlotte came home regularly on her days off, and spent much of her leisure time in our clubs. She had brought from Mississippi to Georgia, and thence to Cleveland, almost a wagon load of household furniture which she had placed in storage. Each week as she drew her weekly wages—this we did not learn until too late to warn her of her folly—she went to the storage depot and placed almost the entire amount in a washtub which was part of her heterogeneous collection there.

Unfortunately, she confided the secret of her little hoard to one of her employers who, forthwith, set up a scheme to rob poor, trusting Charlotte. She accused the maid of stealing a bedspread valued at $700, exactly the amount of Charlotte's savings. Employing a detective, she had him accompany Charlotte to the storage depot, where they seized Charlotte's money and held it for the spread.

I engaged an attorney and entered suit against the employer; but when the case was called, we could not persuade Charlotte to go into court. None of her family had been before a judge, and she would not disgrace her people. Her employer could keep the $700—she knew that some day she would appear before a Righteous Judge. Poor Charlotte was so beset by fear of what a court might do to a Negro plaintiff who appeared against a white defendant, that she refused to trust a court which would doubtless have given an unbiased hearing of her case.

Several years later, Charlotte came to say goodbye.

"Ah's save' enuf money to buy a hawse, and ah's goin' back ter Mississippi," she announced. "Me an' mah sister goin' to fahm." Charlotte left Cleveland just in time to escape the bread line of the depression.

No undertaking can measure its success solely in terms of financial achievement. Some of our best girls struggle bravely against adversity, barely able to keep their heads above the waves. The measure of their success is in the courage of their struggle, and in their preservation of high ideals.

The life of Pallie has been like that. She was brought to us some years ago by her widowed father, a laborer in the steel mills. Unable to make a home for his six children in the wretched shanty where he lived, he "farmed them out."[8] Pallie, a girl of twelve, attended Central High School and worked after school as a waitress in our cafeteria. Her pleasant manners and service soon made her very popular with the patrons. Pallie was with us for seven years. Then she fell in love with a worthless boy; and, in spite of my efforts to dissuade her, married him. There followed disillusionment, poverty, and desertion of his family by the irresponsible husband. Now Pallie is supporting her five children, sending them to public and Sabbath Schools;[9] she herself sings and works in a mission in our slums. Undefeated by ill fortune, she is the faithful guardian of her poor home, and an influence for good in her own small group.

In many instances the investment which the Trustees have made in the life of the colored girl is doubled and trebled again in the lives of her sisters and brothers, and multiplied again in the lives of her children whom she protects and encourages by her example.

When Lois came to us, she was not strong physically. Her mother, also poor in health, was sent to the hospital; but Lois, by special permission because of her youth, was placed in Camp Merriam, which bears the name of Mrs. Walter H. Merriam,[10] a former president of our Association. We cared for her through elementary and high school days. Meanwhile, both mother and daughter were restored to health. Lois fought her way through Ohio State University,[11] received library training, and is now directing the reading interests of young people in a branch library.

Among the first Girl Reserves of the Phillis Wheatley was Catherine

Bell. After finishing high school, she took a commercial course and is an efficient secretary for one of the large Negro insurance companies. Catherine is a zealous member of our Association. A few years ago she donated a piano, so that talented children might have an opportunity to practice.

There are difficult problems, investments in time and money, which at first seem to yield but poor results. One of these problems was Josephine. She had worked on a plantation in Mississippi and lived in a two-room shanty with her aged parents. It was the hope of earning money to make life easier for her mother that had brought the girl to Cleveland. The Traveler's Aid[12] had sent her to us—penniless, ignorant, and untrained. Eager to work but utterly uninformed of the requirements necessary for local employment, she was placed under the supervision of our matron, who instructed her in practical home making.

To such a marked degree did Josephine demonstrate her willingness to work, that when, very shortly, a request for a maid came to us, I recommended our newest charge. I informed the employer that Josephine was definitely raw material, and suggested that she be accepted on trial; she was subsequently employed.

After several months, Josephine improved greatly and won the approval of her employer. Visiting us on her "day off," she asked to see me.

"Missus Huntah," she began, "ah laks Missus Greene. Ah does her wuk, an' she say ah'se good. Now, Missus Huntah, yuh done promise' dat whan ah learns mah wuk, yuh is gwine git mah wages raise'. Wal, ah done learn Missus Greene's wuk. Ah knows whan ah knows a thing ah knows it. Ah laks Missus Greene, but ah'se got to git mo' pay to he'p mah ol' mamma. Ah knows, Missus Huntah, yuh is gwine do what you done say."

In Josephine's eyes I saw the childlike trust which challenged the Phillis Wheatley to do its utmost for her. A brief telephone visit with Mrs. Greene assured me that Josephine would receive consideration commensurate with her improvement.

There was Lila, a mulatto, who felt she was called to preach the gospel. The fact that she had not finished high school was no bar to her ambitions to enter the pulpit. Even though I believed the girl sincere, I could not encourage her ambition. She needed a job, I maintained, and I succeeded in placing her in service. As Lila grew more and more sanctimonious, Phillis Wheatley's Bible Class failed to offer her the religious satisfaction she craved. She delighted in loud praise, and our classes did not provide an atmosphere for such outbursts. She invested in a large Bible, without which she was never seen.

Finally, she gave up the job I had secured for her, announced herself a "sanctified evangelist," and was off on a tour to preach. This venture proved unsuccessful; and Lila is now living a successful life working as a domestic, and supporting the church of her choice.

The spirit of the missionary is inborn in the lowly Negro woman. In religious devotion she finds solace for her troubled heart. For the college woman, social service furnishes an opportunity. Members of the humble classes must find satisfaction in leadership in fraternal organizations, in the mission field, in the care of the sick, and in the work of the church. So while we may deplore the misguided zeal of Lila, we can understand and sympathize with it.

Belzona had the intelligence of a child of eight, together with an aversion to labor and a strong vanity bred of the belief that she was born of the "upper stratum." Thus, she was difficult to deal with. When we occupied our new building, I gave Belzona an elevator job. Her repeated tardiness in the morning and constant requests for time off to attend funerals made me decide to give her an indefinite vacation. This dismissal, I felt, might bring Belzona to her senses and make her realize that food and shelter had to be earned.

Her only sister died, leaving no insurance or any means of procuring a decent burial. To the proud spirit of Belzona, this was an unbearable situation. While the undertaker held her sister's body, she went about among friends and neighbors trying to take up a subscription. Failing in this, she asked me, in a most humble and repentant spirit, to grant security to the undertaker. She would take a job and work faithfully until she had repaid every penny. I yielded to her pleading, saved Belzona from humiliation and her sister from a pauper's grave, and attended the funeral as well.

Shortly Belzona forgot her grief and obligations to the Phillis Wheatley

Chapter XII

and to me, and left the home. Such failures as this do not make us cynical; we are saddened by thoughts of the remorse that the poor girl must some day make for her betrayal of trust. Fortunately, such betrayals do not often occur. Patience, faith, and charity bear good fruit, even in unpromising soil.

When Ella, a nineteen year old girl from Alabama, was presented to me by her older sister, I was reluctant to admit her. Especially since the depression, the problem of finding jobs for legal residents of the city had been difficult. But Ella's sister agreed to pay her board, and the girl was enrolled in our training school.

On the third day of her attendance in class, the teacher requested that the new student be dropped because of her inability to grasp the simplest instructions. Ella was honest, neat, clean; but her mental processes were so slow that she was a hindrance to the other students.

My sympathy for retarded[13] girls has always been keen; and I suggested that the teacher give the girl private lessons in bed-making, cooking, and table service. In the evenings, Ella was assigned to my home, where I gave her personal attention. At first this experience with the girl was far from encouraging. Directed to set the table, Ella's response was a cheerful "O. K." And my suggestion that the proper reply was, "Yes, Miss Hunter," brought forth an equally cheerful, "Sho." I began to wonder if the teacher were not right in her judgment that the girl was impossible. "Please, Ella," I expostulated, "listen and remember what I have said to you." But when one evening the pupil said calmly and courteously, "You must give me time; I'll learn," I knew that the seed had not fallen upon barren ground.[14]

At the end of four and a half months, Ella had successfully completed the homemaker's course and secured a part time job, thus earning money enough to attend night school. She studied cosmetology, secured a state license, and is now a successful operator in a thriving shop.

Quiet in manner, tender in her dealings with others, and ever ready to serve was Helen, another member of our first group of Girl Reserves. For eight years I watched her through elementary and high school, observing her splendid qualities. When she was graduated from high school, we made it possible for her to attend college. For two years she made a good record.

Then a young man engaged her attentions and affections. Helen's interest in her studies lagged to such a degree that she failed in her courses. Finally, her marriage to the young man saw the end of her activities in the Phillis Wheatley. I thought her one of my disappointments.

Ten years later, when I was visiting the Josephine Kohler Pre-School[15] one night, I saw Helen and her husband taking an active part in the work of our Junior Mothers' Club.[16] Helen was not, after all, one of my disappointments. She and her husband had established a home and were useful members of the community. The arrow of good intentions I had shot into the air had found a better mark than that at which I had aimed. In rashly assuming that a college education was the highest achievement for Helen, I had erred. She had a right to find fulfillment in her own way.

Much has been said about the tragedy of waste in our country—the destruction of forests, the impoverishment of the soil, the failure to utilize the sources of power in our great streams. Recently, we have recognized that there is a greater tragedy in the waste of human potentialities. There is a great force in the bodies, minds, and hearts of the Negro citizens of this country. Too long this energy has been overlooked or treated with contempt by American society, until in our large cities it has become in many respects a force for evil, breeding disease and crime that has united itself to other evil forces and become a menace to civic life. In this situation the Negro church and the social agencies are the colored citizens' inspiration.

It is the special mission of the Phillis Wheatley Association to discover, protect, cherish, and perpetuate the beauty and power of Negro womanhood.

Thus protected and developed, it will become a regenerating force in American homes; and out of these homes will come an influence of Godliness and devotion to the community in which we live. United to those other longer established forces of the more privileged Negroes, it may become a power that will destroy evil and create that health of body and soul which will establish the Kingdom of God in our municipal life.

It is the "Promised Land" for which we must "work together, children."[17]

CHAPTER XIII

Training for Homemaking and Domestic Service

The story of building a material home, thrilling though it may be, is not the real story of the Phillis Wheatley; nor has the generosity of the people expended itself merely to satisfy civic pride. In all our undertakings of twenty-nine years, we have kept fixed in our hearts the fundamental purposes written in the constitution of the Phillis Wheatley Association:

> To maintain a home with wholesome surroundings, to afford Negro girls and women an opportunity for fuller development, to promote growth in Christian character and service through physical, social, mental, and spiritual training, to create a social understanding which operates unceasingly for the extension of the Kingdom of God.

As a means of carrying out these purposes, a diversity of activities has grown up—each as the need appeared, and as our income would permit. Each new activity has contributed to the abundant life which, in the spirit of the Master, we desire for all girls. Our two most important objectives are the fundamental reason for our existence—"to maintain a home with wholesome surroundings," and, second, to give training for homemaking.

A brief history of the Sarah C. Hills Training School and the Ella Ford Finishing House[1] will explain the nature and purpose of the instruction in homemaking which the Phillis Wheatley offers.

My beliefs are based upon my personal experience in the field of domestic service, plus observation of conditions, and my study of the industrial and social history of the Negro woman. Fundamentally, I subscribe to the first principle of our American democracy—equality of opportunity to all citizens, black and white. The Negro who is fitted by nature to be an executive should be given the training to develop his talents, and an opportunity to serve his country in an executive position; the Negro who has mechanical ability should have a technical education and an opportunity to earn his living as an artisan or an engineer. The Negro woman who has outstanding musical talent should be able to cultivate her gift and use it for the joy of mankind; she who has intellectual interest and a desire to share her intellectual life with young people should be trained in normal schools,[2] colleges, and library schools,[3] and encouraged to secure a position in our public school systems or libraries. To every man and every woman—black or white—according to his capacity to receive. All attempts to develop a potentiality that does not exist will be futile, and will simply add to the number of square pegs in round holes.

It is necessary to consider two terms—natural capacity, and training to develop that capacity. Though we may believe that men are equal before God, and, theoretically at least, before the law—there are individual differences in mind and body which we must accept as permanent. The girl who has no ear for music and cannot carry a tune cannot become a concert singer. She who has little mental aptitude cannot be a stenographer or a teacher. Training must be adapted to the mental and physical endowment of the individual. In apostolic times, St. Paul recognized these individual differences when he reminded the Corinthians that "there are diversities of ministries," and "that though one and the same Spirit worketh all these things, He divideth to everyone according as He will."[4]

Considering the second term—"training to develop the capacity," we shall have to face conditions as they exist, at the same time using our energy and intelligence to improve those conditions. There is no doubt that Negro children are not receiving education equal in amount or excellence to that given children of the white race. This disparity is most marked in Southern schools where the per capita expenditure for white children is almost three times that of the expenditure for the Negroes.

Even in the schools of the North, racial discrimination operates. In Cleveland, for instance, two continuation schools[5] are conducted—one for white girls and one for Negro girls. The Jane Addams School[6] with ninety-nine per cent of its pupils white girls, produces excellent results, because of its high grade equipment and highly trained teachers. Longwood School,[7] because it lacks adequate equipment, has become a mere makeshift provision for colored girls whose mentality and economic difficulties have prevented them from continuing their academic training in regular classes. This discrimination continues in the trade schools for boys; and, unfair and unjust as it is, exists in Cleveland under the hands of the Board of Education. These inequalities of opportunity we must strive to remove; but while they exist, we must make some adjustment to them.

Let us consider the third term of our social problem—opportunity for the Negro boy or girl to find a place in the social and industrial world. Here again we are opposed by racial prejudice, which operates to exclude young boys and girls of the Negro race from positions for which natural ability and training have fitted them. In too many factories there are foremen who permit mechanics to cripple service by keeping machinery out of repair, who refuse to give instruction to Negroes in the operation of certain machinery, and who trump up charges of inefficiency to make possible frequent dismissals and thus increase the turnover of employed Negroes. It is an unwritten law of all garages where white mechanics are employed that Negro workers, even those who have diplomas from technical high schools, shall be excluded from repair jobs and kept busy at all the dirty, disagreeable, and menial tasks which the white workmen scorn.

To these discriminations and injustices we must offer opposition that is intelligent and persistent; but, as long as these conditions last, we must provide in some way for the employment of those who are denied entrance to trade schools, industry, business, and the professions.

To recapitulate, I believe that we must find a place in the world for those Negroes whom poor endowment, inadequate training, and racial prejudice bar from certain occupations. Let us not accept injustice; but while we are trying to remove unfair conditions, let us ameliorate as far as possible the conditions of those who are its victims.

Upon these considerations in 1931 a training school for more thorough homemakers was established at the Phillis Wheatley Association. This school grew out of "The Unemployment Sewing Circle,"[8] organized by Mrs. Alexander H. McGaffin[9] and Mrs. T. McC. Black,[10] members of the Church of the Covenant,[11] to assist women and girls of the neighborhood who were out of jobs. These women were given a bowl of soup; they were instructed in the making-over of old garments; and as they worked, they sang. It was a way of keeping their hands and minds occupied—of building up their morale with a little warm food, pleasant society, and friendly advice.

On visiting our employment office to chat with them one day, I was struck with their unkempt and untidy appearance and their air of helplessness. I wondered whether they were able to do the work of their own households. Calling the home economics instructor to my office, I asked her to give the girls some simple tests. Out of a group of eighteen it was found that not one could do even plain cooking, and only one could set a table. Here was a real need at Phillis Wheatley's door. We must do something to improve these incompetent girls whose poverty made it necessary for them to leave school and find a job, but who were incapable of performing the simple tasks of household work, much less of earning a livelihood.

We opened a school for homemakers with a group of nine girls from sixteen to eighteen years of age, daughters of some of the poorest and most wretched families. In this group and in later classes we found that many of the girls were untidy and neglected in every human respect. Even though reared in a city, some of them had never used a bath tub; and most of them knew nothing of personal sanitation and hygiene. Our first duty then was to give to each class an elementary course in personal regimen, stressing especially the importance of the use of soap and water and clean linen. The girls were given uniforms of green Indian Head,[12] attractively made and so becoming that they were an inspiration and a great aid in restoring self-respect. The students were quite reluctant to put them aside for their own garments when the class was dismissed for the day.

By this approach, we restored in part the morale of these girls and engaged their interest. Then we gave attention to improving their manners and to laying a foundation of right attitudes toward work in their own homes and those of their employers. Once Mrs. D. W. Frackelton, a former President of the Association, remarked to me that she believed that right attitude toward work was the most important element in the training of the homemaker. She felt that no degree of skill which the girl may acquire can take the place of a faith in the importance of her work and an earnest desire to make her contribution to the happiness of the family she serves, whether it be her own or that of her employer. We stressed this fundamental theory throughout the course. Mrs. Frackelton, who was greatly interested in these girls, often visited our training school, until a well organized committee relieved her of the supervision.

In answer to the criticism that our undertaking is degrading to the Negro girl, because it deprives her of ambition to reach a higher economic status, I would call attention to these considerations:

1. The course is not intended for those girls whose intellectual capacity or previous training plainly indicates that they are better fitted for other kinds of work. Every effort is made to discover latent ability in other fields, to direct it, and to find some way of getting training to develop it.

2. Our aim is to give Negro girls an opportunity for fuller development. We shall continue to work for this in the political, social, and economic life of Cleveland. We do not seek to fit the Negro girls to the mold of the Phillis Wheatley; rather, we use the Phillis Wheatley Association as an instrument for her social and moral redemption.

3. In the school our primary purpose is to equip girls for homemaking, and, incidentally, use the training to solve their economic problems. This, when it includes the rearing of children, is the finest contribution that most women can make to the sum of human happiness. And in studying home management and applying our solution to the lives of girls who manifestly need it, we are simply

following the example of the best schools and colleges of the United States. If in the period before her marriage and the conduct of her own household the young colored woman can use her ability as a means of livelihood, she can, if properly trained, do so with profit to herself and those whom she serves. Let us not forget that race prejudice still operates to exclude many a capable Negro girl from positions in offices, department stores, etc. We intend to assist these young women to earn their living with efficiency and dignity, wherever there is opportunity to place them in positions of trust.

This is the story of our modest beginning, and a statement of our purposes. At first we gave only a six weeks' course. With the leadership of the new committee, it was soon felt necessary to lengthen it to nine weeks, then to four and a half months. Now we are convinced that a six months' course is advisable to improve our standards and extend our usefulness.

In September, 1937, the Board of Trustees was so impressed by our experiment that they purchased an old house adjoining our building, remodeling and transforming it into a practice cottage, thus enabling the girls to get the spirit of family life, rather than that of an institution. Here we have four bedrooms attractively furnished; a spotlessly white bathroom with curtains of cross-barred red and white; a cozy, homelike living room and reception hall; a dining room equipped with a medium supply of china, linen and silver; an up-to-date kitchen with U-shaped working units, thermostatically controlled range, and other modern equipment; all approximating the kind of home in which the girl may be employed, and giving a good model for the arrangement and furnishings of her own home.

Here she learns how to take prideful care of walls painted or papered; of painted and varnished woodwork; to clean waxed and painted floors, as well as those covered with linoleum, rugs, or carpets; to keep in good condition upholstered and highly polished furniture, porcelain, and metals; and to use all electrical equipment. This training is in addition to lessons in planning, cooking, and serving meals, and instruction in the most scientific methods of laundry work.

We believe the results, as shown by our records, justify the experiment.

Out of the one hundred-seventy-eight girls admitted from 1931 to 1938, one hundred and two completed the full course, received certificates, and secured immediate employment. Seven were married and are managing their own homes. Two entered college. Ten left the city; five were in poor health; twenty-one were dismissed or left the training school because of inability to adapt themselves; twenty-two did not qualify for certificates. Nine were in training at the time this study was made. We must continue at all costs this much needed work, especially since most public schools have failed our girls in many well known Negro districts. I cite these facts with the hope that the public may realize how few of our girls are receiving the type of training they need.

Observation of the children who come after school hours to take part in the activities of the Phillis Wheatley has convinced me that it is futile to force upon many of them an academic training, when they are best adapted to some form of industrial training. Sewing, cooking, and dramatics are far more attractive to some children than the Latin, algebra, and history which they study at school. A book education is the cheapest; but, in terms of its results for citizenship, it is for many boys and girls the most inefficient. To make our children worthy members of their community, we must develop character in them through the art of doing.

The responsibility for this undertaking, to be sure, lies with educators and the public school system. For a quarter of a century there has been a gradual getting away from strictly academic courses and a development of vocational training for the industrial-minded child. The Jane Addams School is a fine experiment in vocational training for white girls. Whether the Cleveland Board of Education will continue a policy of depriving Negro children depends upon the leadership of the Negro citizenry. Social agencies such as the Phillis Wheatley, supported by private funds and limited as we are in the number of teachers and equipment, cannot meet in any large degree this need of training young women for homemaking. However, it is our duty to pioneer and experiment in this field, and to compensate in a small way for the neglect of industrial training of Negro girls by public schools.

From our experiment, limited in scope though it is, and from the experience of earlier years in domestic service, I have come to certain conclusions about the problem of domestic service. As I think back over the history of the Negro woman in personal service, I realize a difference between the older and newer traditions. The older, self-made Negro servant eked out meager existence through service in the kitchen or laundry of her employer. Often she divided her strength between two homes. The sacrifice she made in so doing weighed heavily on her heart and is reflected in a high death rate among Negroes, especially among the children.

The Negro servant heated the water for the white man's bath, cooked his meals, washed and ironed his clothes, cleaned his house, got his children off to school, and in the absence of the parents was charged with the serious responsibility of caring for their children. Her wages were poor, and the equipment with which she worked made her labors burdensome. In the last twenty years, improved methods and modern tools have tended to lighten the burdens of the servant, and the meager wage has grown to something nearer compensation that would permit the right sort of living.[13] But the most important factor in successful domestic service is a happy and human relation between the lady of the house and the maid—on the part of the maid, respect and affectionate regard for her employer; on the part of the employer, sympathy and imagination. Perhaps it is not going too far to say that the lady of the house should stand in the relation of a foster mother to the young woman who assists her in the household tasks. Imagination she must have to compare her strength with that of her servant, and assign no task beyond the powers of endurance; foresight to plan the work over a fairly long period of time, and not to regard the housemaid as one whose day she has purchased from sunrise to sunset—or beyond; sympathy and interest in the problems of her young domestic, realizing her loneliness, gaining her confidence, guiding her reading by placing good books within her reach, and providing a place where she may entertain her friends.

This is the ideal state of affairs. When the employer even approximates it, the girl who is fairly well-trained and well-disposed will become interested in the life of the family that she serves, and will be devoted to its happiness.

How far short the modern housekeeper falls of this ideal we see when we note the decrease of the number of servants who live in the homes of their employers. In Cleveland, sixty-five per cent of the servants go home at night. In some cases, of course, the preference is that of the employer, who has no extra room for the maid. Or it is the result of necessity—the maid has obligations in her home which require her to return to it at night. But in too many cases it is an expression of the servant's own dissatisfaction with the living conditions offered her, and a desire to escape for a time a relation which is irksome and irritating. This living-out of the servant is a complication of her own economic problem, since in many cases there is no increased allowance for car fare and for room rent.

These deficiencies and defects, due to a lack of mutual regard between employer and employee, the Phillis Wheatley seeks to remove—first, by training the maid in the skillful performance of household tasks and by giving her a respect for the importance of her work; second, through the careful follow-up system of a committee from the Board of Trustees and the Employment Bureau, which notes the progress of graduates of the training school, seeks to adjust differences, and makes tactful suggestions to employer and employee.

With these purposes and methods we hope to increase our usefulness in the years to come. That we may do so, we have set up certain objectives which, with the support and confidence of friends, we hope to achieve.

1. The first of these objectives is an extension of our training course to six months. Such an extension would not only mean more advanced instruction and a longer period of practice, but it would enable the teachers to become more thoroughly acquainted with the dispositions of their pupils and to develop more fully the right attitudes toward work. More thorough and frequent medical examinations of all students entering our training school could also be made.

2. We seek to organize an alumni association of home builders, representing the finest of the young women who have completed our course. Such an organization would inspire the students of the training school and be an effective means of raising the standards of our work.

3. We desire to build a hospitality house where the more advanced and capable students may spend half of the term learning the more difficult techniques of food preparation and table service. This house will provide a residence for the teachers, a place where teas, luncheons, and other social affairs might be held, and serve as a finishing school in the art of homemaking.

This is our vision of greater usefulness for the Sarah C. Hills Training School and the Ella Ford House, which was made possible by a gift of The Cleveland Foundation from The Thomas H. White Trust Fund.[14] We have faith, too, from the accomplishments of the past years.

We believe:

1. That this department of the Phillis Wheatley Association has demonstrated the need of specific training for Negro girls in the art of homemaking; that, as a pioneer, it may point the way for a more adequate education of this sort in our public schools.
2. That it is breaking through the opposition of Negro women to training in domestic arts.
3. That it is one of the strongest ties between the Negro and white races in America.
4. That it has improved conditions in the homes of the Negroes, and has helped them to realize that one of the best ways by which they may raise their social and economic status is to improve the conditions of their own homes. How to continue this worthwhile service to Negro girls is a challenge to all who are concerned about the future of the American home.

CHAPTER XIV

Friends Along the Way

The frontier of my struggle did not lead me into money-raising, for financial assistance was not then and never shall be the cure-all of our problems. Past experience has taught me a different philosophy, for friends have done more to broaden my education and encourage me in self-development than any financial assistance could have done. I have learned that the right kind of friends can be of the greatest help in creating better relations between the races. Their attitude toward the Negro and their understanding of the peculiar social problems which I faced, brought about an interest in my efforts that was city-wide. Through these fine associations, we derived most of our moral support.

The world-wide near famine brought shocking losses to me. The strain of economic and social changes caused many fatalities. These dreadful years left their mark upon my heart, when I realized that the great chain of friends which I had claimed had been weakened by death.

Speaking as I did in the churches throughout the city, county, and state, I was brought into contact with many distinguished leaders who were so touched by the presentation of the work that many of them joined our Association. Mrs. Frank Arter[1] a great Methodist leader of women, became a pillar of strength upon which I depended. It was her help in many ways which opened the hearts of The Methodist Church women to us.

On many occasions Mr. Arter[2] related to me the story of the underground railway, and of his service to help the slaves escape into Ohio and across the border. In recent years, when passing through Harper's Ferry, I noticed the shabby memorial to John Brown;[3] and I was able better to appreciate Mr. Arter's interest in the struggle to free my people during the Civil War.

A young Board member, in speaking of Mrs. Arter, said, "I like to remember her for the beautiful prayers she offered up in the meetings." To me, her prayers were like my Grandma's prayers—so meek and lowly—although Mrs. Arter was a woman of great wealth and social position. In memory of these two great friends, the Trustees named our largest branch the Kingsley-Arter Center.[4]

As the news of training Negro girls spread to the four corners of the city, many large churches invited me to tell my story. In school I had acquired some ability to address audiences, as a member of the dramatic classes; and now I was able to grip and hold the attention of my listeners who, in many cases, urged me to remain after the lecture to answer questions.

The Phillis Wheatley Home was proving a blessing in disguise to Negroes, although few of them saw the need for the work at the time of its establishment. One of my pleasant memories was the visit of our home by Mrs. Solon Severance, a woman of social prestige and strong convictions. She was moved by the reports which she had learned concerning our efforts. I was not surprised when she called, for I had long known of the missionary and philanthropic work her distinguished family was carrying on in the mission fields of China. One evening I attended a stereopticon lecture[5] presented by Mr. Severance at St. John's A. M. E. Church, in which he told of their interest in the underprivileged of the Orient. The knowledge I gained from his lecture enabled me better to understand how easy it was for his wife to find her way to our doors, where she shared Christian love and charity with another underprivileged group.

I guided her through the Home, interpreting to the best of my ability the need for training of Negro girls. In the course of conversation, she remarked, "People like yourself seldom provide for their own comfort. Someone should see to it that at least the comfort of a decent bed is provided for you." After inspecting every nook and corner of the building, she shook my hand and departed. Never once suspecting her motive, I felt strongly that another Angel of Mercy had crossed my path. Within a few days there arrived for me a handwoven, blue and white woolen spread, an art design of Mrs. Severance's own mother. Each year while she lived, I looked forward to her annual visit to our home. Fortunate, indeed, it was for us that her noble daughter, Mrs. Benjamin L. Milliken,[6] took over her mother's interest in the Phillis Wheatley.

At one of our Sunday Vesper Services, Mr. Raymond Clapp[7] of the Welfare Federation delivered the address and remained to visit awhile with me. Among the many things he said was, "We do not want to see you spend your time worrying about finances. If you can duplicate yourself in leadership here at the Phillis Wheatley Association, I believe that the Welfare Federation will see to it that the money is provided to carry on this work." This challenge, coming from one of the country's foremost welfare leaders, has been a guiding force in selecting young women to serve in our institution. With the continued interest and support of the Community Fund and the Welfare Federation of Cleveland,[8] the Phillis Wheatley Association has been able to carry on its work.

HOW I WAS TAUGHT SOCIAL SERVICE

In 1918 an incident occurred that brings to me again the fine attitude of Mr. Clapp. I was asked by the Welfare Federation to appear for the first time before its committee. Around the table were seated several ladies, none of whom I knew; I assumed that they were executives who were waiting to be heard, as I was. One lady in particular asked many questions, smiled, and chatted with me. She seemed to know more about social work than I; and all the time I was learning and gaining new ideas from the questions asked by her and others. Somehow, I kept wondering when they were going to call me before the Committee. Suddenly everyone began to smile, and I smiled, too. Then Mr. Clapp arose and kindly said to me, "That is all." I was rather stunned, disappointed, and puzzled to think I had not been permitted even to present our work to the Committee. I was greatly bewildered, as I left that building, and quite undecided as to what could have happened that I had not been given a hearing.

Lo and behold, the next day I heard that a great philanthropist, the lady who had asked most of the questions and who had seemed so interested in my story, had given her blessing to the Phillis Wheatley. Later, by chance, I met this splendid woman and remembered that it was she who so tactfully drew from me all that she wanted to know about my work, without my realizing that I was before the Welfare Federation Committee. This kind friend and her late husband have remained supporters of our work. In after years, other members of the Committee were not so sympathetic.

In one of our most severe winters the Home did not have sufficient bed covering for the girls. An open house party brought many friends to inspect the building. The walls of the halls were placarded with printed rhymes. On this particular occasion we were honored with the presence of Mrs. Benjamin L. Milliken. Being a close observer, she read one of the rhymes which said:

The winter winds blow, the ground is covered with snow;
We to bed are afraid to go, because the covering is so low.

Mrs. Milliken had not been gone from the home a few hours before a truck, laden with quilted comforters, came rolling up to our door. What a shouting there was among the girls who expressed their true gratitude for this unselfish friend! Like her mother, Mrs. Solon Severance, Mrs. Milliken desired that no one, however humble, should suffer.

There were times when the coal bin was empty; and another of our friends, Mr. M. A. Bradley,[9] saw to it for many winters that coal was supplied. One Sunday morning after a meeting in the Unitarian Church,[10] where I presented the story of our struggle, Mrs. Bradley[11] quietly slipped a very comforting note into my hands. This expression of sympathy has remained with me.

By chance I met the Honorable Maurice Maschke,[12] who had befriended my people in their political rights for a quarter of a century. He arranged for me to meet Mrs. Maschke,[13] who cordially received me and continued her interest in my race. In memory of her husband, after his death, Mrs. Maschke furnished a room in the Sarah C. Hills Training School.

The "come and see us" program so imbued Mrs. Josephine B. Kohler[14] that she made possible the enlargement of our pre-school service. With the spirit that the least of His little ones should not be denied, she assisted us in our efforts to standardize this work for Negro babies. Food, medical service, and equipment are provided by her for the underprivileged babies of our community. Because of the application of this professional service, we have assurance that the future will produce better and more useful citizens.

When we are in distress and needs pile high, it is a natural inclination to turn to friends who will give assistance. One noble lady, who later became a member of the United States Congress, wrote:

My dear Miss Hunter:
Your letter regarding Phillis Wheatley needs has lain all too long, unanswered; but being my own secretary makes replies unavoidable.

As I re-read it, I cannot help thinking once more that the problems of one race are very much like the problems of another! Of course, there are gradations in both; but is it not so that living standards, reducing mortality and unmarried mothers are common to both? Oh, of course, I know that there is perhaps a more acute situation for your people than for the greater part of mine; yet, I sometimes wonder. It seems as if all of us need to manage to see that humanity lifts itself a little faster from the mire!

I wish I might make a truly substantial contribution, but the inclosed [sic] check for fifty dollars is all I dare add to my already desperately heavy budget. But I hope it will carry to you my interested good wishes for the fine work you and those working with you at Phillis Wheatley are doing.

Very cordially yours,

Signed—FRANCES P. BOLTON[15]
(Mrs. Chester C.)

Before I learned to read, my mother taught me from a Sunday School card a little verse:

Lord, make my life a little light within this world to grow,
A light that will burn bright wherever I may go.[16]

I did not get the full significance of these words until I learned to know Miss Bertha L. Bailey,[17] an Oberlin College[18] woman whose life has been a shining light to Negro girls.

Another great honor which I cherish is my acquaintance with Mrs. F. W. Stecher,[19] in whose home I visited many times. She was an interesting personality, and had a way of making the humblest person feel at ease in her presence. She was sympathetic in wanting to see lifted the mortgage notes on our Home, so that my time could be utilized in training useful citizens. She so thoroughly shared my philosophy of life, that I never left her presence without feeling spiritually rewarded. She was known and loved by many friends for her quiet, yet forceful influence for good.

In an effort to arouse the folk to the needs of better sanitation and better health, I undertook to assist in the task of getting a bond issue passed to increase hospital facilities which, in a measure, would serve the district largely inhabited by Negroes. In this, I found the leaders of my race unprepared to accept the challenge.

The following letter came to me, as a result of my efforts:

My dear Miss Hunter:

In this morning's paper I noticed an item which stated that you had participated in a public debate advancing the passage of the hospital bonds. Knowing the situation as I do, I want to congratulate you on the position you are taking in this matter. It requires courage for one in your position to do it. I just wanted to tell you that I recognize that fact and wanted to give you a word of encouragement.

Very truly yours,
Signed—J. E. Cutler,[20] Dean,
School of Applied Sciences
Western Reserve University
Cleveland, Ohio

Dr. Cutler's recognition of my service was sufficient encouragement for me to continue my effort to better conditions. The hospital would have served a mixed clientele, and also have given professional training to Negro physicians and nurses on an equal basis with that given to the whites.

The values of these efforts spread themselves far beyond the boundaries of Ohio. A letter, typical of many I received, follows:

Greenville, S. C.

Dear Madam:

I take pleasure in enclosing you herein a copy of the Constitution and By-laws and a statement of the purpose and some other information concerning the Phillis Wheatley Association of Greenville,[21] thinking that possibly this literature would be of interest to you.

You will notice that the Constitution and By-laws, to a considerable extent, are modeled on those of the Phillis Wheatley Association of Cleveland.

We had one of your booklets which has been a great help and inspiration to us. Your work is more on the lines of what we are going to attempt here than any other work for Negroes with which we are familiar. Of course, each place has its own peculiarities and needs.

We want to express to you our sense of obligation for the inspiration and help received from your institution, and to wish you much success in your future work.

Faithfully yours,

Thomas F. Parker,[22]
President of the Board

And so it is joy to see the program—humble as it is in Cleveland—of interracial service, finding its way into the hearts of both white and Negro citizens in many deserving communities.

CHAPTER XV

———◆———

Harvest of the Years

As the work of the Association expanded, I saw the need for further improvement in my own education. This urge for further self-improvement suggested itself from my association with members of the Boards of Trustees in the administrative work of the institution.

The Central High School, located within two blocks of our first home, kept beckoning me to come within its portal. Busily engaged as I was, trying to meet the needs of bewildered young women, I nevertheless, entered the evening classes of Central High School, and pursued courses in English under the fascinating influence of Mrs. Viola Smith Buell[1] one of Cleveland's best known English scholars. Once Mrs. Buell visited our Association; and as she was leaving the building, remarked, "My child, you have something far greater in your work here than you can now see. God bless you in your efforts." These kindly words of wisdom from my teacher have remained with me since we parted at the gate.

In the summer of 1914 Miss Florence Simms,[2] Field Secretary of the Young Women's Christian Association, discovered me while sharing in the discussions at the Girls' Industrial Conference,[3] held at Summerland Beach, Ohio. She was impressed, I learned, by my deportment and activity. It was her suggestion that I be given additional training. Mrs. W. P. Champney, Sr.,[4] then President of the local Young Women's Christian Association, was instrumental in my availing myself of the opportunity to study with the

National Board of Young Women's Christian Association in New York City. The course in Religious Pedagogy definitely enlarged my vision and helped to shape and crystallize my thinking for the work I am doing today.

When the activities of our Association were better organized and additions were made to the staff, my duties as executive secretary were so planned that I was able to take extension courses in social planning, political history, psychology, and other subjects offered at Western Reserve University. These opportunities for self-improvement prepared me for four years' study at Baldwin-Wallace Law School,[5] where I was graduated in 1925 with the degree of LL.B. In that same year I successfully passed the Ohio Bar. One of my cherished memories is that of being admitted to the Bar by Judge Florence E. Allen,[6] while she was a member of the Supreme Court of Ohio.

Two honors in recognition of civic service have come to me from institutions of learning conducted by Negroes—honors which served to spur me on to greater activity. The first came when the faculty of Wilberforce University[7] conferred upon me the degree of Master of Arts. The second followed a visit to our institution by Dr. Frederick D. Patterson,[8] President of Tuskegee Institute, who declared the interracial co-operation manifested in the development of the social and vocational program conducted at the Phillis Wheatley Association to be the embodiment and essence of the industrial philosophy maintained by Dr. Booker T. Washington. For this achievement, Tuskegee Institute in 1938 conferred upon me the honorary degree of Master of Science.

In furthering my education, I learned much by observing the smooth and systematic operation of the women's groups in the churches. Their year-round program planning made most churches a beehive of activities. One of my moments of lasting inspiration came by an invitation from Mrs. Ralph L. Fuller[9] to speak to the women of the Willoughby Methodist Church[10] in her palatial home. From such gatherings I learned to plan adult programs, which served to hold the interest of hundreds of women in our institution.

In the field of social service, there was much to gain by association as a member of the American Association of Social Workers,[11] and as a member of the National Conference of Social Work[12]—attending conferences of these two organizations, reading the best literature, and following the activities of social leaders through the "Survey"[13] and other interesting magazines on social work.

Having once attended Central High School, I naturally became interested in its future. I knew the history of the school, and had often heard it referred to as the pride of the Western Reserve, numbering as it did among its graduates some of the greatest men and women of the nation. I have watched the student body grow; and, on the other hand, have observed the deteriorating condition of its physical structure. At one time Central High School was the finest building in the city, but in later years the school became the most unpopular unit in the entire school system. Many parents, in order to avoid sending their children to this school, moved out of the community or devised ways to secure transfers so their children might attend high schools in other districts. Such deplorable conditions challenged my community pride, and prodded me into doing something to remedy the situation. In 1933, I invited other interested citizens and formed an interracial committee to study the physical and environmental needs of Central High School. As a result of this study over a period of some two years, recommendations affecting the school were submitted to the Cleveland Board of Education.

Today there stands a new Central High School building, erected at a cost of one and a quarter million dollars, beautiful in design, modern in equipment, and inspirational to behold.

Another civic satisfaction to me was that of sharing largely in the election of the first colored woman[14] to membership on the Cleveland Board of Education. The increasing participation of my people in the civic and political life of Cleveland was a challenge for my own larger participation. I availed myself of every opportunity to co-operate in promoting the matters affecting the welfare of individuals and groups whose ambitions would bring greater respect for the entire race.

For twenty years, delinquent Negro girls, incarcerated in the Ohio State School at Delaware, [15] have suffered under horrible living conditions and from the lack of proper training to fit them for better citizenship, when they return to their communities. In 1936 the Ohio Federation of Colored Women's Clubs[16] authorized a committee to investigate conditions affecting Negro girls at Delaware, and named me as chairman. Facts were established by the committee and reported to the Governor of Ohio. Some relief was obtained in 1937, when one additional cottage was provided. However, this proved insufficient, and the committee made further representation to the state authorities. In 1940 changes were made, thereby alleviating in part the conditions which were brought to light in the study. The plans are that in the future, Negro girls so incarcerated will share the educational and recreational advantages there provided by the State of Ohio.

More and more the results of past efforts exhibit themselves. Recently a Negro doctor, Charles H. Garvin,[17] was appointed to membership on the Cleveland Library Board, and in 1940 was elected President of that Board. For years I have had the honor of serving on various committees appointed by the Mayors of Cleveland. It was my purpose to use these opportunities for service to my city and to my race. In the years ahead I trust that the harvest of my efforts will be better-trained leadership, which will insure a larger life for others yet to come.

CHAPTER XVI

---•◆•---

Looking Ahead

Thirty-four beautiful, fragrant roses! It was a thoughtful to-
ken coming from my Board of Trustees commemorating the
thirty-four years of the life I had spent in Cleveland. To me it
was a symbol of the loyalty and love of my coworkers, which illuminates
"looking ahead."

I believe Providence sent me here that tenth day of May in the year
1905; and a gracious Heaven enabled me to win my way against the temptations that beset the Negro girl, that I might save others by becoming their
champion and counsellor.

The work of the Phillis Wheatley must go on; and for its continuance,
two things are necessary—trained leadership and an endowment which
will make it independent of the fluctuations of public favor and periods of
economic depression.

TWO BROTHERS POINT THE WAY

My great dream of later years has been to lay the foundation for the
perpetuation of the work of the Phillis Wheatley Association. Having
kindled the flame of service and built a workshop, my next hope was to
provide assurance for its continuance. When the wills of Mr. Henry C.
Richman and Mr. Charles L. Richman[1] disclosed the fact that the Phillis

Wheatley Home was a beneficiary, there was unfolded before me a larger vision of what part friends like these two would play in bringing into realization my dream—an adequately endowed Phillis Wheatley Association. The gifts of these gentlemen are the first sproutings of the seeds of service sown with "A Nickel and a Prayer" in the hearts of the people for the work with Negro girls.

The Fiscal Board of Trustees,[2] in visualizing the future of our work, created an endowment fund with the thirty shares of stock in the Richman Brothers Company[3] and the $2,000[4] provided in the wills of these benefactors. Everlasting will be the gratitude of Negroes for the deep human sympathy received from friends who have helped along the way.

While this work has been very specific and definite, its influence has extended far into the economic and religious life of the Negro race. As secretary of the organization, I have studied many of the problems of the Negro population in great urban centers, and this study has led me to some very definite conclusions. Love of my people, born of the days when I picked cotton with them on plantations in South Carolina, has given me a fervent hope and desire for their permanent progress.

THE NEGRO AND INDUSTRY

The stake by which the Negro tied himself to earth in the golden days of agricultural independence weakened when he migrated to industrial centers. His leaving the field of agriculture marked the beginning of a serious setback to his economic progress. Today, he is wedged between two conflicting forces—a lack of urge to return to the agricultural centers, and unwillingness to remain under the grindstone of continual unemployment. It is my belief that had the Negro remained in agricultural endeavors, he would have adapted himself to changing conditions and continued to be one of America's greatest assets. We are groping around in ignorance of the great potentialities of undeveloped resources which stare us squarely in the face, while the masses of our people accept state and federal dole.

To ponder the question of who may be responsible for the Negro's leaving the South is useless. He is in the North, two million strong. The niche into which he fitted himself is no longer open.

In America we have two different philosophies of social justice with but one standard of living. The white man's philosophy holds that the Negro needs only a third of the income required by the average white man. This takes no account of the fact that the black laborer has the same living necessities as does the white laborer. A white chauffeur will receive one hundred and twenty-five dollars, while the black chauffeur receives sixty-five dollars a month. Throughout industrial and other pursuits this disparity prevails. Despite this inequality of income, the Negro must pay the same for clothing, food, and often more for shelter and insurance. Such a condition indicates a blindness to the human rights of colored citizens.

Labor unions have measurably succeeded in establishing wage levels in the major industries; but these benefits have been available only in a limited sense to the colored man. He has had to overcome barrier after barrier; some erected for selfish motives, and others born of the desire to prohibit him from entering a particular industry under any circumstances. White labor, in its mad rush to protect itself, seems to have forgotten that its black fellow laborer, if left out of consideration, proves a menace to any permanent adjustment of its struggles with capital.

In this situation is to be found a challenge to our leadership. Leaders must help the Negro laborer to hold such opportunities as he now has, and to discover new fields of service. The way to attract interest is to do something worth while, to create through joint efforts a demand for our commodities. The National Housewives'[5] League[6] is a notable example born of a grave necessity to save the Negro's pride, and to prevent many from dire want in the midst of the deepest depression.

The genius of Fannie B. Peck[7] disclosed that the Negro housewife spends 80 per cent of the earnings of the family, and that a large percentage of these earnings is spent with merchants who do not and will not employ Negroes. It did not seem wise to Mrs. Peck to spend her time in trying to abolish this unfair and unjust American policy, but she set herself to the task to make a way to help the Negro find employment.

Negro women were called together. They organized a National Housewives' League, with headquarters in Detroit, Michigan. Women there were convinced of the need for such an organization. It seemed an excellent plan to pool the interests and buying power of the race. The idea spread into the Eastern and Midwestern States where other groups were organized. The slogan, "Do not buy where you cannot work," was adopted.

The Rev. Mr. Peck[8] organized the men into trade associations. Many of the organizations adopted the name "Booker T. Washington Trade Association," while others are known as the "Progressive Negro Business League."

From these efforts have come to the race additional shoe and grocery stores, laundries, furriers, and several credit loan associations. The refusal of store managers to employ Negroes as clerks, and the wholesale discharge of porters and maids, of necessity awakened the best in the leadership of the Reverend and Mrs. Peck. They realize that the idea has not only provided jobs and re-awakened in the Negro a sense of self-respect; but the best thing that has come out of the movement has been the training of young men and women for useful citizenship.

George Carver,[9] a Negro scientist, has demonstrated that the world will make a beaten path to your door, if you have what it wants. Once we place ourselves in the position of producers, we will not only draw white capital, but will find less racial prejudice. Many people, especially of my race, may never again be self-supporting or enjoy good health, unable as they are to find steady employment.

At present we are suffering from social and economic paralysis. For example: Negro insurance companies have approximately $15,000,000 of insurance in force and employ 8,000 Negroes. One large life insurance company has in the neighborhood of $300,000,000 of insurance from Negroes and employs no Negroes. This is one aspect of the causes which are threatening our economic future and especially the future of Negro youth.

In the field of social welfare for the Negro, two approaches exist. One places administrative leadership in the hands of white people, and the other gives the leadership to Negroes. Both approaches provide an opportunity for interracial co-operation.

The most important difference to be noted between the two methods is in the salary provided for Negro officials and that provided for white administrators. In one city the salary available for a white director of an agency for Negroes is approximately 25 per cent higher than that paid the Negro executive of an agency doing the same kind of work and serving an equal number of persons.

LEADERSHIP

The ideal of Negro leaders in this changing social order must be an unswerving desire to inculcate in their race self-esteem, created of the inner conviction which intelligence dictates.

The Negro in northern states has remained indifferent too long to the call for intergroup action. He has contended for mixing of the racial groups. He has failed to visualize the opportunities within his race and reach. The Biblical injunction that "where there is no vision the people perish"[10] applies to many of our leaders. As a race we can no longer depend upon the other race for our economic freedom. We may as well acknowledge that the white man is too busy with his own endeavors to be interested in the Negro. In most cases his interest does not extend much beyond that of a charitable impulse. Few are concerned with the economic improvement of the Negro. Thus the charity which he gives, at the same time in which he withholds economic opportunity, reduces the Negro's status almost to that of servitude.

Too often, alas, has the Negro been misled by leaders of his own race. There are those false prophets who would persuade us that some day the

Negro will be absorbed by the white race. What the Negro really desires is a change of industrial and economic status so that he may enjoy the privileges and culture that other men possess. By thorough and complete miscegenation we should lose our richest heritage. The Negro must continue to make his distinct contribution to the world—as a Negro.

EDUCATION THE WAY OF ESCAPE

The foundation stone on which to build strong American citizens—whether the race be black or white—in my judgment, must be a thoroughgoing education, adapted to the peculiar needs of the individual. The masses of the Negro youth are today being trained without directed purpose. I observe them as they struggle through the elementary schools, junior and senior high schools, and, finally, through the colleges of our country. Most of them return to their communities unfitted for the work the modern world needs to have done. I have considered over and over again plans for the proper education of the Negro youth in our American democracy. He has been more or less confused in two schools of thought. One idea is that a classical education is the means by which the full salvation of the race will be attained. The other emphasizes the need for vocational training, contending that practical education will enable the Negro to meet the challenge of our highly competitive society.

Across these two ideas of the proper training of Negro youth runs the peculiar American policy of racial segregation. I have found that in many northern communities in which exist the mixed school and the non-mixed faculty little concern is shown for the future of the Negro child. The personal interest so vital to inspirational growth seems wholly lacking. Also in certain northern communities' schools, presumably mixed but whose enrollment is predominantly Negro, show a woeful lessening of the teacher's interest and discipline. Under these circumstances the Negro child completes his public school work without receiving the well-rounded education to which he is entitled. It is this situation that persuades me that Boards of Education in northern States, in their attempt to segregate nationality and racial groups and to wage economy programs upon such groups, themselves would do well to restudy the purpose and meaning of public school education. Where segregation arises out of a natural and normal migration to a community, and when in such community there exists a need for a specialized school because of over-aged and handicapped pupils, there should be provided by the Boards of Education the best experts in practical teacher training for that group. In the grouping of pupils on bases of nationality and race, there exists an opportunity for the development of group and race consciousness. This may prove an advantage, provided it is properly directed.

However, attempts to segregate nationalities and racial groups are generally used to afford opportunity to train cadet teachers and new principals, many of whom have little knowledge of the social and economic background of the students whom they attempt to serve. In the old American way of Negro segregation students are not only handicapped by denial of proper educational facilities but are victims of social and industrial prejudices. In recent years Negro teachers are gradually being inducted into public school systems in northern states, due to migration of Negroes from southern states. As the number of pupils increases, Negro teachers are regimented into a district where buildings are aged and worn, equipment is meager, and liberal education is withheld. Despite the curtailed financial support in schools where pupils are predominantly Negroid and where teachers are properly trained, regardless of race, students develop in a curriculum adapted to their ability and capacity. In my opinion, nationality plays an important part in group education when all things are equal. For instance, the Negro teacher reaches beyond the stereotyped, prescribed system and endeavors to inject into a Negro student that fuller meaning of education which lifts him above mere academic procedure to a richer realization of the needs of his soul. He inspires the child through the intimate and sympathetic relationship growing out of the suffering in which, as fellow Negroes, the teacher and pupil share.

In America the law of the land definitely prohibits discrimination because of race, creed, or religion; therefore, segregation that is based on race or religion should not exist. The Supreme Law of the Universe teaches that all men are created equal; and from this Law America wrote and established a Constitution giving birth to a democracy which has no color barrier when lived and practiced. Negroes in America do not acknowledge segregation, but suffer it only when administrators of the local and national laws, through prejudices, force these evidences of segregation upon them. The best example of forced segregation in public school systems of education is seen in three borderline cities—Baltimore, St. Louis, and Washington. The experiences of these cities, with the dual system where a more or less equitable distribution of teacher remuneration and physical equipment exists, afford an object lesson to those cities which segregate nationalities and racial groups to the exclusion of American principles.

In these cities both the teacher and the pupil receive wide opportunity for initiative and a well-rounded development. In Baltimore, where the separate school system exists, an opportunity for interchange of educational ideas is promoted in the joint city-wide meeting of all principals of white and colored schools once each month—all receiving the same advantages offered by the Board of Education. In the presumably mixed schools of the Midwest Negro teachers rarely have these advantages; nor are they given an equal chance to serve in the grades above the elementary level, even though the upper grades in these schools are crowded with Negro students.

While separate schools are prohibited by statute in Ohio, Cleveland has evaded the law by a system of gerrymandering districts[11] that round up Negro pupils and restrict their attendance to schools in the "black belt."[12] Since 1929 the Cleveland Board of Education, even though for four years it had a Negro member, has succeeded in transferring approximately 85 per cent of the Negro teachers into the Negro district. Let us assume that the school authorities felt justified in following this procedure. Yet it does seem that the resentment which certain Negro citizens feel might have been appeased had the buildings and equipment provided been of the same type and quality as those maintained in other sections of the school district, since segregation is forced upon this particular group.

Schools in which the enrollment is predominantly Negro should have a much larger proportion of Negro principals and teachers. Having had no observation or direct contact with Negro life, and not sufficiently realizing his economic struggle, few white teachers can appreciate or interpret to the Negro child his possibilities. I do not wish to imply that the white teacher does not do his best; but he cannot feel the yearnings of another race whose social deprivations and sufferings are not within his own personal experience. The earnestness of a trained Negro teacher in his desire to raise the economic level of his race cannot possibly be assumed by any other nationality. The Negro teacher has learned from the grave necessity of struggling for mere existence. He is willing to pay the supreme price to educate the youth of his race, knowing full well that his salvation depends upon the light he receives from such sacrifice.

I am, therefore, fully convinced that we cannot make real advancement in our pursuit of education in cities where Negroes are segregated and their children are deprived of Negro leadership until Boards of Education provide equal educational facilities under the law. American democracy definitely promises equality of opportunity in public education. When she openly denies the Negro child this fundamental right, American democracy becomes a sham.

Richard Allen,[13] the spiritual figure of his generation, was the first to point the way. He did the unprecedented thing. White Christians at Philadelphia refused to permit Afro-Americans to participate in the Lord's Supper. Instead of whining and protesting their un-Christianlike attitude, he walked out of that church building, rallied his brethren and established the African Methodist Episcopal Church,[14] the largest and strongest Negro organization in the world. The Baptist Church could approach the Methodist strength and become a greater force, once they were united.

Dr. Booker T. Washington, with his burning desire to help his people, made putty of racial barriers and broke through organized prejudice and discrimination in the Black Belt of Alabama.[15] He built an educational highway from Tuskegee Institute[16] to the four corners of the world by his industrial philosophy, which gave to white men a medium through which they could get an understanding of the needs of the Negro.

These two leaders did not waste their energies in futile attempts to abolish segregation, but addressed themselves to the task of educating Negroes to find a way to better citizenship.

Better citizenship—this is the goal to which the Negro may advance only under intelligent and brave leaders. But between us and this goal are many paths to be made straight; many rough ways to be made plain.[17] In a wilderness of indifference, intolerance, misunderstanding, and organized vice, the Phillis Wheatley Association has cleared one path—has made one rough way plain by giving physical and spiritual aid to thousands of homeless Negro girls and women in Cleveland and other cities. But its finest accomplishment has been the ideal of interracial co-operation which it has established—an extension of Christian comradeship beyond the hearthstone; beyond the barriers of class; beyond religious differences, or more of race.

May that spirit of comradeship which is a reflection of the Eternal Love be carried far beyond our life and our times into regions as yet unexplored—to those far horizons where good will and the brotherhood of man may become the sovereign law of life.

CHAPTER XVII

---·◆·---

"Fireside Musings"

My sister, the battle is so hard;
My sister, the battle is so hard;
My sister the battle is so hard;
Thank God I'm in-a this field.[1]

Thank God I am in this field—in the heart of the Southland where I spent my childhood days. This song, with its sweet melody and plaintive note, turns back the years, and at home with Mother's sisters I feel like a child again.

In all of God's children there is that sincere longing for peace. My own worn and weary soul sought rearmament of faith in the quiet of the wilderness where I first saw the light.

While traveling along the highway, I viewed the countryside. Here and there acres of land under cultivation awakened in me memories of the days when I labored in these fields. I saw a plow drawn by husky mules. It seemed but yesterday that the man behind the plow was the father I loved so dearly.

Gathered around the fireside in the home of my aunties the evening after my arrival at Pendleton, there were old friends who had come from near-by farms to welcome me home. Hearing them sing the spirituals in their native tongue, I could not keep back the flood of recollections which carried me from this, my birthplace, to the far-away field of my present endeavors. It was touching to worship in the church of my childhood and to speak from its pulpit and to pause at the ballground where we children played the game. Instead of the shanty schoolhouse through which the rain dripped upon my apron and where the sun peeped in at noon, there stood a modernly equipped school building.

At the time of this visit I met Superintendent George A. Brown[2] of the county public schools. I learned of his profound interest in the youth of my race, his work with them for higher standards of education, and his leadership in interracial fellowship. I realized that a new spirit had permeated the old Southland, and felt that the teachings of the early missionaries were bearing abundant fruit. How close I felt myself to this new South! Booker T. Washington I had known, and his teachings I had followed.

It had been my privilege to meet Julius Rosenwald,[3] whose benefactions were evident in all this new attitude toward my people in the South. There was no doubt that the interest of the philanthropist in the improvement of Negro education had played its part. I recalled my visit with him at the time of the proposed expansion of the Phillis Wheatley work in Cleveland when I was in a quandary over financial difficulties encountered in our building needs. Having learned of Mr. Rosenwald's interest in Tuskegee and having seen many of the schools erected in the rural South by the Rosenwald Fund,[4] I believed that he would help us. Fortunately, I knew Mr. Samuel H. Halle,[5] a distinguished business man of Cleveland and a personal friend of Mr. Rosenwald, and did not hesitate to request Mr. Halle to pave the way for an introduction. His splendid letter enabled me to reach Mr. Rosenwald in his summer home and later, by appointment, I saw him in his office. He seemed to be pleased with our progress and indicated his willingness to help us. The conditions attached to his gift made it impossible for the Phillis Wheatley Association to accept his generosity, but his gifts to the Young Men's Christian Association[6] and Negro schools, and his contribution to interracial understanding have made him a good friend. Any contribution of intelligent sympathy and material support to the education of the Negro, whether it be in my chosen field in the North or in my old home in the South, is a heartening assurance of our progress toward the goal of a truer democracy.

And thus the thoughts suggested by the spirituals chanted by the group around the fireside led me far afield. But now the evening grew old and the women and children of the neighboring farms bade me goodnight in their usual gleeful manner. I said to myself, "How dear to this heart are the scenes of my childhood." Aunt Nan,[7] with her close companion, the cob pipe, left the warm log fire and went off to bed humming another spiritual:

Soon-a will be done-a with the troubles of the world,
Troubles of the world, the troubles of the world,
Soon-a will be done-a with the troubles of the world,
Goin' home to live with God.[8]

These comforting words and the music might have lulled me to sleep had it not been that they impelled me to muse upon the national activities of Negro women. Thoughts, flashing like airplanes over the good earth, led me first to Wendell Phillips High School[9] in Chicago, where pioneers of the National Association of Colored Women were in session in 1924. I remembered that a thousand brown women represented forty-six states on the occasion of their Thirteenth Biennial Convention. This organization was the outgrowth of the consolidation of groups of organizations sponsored by Josephine St. Pierre Ruffin[10] and other pioneering women, many of whom had in a short while lifted the veil of illiteracy from their own uplifted souls. I recall how amazed I was at the activity of the delegates with their badges and banners of identification, their humble, yet appealing motto, "Lifting as We Climb."

It was here I witnessed the first national demonstration of activity by illustrious women of my race. It was interesting to hear reports by Hallie Q. Brown,[11] Emma Miller,[12] Lucy C. Jefferson,[13] Rebecca Styles Taylor,[14] and other delegates to the Conference. For me, a spectator, this afforded opportunity to observe the manner in which these women were attacking the problems of their day! I had seen, in my work, the activity of cultured white women and I marveled that the descendants of Negro women so recently removed from bondage could have displayed such dignity and culture in their deliberations.

The program to give to Negro children those activities in the field of social service not provided for them by the states was of paramount concern to the Southern women. Their intense interest in these matters impressed me seriously. Their establishment of a scholarship fund to assist worthy girls, their desire to provide institutional care for delinquent and deserted children not provided for by the state appropriation board, their effort and emphasis upon home training, arts and crafts, and the building of clubhouses were of vital importance in the upward struggle to brighten and better the lives of Negro children.

I recall most vividly the inspiring address of Mary McLeod Bethune,[15] the dynamic personality who in her forceful and intelligent address secured approval of the delegates to establish headquarters in the nation's capital with a secretary to further develop the work of the National Association. She won that year the election to the presidency. Four years later, after the meeting in California, Sallie W. Stewart[16] was unanimously elected to this high office and with her leadership, great emphasis was placed on the program for mother, home, and child, together with more business-like methods in the management of the organization's affairs. Dr. Mary F. Waring[17] became the torch-bearer in the deepest of the depression, and nobly and courageously kept the organization together, meeting payments on headquarters under severe financial strain. In 1941, with Mrs. Robert R. Moton[18] as President and Mrs. Stewart as National Executive Secretary, the complete liquidation of the $25,000 debt on national headquarters in Washington was accomplished. Mrs. Moton served the girls at Tuskegee for many years as Director of Industry.

Somehow the zeal of these older women has touched off the fire of useful service in the young women of my race. Throughout the nation in our colleges and universities, young women have directed their sororities to undertake the promotion of definite programs of racial helpfulness. A far-reaching and successful health program is being fostered by the Alpha Kappa Alpha Sorority[19] through the Southland. In the nation's capital this sorority maintains an efficient lobbying service for the promotion of those issues affecting the national life of the Negro. The Delta Sigma Theta Sorority[20] has special interest in providing a traveling library for the people of the rural South, and a national vocational guidance program for young women. Zeta Phi Beta Sorority[21] emphasizes the need and service for nobler womanhood in the Negro race. Iota Phi Lambda Sorority[22] encourages young women to pursue commercial training. Each of these four national groups maintains scholarship funds and is helping worthy girls through college. My admiration for these important and sacrificing services caused me to accept honorary membership in the Alpha Kappa Alpha Sorority. A sisterhood banded together in the spirit of co-operation, well may we sing,

Facing the rising sun of our new day begun,
Let us march on till victory is won.[23]

Inspired though I was by the achievement of Negro women, I found my eyes heavy with sleep and unwilling to guide my wavering pen to further musings on past events. The clock on the mantel struck a wee hour of the morning. The log fire had spent itself; there remained only the gray cold ashes in the fireplace. When the light shone no longer, I found comfort in humming to myself a favorite song that I have often heard over the radio from the voices of the Southernaires[24] and the Wings Over Jordan Singers[25]:

O Lord, I couldn' hear nobody pray
And I couldn' hear nobody pray;
O 'way down yonder by myself,
And I couldn' hear nobody pray.[26]

As I sat at the breakfast table next morning and enjoyed fried chicken, corn grits, and gravy, I was much amused by the humble comment of a neighbor woman. Looking seriously upon me, she remarked, "Janie, I's just sitting hare thinking to myself, whar you done git all dat sense. I done sed you sho' must have inhaled all your sense." Of course, her remarks touched a responsive chord and brought forth from me deep and hearty laughter. How she enjoyed the joke after the words had been explained to her! The good humor and hospitality of the South are profoundly felt in the unlettered folk who teach us the true courtesy which meant so much in the struggles of the early days. Breakfast over, a kindly man knocked upon the door, asking the women to come to the College farm[27] to pick the chickens for the students' dinner. The women seemed to be pleased to get the extra work.

I wandered down the red clay road to the Old Stone Church,[28] originally known as Hopewell on Keowee. The organization dates from 1785, the present church building from 1797. This is one of the oldest Presbyterian congregations in northwestern South Carolina and is situated midway between Pendleton and Clemson. General Andrew Pickens,[29] one of the founders, named this house of worship after his old church in Abbeville County. There I noticed the inscription on the age-worn tombstones in the churchyard. I learned the genealogy of the Pickens family, in whose home Grandmother Milliner was reared a slave before she was sold to Captain Adger. I visited the home of General Andrew Pickens, and as I climbed the stairs of that old mansion, I imagined that I could hear my grandmother humming, as she served her mistress in that home,

> Must Jesus bear the cross alone,
> And all the world go free?
> No, there's a cross for every one,
> And there's a cross for me.[30]

These words must have been comforting to her weary soul. The remembrances of those early days we spent together and her stories of struggles and hardships during the reconstruction period were filled with wisdom and understanding. How well I remember her stories of the separation of families by chattel sale; of the tearing apart of her own soul when her mother was sold down the river to a new and unknown master.

When the slaves were at last set free, many of them sprang to their feet, clapping uplifted hands and singing:

> Free at last, free at last,

Thank God Almighty, I'm free at last,
Free at last, free at last,
Thank God Almighty, I'm free at last.[31]

Great-grandmother, who was more than a hundred miles away when the Proclamation was signed, walked from Newbury to Pendleton to be reunited with her family. Hungry and thirsty, she and a companion caught wild game, and after begging a coal of fire from a house by the side of the road, cooked a meal.

The thought of these trials of the old people, and the comparison of their hardships with the opportunities afforded in this day and generation, make me thankful for the privilege of sharing the blessings that have come my way. I have often heard white friends marvel at the fact that Negroes do so much for their own people on the little they receive. Our getting and giving is much like the miraculous bestowal of loaves and fishes[32] which Jesus blessed.

The contribution of these noble characters, with the love and advice they gave to all of us, is an inheritance I wish to cherish and perpetuate.

On my way down through the section which great-grandmother traveled on her return to familiar land, I was glad to see again the beauty of the trees, dripping with moss. And in Summerville I greeted the friends I knew long ago. The approach to Charleston from Meeting Street was strange but attractive. There were throngs of soldiers and workmen busily engaged in national defense projects. Land that once produced vegetables is now a suburb of Charleston. The federal housing projects, new and spacious, provide decent homes for Negroes and whites alike. One of the projects bears the name of the United States Senator Benjamin Tillman.[33] Charleston has undergone many physical and social changes, but the improvements have not marred the beauty of that ancient city. It was good to see that much of the old slum district in which I had gone about as a nurse had been cleared away. With improved living conditions for the poor, better health seems assured. Although partly hidden by the pressing need for modern dwellings,

South Battery, with its stately old mansions, still remains to tell its history.

Recollections of the quaint old Market House off Meeting Street, where my people were once sold on the auction block, are carefully preserved. One reverberation of the social changes is that not far from this ancient slave market is a library for Negroes,[34] with Susie Butler[35] as librarian. Avery Institute[36] continues its effective work with the youth of my race. Burke Industrial School[37] for Negro youth was founded in 1910 through the far-sighted vision of the school commissioners, of which Major Augustine T. Smythe was a member. To see these social and educational improvements made me feel like singing:

It makes me love everybody.[38]

On Legare Street the answer to the shiny brass knocker on the door was a cordial welcome into the home of Mr. and Mrs. John Bennett.[39] "Miss Susy's" reminiscences of the years when we were young on Woodburn Farm gladdened our hearts. To learn anew of the enduring interest, interracial service, and sympathy of this family in helping to provide better schools for Negro children meant much to me. The unavoidable absence from home of Mr. Bennett was deeply regretted, but Mrs. Bennett told me how pleased he was over my humble success in the North.

St. Michael's Church,[40] with its historical record of Christian service, standing as a monument to the faith of Charleston, seemed more sacred than ever before. How beautiful and stately stood old St. Phillip's[41] Church, with the oldest congregation in town! It has served the people in Charleston since 1735. In olden days the spire was used as a lighthouse to guide the vessels coming into the harbor. The story is told that St. Phillip's Church was saved from burning during one of the disastrous fires which swept Charleston in the past, by a courageous Negro man who climbed up the outside of the steeple and with his cap beat out the fire which had caught on the woodwork. The grateful people of Charleston were so pleased with the heroic efforts of the man that they raised enough money to purchase his freedom from his master. Age has not changed the dignity of old St. Phillip's nor lessened its humble ministry of faith, hope, and love.

In this love so truly divine I could see the marvelous change of attitude of the white race in the Southland toward my people. The education of both races has transformed much of the traditional misunderstanding into a growing working fellowship for a happier and nobler South. This love which passes all understanding,[42] uniting Negroes and white people, North and South, shall "crown our good with brotherhood" and we shall hear America sing:

Thank God I'm in-a this field.[43]

APPENDIX A

The following letters chronicle the remarkable exchange between Jane Edna Hunter, the founder and the general secretary of the Phillis Wheatley Association in Cleveland; Booker T. Washington, the African American power broker and principal of Tuskegee Institute; and George A. Myers,[1] a prominent black Republican and prosperous barber in Cleveland, regarding Hunter's desire for Washington to endorse the PWA. Although Myers initially opposed the PWA and convinced Washington not to support the institution, he made financial contributions and lent his influence to the PWA after efforts to integrate Cleveland's public facilities stalled.

JANE E. HUNTER TO BOOKER T. WASHINGTON
Cleveland, O., June 17th, 1914
Hon. B. T. Washington Pres.
Tuskegee Inst.
Tuskegee, Ala.

Dear Mr. Washington,

The Phillis Wheatley Association of Cleveland desires and would greatly appreciate if it is possible to have you come here and lecture for our Association any time during the winter when convenient to you.

Our work is endorsed by the Chamber of Commerce and many of the leading and best citizens of Cleveland.

We are endeavoring to help and encourage the young Colored women who come to this city as strangers and without friends.

We believe that you are in sympathy with every good effort made to improve conditions among the race.

We know of no one that we are more anxious to have than yourself.

Please if possible grant us the honor of your presence and encouragement.

Mr. Powell advised this course of interview and we are sure will be pleased to speak for the good we are doing.

Awaiting your reply.

We are very truly yours,

The Board of Trustees
Jane E. Hunter, Gen. Secy.

GEORGE A. MYERS TO BOOKER T. WASHINGTON
Cleveland, July 20, 1914
Dr. Booker T. Washington,
Tuskegee, Ala.

My dear Doctor Washington:

Your favor of the 15th being confidential prevents me from making diligent inquiry into the matter about which you wrote. The Institute is here, fostered by a few misguided whites endeavoring to relieve their conscience of the discrimination by the Y.W.C.A. against our women. The young woman at the head of this Institute (located in the house next to and owned by St. John's A.M.E. Church, where you spoke to our people the last time you were here) has no standing among our better class of women.

Personally as you know I am broad minded and interested in every movement for the uplift of our people. I have had nothing to do with this, because I cannot consistently see the need of any segregated movement in Cleveland. Segregation here of any kind to me is a step backward and will ultimately be a blow to our Mixed Public Schools (in which there are now thirty-three of our colored women employed as teachers, many not having a colored child in their classes). All of the older inhabitants here frown upon segregation and we are honest about it.

I would therefore advise that you take the matter up directly with the Board of Trustees of this Institution and ascertain if they authorized this woman to write you for a meeting and the kind of a one they contemplate. It is my private opinion that the lady in question conceived the idea herself, in order to further her own aggrandizement and profit by the prestige of your approval and endorsement, holding the meeting in some one of the colored Churches and charging an admission thereto.

Our people as a rule do not appreciate our noted Men and Women as they should. They would use anyone to further their own selfish aims or aggrandizement. Mr. Powell informs me the lady spoke to him about the advisability of securing either you, Prof. Du Bois, or Miss Jane Adams; [sic] he advised her to write you, which she did.

If you further desire, I will make inquiry from the white Trustees and advise you. With best wishes and kind regards to Mrs. Washington, I am very truly yours,

George A. Myers

....

JANE E. HUNTER TO GEORGE A. MYERS
Cleveland, Ohio, March 28, 1921
Mr. George Myers
Hollenden Hotel
Cleveland, Ohio.

Dear Mr. Myers:

Even though I tried to thank you personally for the $50.00 which you gave me to use in feeding some of the poor people who came to our door, I am taking this opportunity to thank you again.

It has put me in position to do a good deal more for people whom I know are worthy and in destitution. I am sure it makes them feel better towards the institution when through you the institution is able to do something for them.

I spoke of your contribution at the Colored Minister's Alliance last Tuesday. They seemed to have appreciated your generosity. I wish we had more such men in our race like you who believe in helping the poor.

Surely God will help and bless you with a long and happy life is the prayer of
Your humble servant,
Jane E. Hunter
General Secretary

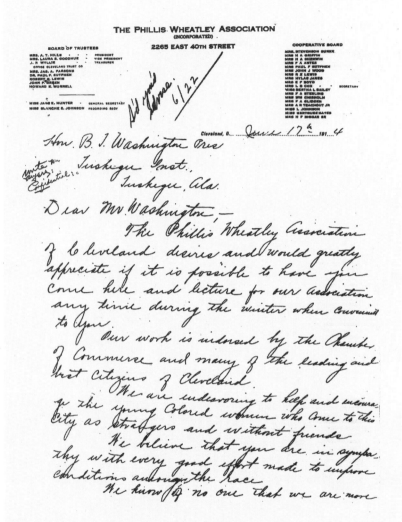

THE PHILLIS WHEATLEY ASSOCIATION
(INCORPORATED)
2265 EAST 40TH STREET

BOARD OF TRUSTEES
MRS. A. T. HILLS · · · PRESIDENT
MRS. LAURA S. GOODHUE · VICE PRESIDENT
J. R. WYLLIE · · · TREASURER
OFFICE CLEVELAND TRUST CO
MRS. JAS. A. PARSONS
DR. PAUL F. SUTPHEN
ROBERT E. LEWIS
JOHN P. GREEN
HOWARD E. MURRELL

MISS JANE E. HUNTER · GENERAL SECRETARY
MISS BLANCHE E. JOHNSON RECORDING SECY

COOPERATIVE BOARD
MRS. STEVENSONS BURKE
MRS H A GRIFFIN
MRS D A SHERWIN
MRS F A ARTER
MRS PAUL F SUTPHEN
MRS JOHN J WOOD
MRS R E LEWIS
MRS HYLAS JANES
MRS E F BOYD
MRS L S COX · · · SECRETARY
MISS BERTHA L BAILEY
MRS F A STERLING
MRS WM CHISHOLM
MRS F A GLIDDEN
MRS A R TEACHOUT JR
MISS L JOHNSON
MISS GERTRUDE HAYES
MRS H F BIGGAR SR

Cleveland, O. _June 17th_ 191 4

Hon. B. J. Washington Pres

Tuskegee Inst.,

Tuskegee, Ala.

Dear Mr. Washington, —

The Phillis Wheatley Association of Cleveland desires and would greatly appreciate if it is possible to have you come here and lecture for our association any time during the winter when convenient to you.

Our work is indorsed by the Chamber of Commerce and many of the leading and best citizens of Cleveland.

We are endeavoring to help and encourage the young colored women who come to this city as strangers and without friends

We believe that you are in sympathy with every good effort made to improve conditions among the race

We know of no one that we are more

THIS PAGE AND FOLLOWING: JANE E. HUNTER TO BOOKER T. WASHINGTON, June 17, 1914, Booker T. Washington Papers, Container 883J, Manuscript Division, Library of Congress, Washington, DC.

THE PHILLIS WHEATLEY ASSOCIATION
(INCORPORATED)

2265 EAST 40TH STREET

BOARD OF TRUSTEES
MRS. A. T. HILLS
MRS. LAURA B. GOODHUE
J. R. WYLLIE
OFFICE CLEVELAND TRUST Co
MRS. JAS. A. PARSONS
DR. PAUL F. SUTPHEN
ROBERT H. LEWIS
JOHN P. GREEN
HOWARD E. MURRELL

PRESIDENT
VICE PRESIDENT
TREASURER

MISS JANE E. HUNTER   GENERAL SECRETARY
MISS BLANCHE E. JOHNSON   RECORDING SECY

COOPERATIVE BOARD
MRS. STEVENSON BURKE
MRS H A GRIFFIN
MRS H A SHERWIN
MRS F A ARTER
MRS PAUL F SUTPHEN
MRS JOHN J WOOD
MRS R E LEWIN
MRS HYLAS JAMES
MRS E F BOYD
MRS L B COX   SECRETARY
MISS BERTHA L BAILEY
MRS F A STERLING
MRS WM CHISHOLM
MRS F A GLIDDEN
MRS A R TEACHOUT JR
MISS L JOHNSON
MISS GERTRUDE HAYES
MRS H F BIGGAR SR

Cleveland, O. _____ 191___

anxious to have than your self
Please if possible grant us the
honor of your presence and encouragement
Mr Powell advised this course of
interview and we are sure will be
please to speak for the good we are
doing
Awaiting your reply
We are very truly yours,
The Board of Trustees
Jane E. Hunter, Gen. Sec

....

OPPOSITE, TOP AND BOTTOM: GEORGE A. MYERS TO BOOKER T. WASHINGTON,
July 20, 1914, Box 16, Folder 5, George A. Myers Papers, Ohio Historical Society
Archives/Library, Columbus, OH. Used with permission.

The Hollenden

EUROPEAN PLAN
EIGHT HUNDRED ROOMS
JAMES H. THOMPSON, Manager.
ADAM W. KUECHLE, Treasurer.

CLEVELAND, ___July 20, 1914.___

Dr. Booker T. Washington,
Tuskegee,
Ala.

My dear Doctor Washington:

Your favor of the 15th being confidential prevents me
from making diligent inquiry into the matter about which you wrote.
The Institute is here, fostered by a few misguided whites endeavoring
to relieve their conscience of the discrimination by the Y.W.C.A.
against our women. The young woman at the head of this Institute (located in the house next to and owned by St. John's A.M.E. Church,
where you spoke to our people the last time you were here) has no
standing among our better class of women.

Personally as you know I am broad minded and interested in
every movement for the uplift of our people. I have had nothing to
do with this, because I cannot consistently see the need of any
segregated movement in Cleveland. Segregation here of any kind to me
is a step backward and will ultimately be a blow to our Mixed Public
Schools (in which there are now thirty-three of our colored women employed as teachers, many not having a colored child in their classes).
All of the older inhabitants here frown upon segregation and we are
honest about it.

I would therefore advise that you take the matter up directly with the Board of Trustees of this Institution and ascertain if
they authorized this woman to write to you for a meeting and the kind
of a one they contemplate. It is my private opinion that the lady in
question conceived the idea herself, in order to further her own aggrandizement and profit by the prestige of your approval and endorsement, holding the meeting in some one of the colored Churches and
charging an admission thereto.

Our people as a rule do not appreciate our noted Men and
Women as they should. They would use anyone to further their own
selfish aims or aggrandizement. Mr. Powell informs me the lady spoke
to him about the advisability of securing either you, Prof. Du Bois
or Miss Jane Adams, he advised her to write to you, which she did.

If you further desire I will make inquiry from
the white Trustees and advise you
With best wishes and kind regards
to Mrs. Washington I am very truly yours

BOARD OF TRUSTEES

Mrs. W. H. Merriam - - President
Mrs. Robert E. Lewis - Vice President
Mrs. A. R. Teachout Jr 2nd Vice President
Mr. J. R. Wyllie - Treasurer
Mrs. Adin T. Hills
Mrs. Laura S. Goodhue
Mrs. Robert H. Bishop, Jr.
Mrs. Harry E. Davis
Mrs. Arthur S. Scott
Mrs. U. S. Tarter
Miss Marie Wing
Mr. M. A. Bradley
Mr. Howard E. Murrell
Dr. Paul F. Sutphen

Miss Jane E. Hunter, - General Secretary

The Phillis Wheatley Association

INCORPORATED

EAST 40TH ST. AND CENTRAL AVE.

CLEVELAND, OHIO March 28, 19 21.

Mr. George Myers,
   Hollenden Hotel,
   Cleveland, Ohio.

Dear Mr. Myers:

Even though I tried to thank you
personally for the $50.00 which you gave
me to use in feeding some of the poor people who came to our door, I am taking this
opportunity to thank you again.

It has put me in position to do
a good deal more for people whom I know are
worthy and in destitution. I am sure it
makes them feel better towards the institution when through you the institution is
able to do something for them.

I spoke of your contribution at
the Colored Minister's Alliance last Tuesday. They seemed to have appreciated
your generosity. I wish that we had more
such men in our race like you who believe
in helping the poor.

Surely God will help and bless
you with a long and happy life is the prayer
of

                    Your humble servant,

                    Jane E Hunter

                    General Secretary.

ABOVE: JANE E. HUNTER TO GEORGE A. MYERS, March 28, 1921, Box 17, Folder
5, George A. Myers Papers, Ohio Historical Society Archives/Library, Columbus,
OH. Used with permission.

APPENDIX B

In 1924, PWA trustees appointed Dr. Robert H. Bishop Jr., a white hospital administrator and public health advocate, as the chairman of the capital campaign to raise $600,000 for a new PWA facility and campground. The following fundraising letter signed by Bishop reflects both the promise and peril of white patronage for black institutions in the early twentieth century. By asserting that Clevelanders could avoid the "more serious phases" of the "Negro problem" by funding a social welfare facility for black girls and working women, Bishop seems to shift the blame for the city's sociological ills on new black female residents. The PWA appointed twelve fifty-member teams to carry out the fundraising drive. In January of 1925, Hunter began publishing lists of donors who contributed more than $100 in *The Open Door*, the PWA's newsletter. One month later, the committee reported they had surpassed their goal with $643,000 in pledges.[1] The nine-story building with two underground levels that served over one hundred black women opened in 1927.

ROBERT H. BISHOP, JR. TO MRS. B.A. SPANYE
Jan. 9th, 1925
Mrs. B. A. Spanye,[2]
11338 Bellflower Rd.,
Cleveland, Ohio.

> *Dear Mrs. Spanye:*
> *In our midst there are those who serve the community daily in many ways, yet are not fully and properly served by the community in return.*

I refer to the colored residents of our city.

Today Cleveland ranks third in American cities in percent of increase in colored population. In fact there are now nearly 50,000 Negroes living in Cleveland, as against 8,500 in 1910.

This great group presents what is probably Cleveland's greatest immediate sociological problem. Improved conditions in housing, education and recreation must be provided or disease, moral laxity and crime will increase. The situation is full of danger to the community and to the colored people themselves.

To meet some of the more serious phases of this problem, The Phillis Wheatley Association, which is a boarding home and training institution for colored girls and women, is about to conduct a campaign to raise $600,000.00, largely for a new building.

In the history of the 112 Community Chest agencies this is the first campaign on a large scale for a colored institution and Cleveland must not fail in this important undertaking.

The situation is so unusual and so very serious that as this campaign progresses we bespeak your sympathetic interest and your active support.

Yours very truly,

R. H. Bishop, Jr.
Chairman

Jan.
9th,
1925

Mrs. B. A. Spanye,
11338 Bellflower Rd.,
Cleveland, Ohio.

Dear Mrs. Spanye:

In our midst there are those who serve the community daily in many ways, yet are not fully and properly served by the community in return.

I refer to the colored residents of our city.

Today Cleveland ranks third in American cities in per cent of increase in colored population. In fact there are now nearly 50,000 negroes living in Cleveland, as against 8500 in 1910.

This great group presents what is probably Cleveland's greatest immediate sociological problem. Improved conditions in housing, education and recreation must be provided or disease, moral laxity and crime will increase. The situation is full of danger to the community and to the colored people themselves.

To meet some of the more serious phases of this problem, The Phillis Wheatley Association, which is a boarding home and training institution for colored girls and women, is about to conduct a campaign to raise $600,000.00, largely for a new building.

In the history of the 112 Community Chest agencies this is the first campaign on a large scale for a colored institution and Cleveland must not fail in this important undertaking.

The situation is so unusual and so very serious that as this campaign progresses we bespeak your sympathetic interest and your active support.

Yours very truly,

R. H. Bishop Jr.
Chairman

ABOVE: ROBERT H. BISHOP, JR. TO MRS. B.A. SPANYE. Phillis Wheatley Association Papers, Phillis Wheatley Association, Cleveland. Used by permission of the Phillis Wheatley Association of Cleveland, Ohio.

APPENDIX C

Hunter placed the majority of the PWA residents in domestic service positions, the most readily available work for African American women in Cleveland in the early twentieth century. Through the development of the Sarah C. Hills Training School, a well equipped home where "girls learn(ed) to keep house in the modern way," Hunter sought to elevate the status of domestics by equipping trainees with professional techniques for polishing furniture, setting tables, preparing and serving meals, cleaning homes, and washing clothing.[1]

....

OPPOSITE TOP: CLASS OF THE SARAH C. HILLS TRAINING SCHOOL, SEPTEMBER 12 TO NOVEMBER 10, 1938 (CA. 1938). Front row (l to r): Frances Scott, Cora Tucker, Julia Fellows, Mary Alice Chapel, Lillian Mitchell, Metiska James, Jessie Lee Melton; Second Row (l to r): Elsie Sherod, Cathryn Bell, Emma Jean Pratt, Dolly Hodge, Elizabeth Johnson, Inez Cantrell.
Used by permission of the Phillis Wheatley Association of Cleveland, Ohio.

OPPOSITE BOTTOM: PWA EMPLOYMENT OFFICE (N.D.) Used by permission of the Phillis Wheatley Association of Cleveland, Ohio.

APPENDIX D

Hunter seems to have considered omitting details of her brief marriage and permanent separation from her husband at this point in her writing process. Ultimately, she decided to briefly mention this relationship at the end of Chapter 4 in A Nickel and a Prayer. In *Jane Edna Hunter: A Case Study of Black Leadership, 1910-1950*, Adrienne Lash Jones notes that Hunter's experience was atypical in early twentieth-century America and describes her attitude toward the separation as "fearlessness." This excerpt from the manuscript complicates Hunter's representation of this pivotal decision in her life, however. As a proponent of African American womanhood and traditional families, she may have been more reluctant to share this part of her life story than scholars have believed.

ORIGINAL VERSION OF MANUSCRIPT:

My poor mother did not know the value of an education, and when she learned that I planned not to come home but to stay in Abbeville where I could earn $5.00 a month in the home of White people, she came and took me home where I was supposed to marry an old man whom I did not love, but who was very rich. I ran off from home to keep from marrying, and went to the home of my Uncle in Florida where I attended the Holloman Academy for one year. Upon my return home (I was then quite seventeen years old) I persuaded Aunt Caroline and my mother to permit me to go to Charleston, S.C.

clothes, or to work on an adjoining plantation of a White man to get
extra money. These were happy days, and I enjoyed being with my cousins.
I went to Church on Sundays, and was able to go to school between November
and February.

After being there about two years, an old Missionary came along,
by the name of Rev. E. W. Williams(his wife, Mrs. *Ella* Virginia Chase Williams
is now in Washington). He told my Aunt that if she would get my mother to
let me go to school in Abbieville S. C. that they would permit me to work
my way through school. My mother consented and that summer before entering school in the fall, Aunt Caroline secured work for me in the plantation house of Mr. B. O. Harris. I earned $2.00 a month and my board. I
saved the four months earning and paid my way to Abbieville, S. C. which
amounted to about $3.00. I entered Ferguson and Williams College in the
Fall of 1895. After taking examination, I was admitted to the fourth grade,
and then I made two grades a year. When I left the College, I ~~was in~~ *had finished* the
~~Junior~~ *Senior* Class of the High School. *Mrs. Williams was my ideal of a Christian.*
I accepted the teaching of Jesus one Sunday in my Sunday School Class.
My poor mother did not know the value of an education, and when she
learned that I planned not to come home but to stay in Abbieville where I
could earn $5.00 a month in ~~the~~ *a* home of White ~~people~~ *family*, she came and took
me home where I was supposed to marry an old man whom I did not love, ~~but~~
who was very rich. ~~I ran off from home to keep from marrying, and went~~ *went with my uncle* to
~~the home of my Uncle~~ in Florida where I attended the Holloman Academy for
one year. Upon my return home(I was then quite seventeen years old)(I
persuaded Aunt Caroline and my mother to permit me to go to Charleston S.C.

Revised version with Hunter's edits:

My poor mother did not know the value of an education, and when she
learned that I planned not to come home but to stay in Abbeville where I
could earn $5.00 a month in a̲ ~~the~~ home of White family̲ ~~people~~, [she came

Above: Early manuscript page from *A Nickel and a Prayer*. Jane Edna
Hunter Papers, 1930–1969, Folder 7, Western Reserve Historical Society Library,
Cleveland. Used with permission.

and took me home where I was supposed to marry an old man whom I did not love, [but who was very rich.] I <u>went</u> ~~ran off~~ from home to keep from marrying, and went <u>with my Uncle John</u> ~~to the home of my uncle~~ <u>to his home</u> in Florida where I attended the <u>Harlem</u> ~~Holloman~~ Academy for one year. <u>X</u> Upon my return <u>to mother</u> ~~home~~ (I was then quite seventeen years old) <u>?</u> I persuaded Aunt Caroline and my mother to permit me to go to Charleston, S.C.

APPENDIX E

Hunter published the first edition of *A Nickel and a Prayer* in November of 1940. In the preface to her autobiography, she mentions favorable reviews written by two friends who had provided editorial feedback: John Bennett's in Charleston, South Carolina's *The News and Courier*, which was reprinted in Columbia, South Carolina's *The State*,[1] and Rhoda E. McCulloch's review in *The Woman's Press* magazine produced by the YWCA.

....

BOOK REVIEW BY JOHN BENNETT

S.C. NEGRO WOMAN'S LIFE IS WELFARE DRAMA

A NICKEL AND A PRAYER, BY JANE E. HUNTER; PP. 198; ILLUS.; CLEVELAND, OHIO, ELLI KANI PUBLISHING COMPANY. $2.50.

This is not so much a book review as comment upon a strange story.

The book itself is beyond ordinary, and deserves more than ordinary consideration. It is the story of a South Carolina Negro girl, who pledged her life to wipe out some of the hazards which meet a young colored woman seeking in a strange city for decent employment and an honest living, and has amazingly succeeded in achieving that end.

The author, Jane Hunter, was born in a two-room tenant house on Woodburn farm, near Pendleton, Anderson county, South Carolina. Her parents were sharecroppers, tenant-farmers, field hands; herself a field-hand, stripping fodder, working in the cotton-field and corn, and more than often sleeping on a bare floor with nothing but a quilt to cover her.

Her father, a field-laborer born in slavery and half-white, was the son of an English overseer and a full-blooded Negro woman. Her mother's parents were also tenant farmers, sharecroppers and field hands, in slavery and out, and the first ex-slaves in the district to own the land which their forebears had tilled as slaves. Her early life was often one of hardship and destitution.

WORKED IN CHARLESTON

Her paternal grandmother, an unusually intelligent woman, had been trained by Dr. Thomas Pickens as a practical nurse, and served the entire neighborhood as midwife. Her father, doubtless stirred by his paternity, insisted that his children should secure an education. Her first opportunity to do so was at Silver Springs, where an employer's daughter taught her to write her name and to read simple nursery rhymes.

Opportunity offering, she came to Charleston as a domestic servant in the employ of the Rutledge family. All her references to those who employed her on Woodburn farm and in Charleston are made with grateful remembrance, appreciation, and judicious reticence.

Eager to advance herself, and encouraged by her employers, she obtained admission to Cannon Street Hospital and Training School for Nurses, all instruction there being given by the white physicians of the city. She began her profession under the observing patronage of Dr. T. Grange Simons, chief surgeon at the hospital, and on his recommendation continued her training at Hampton Institute Hospital and School for Nurses.

Planning to practice her profession in Florida, she was carried instead by a queer turn of fate to Cleveland, Ohio, and the practice of her profession there. The disheartening rebuffs she met in that city on account of her color seemed to her more drastic than any she had met in Charleston. One physician told her flatly: "Go back South; white doctors don't employ nigger nurses," a phrase she had never had applied to her before.

The mushroom growth of Cleveland between the years 1910 and 1920, as regarded its Negro population, was 300 percent. Hordes of uneducated, untrained Negro laborers poured in from the South. Drawn from rural communities and country villages by the lure of better wages, the ignorant, friendless Negroes offered a glaring mark for the rapacity of real estate sharks, corrupt politicians, and procurers: Cleveland's Black Belt underwent a vicious degradation of a type familiar to all Northern cities having a large population of primitive black folk.

By her own experience familiar with, and seeing the tragedy of young colored women coming into a strange city alone, beset by temptations and danger, struggling for a livelihood against discrimination, injustice, lack of educational opportunity, wanting a decent place in which to live, in a community where poverty and vice awaited the unfortunate, she set herself the task of providing a home for friendless Negro girls, a refuge for the weak, a guard for the unsophisticated, a training-school for the industrious, offering education to the ambitious, and a place of decent recreation for the young.

Her aim was to rescue and to assist young Negro girls alone and friendless in a great city, without employment, reduced to squalor in disreputable tenements, and well nigh helpless against mental, physical and moral degradation; and to lift the standards of Negro working-women by adequate training for efficient and self-respecting service.

FOUNDED BY OWN RACE

With singular insight she turned for aid not to influential white patronage, but to the poor and lowly of her own race, a group of Negro working-women. Starting literally with "a nickel and a prayer," that small group of poor, hard-working Negro women set out to found a great philanthropic enterprise in a Northern city, led by the South Carolina girl, Jane Hunter.

Difficult year after difficult year their efforts moved forward, resolutely, patiently, courageously, often against stubborn, and sometimes sinister, opposition, to build an agency for the training and guidance of inexperienced Negro girls; to cultivate a reasonable understanding between the white and dark races; and to demonstrate the truth that the only efficient method of dealing with a submerged minority is not paternalistic, but democratic, by helping the underprivileged individual to help himself.

In their first old vacant building these women rolled up their sleeves and did the work themselves of reordering disorder: they "washed the dirty windows, scrubbed the dirty floors, and scraped off twenty layers of old paper from the walls."

Battling upward against prejudice, discrimination, skepticism, distrust, and the malignant treachery of corrupt politics, that home for the friendless has grown into a great and greatly efficient community center supported by both white and black, with cordial cooperation and commendation from the highest and best . . . a notable example of most successful interracial cooperation in the field of social service.

COPIED IN NINE CITIES

Thus, through the devoted work of that small group of Negro working-women, led and inspired by this South Carolina Negro girl, was established the Phillis Wheatley Association of Cleveland, a training-school and refuge for Negro working-girls, guiding the ignorant, protecting the weak, directing the foolish, providing training for service and for home-making, education for the ambitious, recreation for the young, counsel and correction for the wayward, and a home for the homeless.

The National Association of Colored Women has now established like institutions in nine American cities; and Jane Hunter is chairman of that department of the national organization. In just recognition of her accomplishment for herself and her people, Wilberforce University has conferred upon her the honorary degree of M.A.; Tuskegee that of M.S.; and completing a lifelong desire for education, after four years of study, Jane Hunter passed the stringent state examination, and is admitted a full-fledged lawyer at the Ohio bar.

Jane Hunter is a realist. Not blind to discrimination, she confronts race prejudice frankly and sensibly, seeking only justice for capable members of her race; and maintaining, as did Booker Washington, that the way upward for self-respecting, self-supporting Negroes is by adequate education.

Clear-sightedly she perceives that through disregard of the potentialities of the Negro race in large American cities, that potency has become a force for evil, breeding disease and crime, and, uniting with even more malignant forces of evil, has become a menace to civic life.

Claiming nothing beyond merit's honest deserts, shunning the toadstool of political advancement, she asks no privilege beyond that deserved by actual achievement. What she herself has accomplished is extraordinary; what she has enabled other women of her race to do for themselves is no less extraordinary. What is more, while rising to distinction herself, she has not forgotten the kindness and consideration shown to her in her own days of adversity as an underprivileged girl in domestic service, cotton field and corn, but speaks of those difficult days and their condition with sensitive appreciation and grateful remembrance.

The Phillis Wheatley Association is the embodiment of the philosophy maintained at Tuskegee by Booker Washington; and, like Washington, the author concludes, against all crackpot theories, that "The Negro must develop his own abilities, and make his contribution to the world . . . as a Negro."

This book is out of the ordinary, one of the most remarkable books produced by an American Negro. It calls for more than ordinary consideration, and a place beside Booker Washington's "Up from Slavery."

JOHN BENNETT.

Charleston, SC, *The News and Courier*, Nov. 24, 1940. Used by permission of *The Post and Courier*, Charleston, SC.

EXCERPT FROM BOOK REVIEW BY RHODA E. MCCULLOCH

A NICKEL AND A PRAYER
JANE EDNA HUNTER (PARTHENON PRESS, $2)

Jane Hunter's life story is the latest addition to the long shelf of autobiographies of women who have used their own struggles to overcome handicaps as the pattern for their contribution to society as a whole. The story of her own childhood, of her relations with her father and mother, of her patient attempts to become a participating member of her community – all of this will give courage to us all. At many points the style of her writing approaches the best standards of English prose. I hope that this book will run to several editions.

REMC (RHODA E. MCCULLOCH)
12/23/40

JEHP, Western Reserve Historical Society Library, Cleveland, Ohio

APPENDIX F

Hunter's correspondence with family and friends provides important insights into her personal life as well as the challenges she faced in managing a racial uplift organization for black girls and women during the tumultuous early twentieth century. She maintained close ties to relatives in her hometown, Pendleton, South Carolina, by providing financial support and visiting with them throughout her career. Hunter also cultivated close relationships with other race women, Nannie Helen Burroughs and Mary McLeod Bethune, with whom she exchanged letters, gifts, and visits, and developed professional collaborations.

JANE E. HUNTER TO NANNIE HELEN ENGLISH
Dec. 21, 1933
Mrs. Nan English
Pendleton, S.C.

My dear Aunt Nan:

I hope you have not thought strangely of me because of my neglect and my silence, but I tell you the truth that since my return home after visiting you in March, I have had the hardest time. Things were torn to pieces and it has been all I could do to hold things and myself together since last April.

I cannot tell you in this letter what I have gone through, but things seem to be letting up and I can see day light again. Nearly everything I had has been lost through the closing of the banks. Our salaries were cut in half and with the responsibility I have and in trying to keep what little I had, I have lost almost everything.

I am sending you [the] enclosed, not that I can afford it, but because I really want to do it, and I would like to send you more, a check on [sic] the Post Office for $7.00. $5.00 is for you and $1.00 is for Aunt Neat and $1.00 for Aunt Flora.

Please do not try to send me anything. I do not need it, unless later on you see your way to send me a big bag of rabbit tobacco. I am drinking that because I am suffering so with neuritis. I would be very glad if you would gather up the weed and send it to me.

Give my love to Aunt Betty. When I send you a box sometime later you can give some of the things to Aunt Betty. I want you to pray for me for I have had a terrible year, and I am afraid that I am going to break down under the strain.

I want to wish you all a very Merry Christmas and a better New Year than you have had during the past year. Lots of love.

Devotedly yours,

Jane E. Hunter
Aunt Nan $5.00
Aunt Neat 1.00
Aunt Flora 1.00

TEXT TRANSCRIBED FROM CARBON COPY OF LETTER IN PHILLIS WHEATLEY ASSOCIATION PAPERS, Phillis Wheatley Association, Cleveland. Used by permission of the Phillis Wheatley Association of Cleveland, Ohio.

....

JANE E. HUNTER TO NAN BURROUGHS
Sunday after
Nov. 2, 1929

Dearest Nannie Burroughs:
I had the good sense to remain in bed all day and two healthy meals were served.

The return trip home served me worse than my trip to Washington. My only reason for any material difference in the ride I guess was the anticipated joy of seeing you. The fatigue was awful.

It was so nice to see you and to know your real sweet self. Surely we will continue to cultivate a lasting friendship. I want to be your devoted sister in kindred thought and love. You are so deserving and so capable. Your work is unique and remarkable; to me it fulfills a need that [is] not even attempted by other educators. I shall not be happy until I have made a definite contribution in a tangible way to your school.

Things here went on smoother in my absence than when I'm here. I can see these young women growing spiritually larger and more serviceable each day. I notice them more after time away from them for a few days. Needless to say that I had a most delightful time with you and the "Mayor" of Philadelphia. She is a great hero. I do admire her courage so much. It was good to have a chance to renew my acquaintance with her.

I didn't get to talk to you about little Doris Summers from Cleveland. I do hope that you will inspire her to a life of service. However, her background is not all that it could be to assure moral fiber for future growth. She is quite young and has a chance to make it if we can reinforce that which she has.

Let me thank you for the most enjoyable visit in your home and for the privilege to know you better. Remember that it is my sincere wish to always cherish your wonderful self. May His love abide in you and keep you while you think not of yourself.

Fondly yours,

Jane E. Hunter

P. S. There is a motto or rather a poem in your private quarters entitled "Keep A Going." Please have your secretary to copy it and send to me. I meant to have [her] do so myself before leaving.

Janie

Sunday after
Nov 2, 1929

Dearest Nannie Burroughs:-

I had the good sense to remain
in bed all day and two healthy meals
were served. The return trip home served
me worse than my trip to Washington
My only reason for any material difference in the ride I guess was the anticipated joy of seeing you. the fatigue
was awful. It was so nice to see you
and to know your real sweet self.
Surely we will continue to cultivate
a lasting friendship. I want to be your
devoted sister in kindred thought and
love. You are so deserving and so
capable. your work is unique and
remarkable; to me it full fills a need
that not even attempted by other educators. I shall not be happy until I
have made a definite contribution
in a tangible way to your school.
Things here went on smoother in
my absence than when I'm here
I can see these young women growing
spiritually larger and more serviceable
each day. I notice them more after
being away from them for a few days.
Needless to say that I had a most delightful time with you and the

....

ABOVE AND OPPOSITE RIGHT: JANE E. HUNTER TO NANNIE HELEN BURROUGHS.
"Hunter, Jane E." file, Box 38, Nannie Helen Burroughs Papers, Manuscript Division,
Library of Congress, Washington, DC. Used by permission of the Nannie Helen
Burroughs Foundation

"Mayor" of Philadelphia She is a great
Lena I do admire her courage so much.
It was good to have a chance to renew
my acquaintance with her.

I didn't get to talk to you about
little Doris Summers from Cleveland
I do hope that you will inspire her
to a life of service However, her background
is not all that it could be to assure moral
probes for future growth. She is quite young,
and has a chance to make it if we can
reinforce that which she has.

Let me thank you for the most
enjoyable visit in your home and
for the privilege to know you better
Remember that it is my sincere wish
to always cherish your wonderful
self. May His love abide in you
and keep you while you think not
of your self. Fondly yours
                    Jane E Hunter.

P.S. There is a motto or rather a
poem in your private quarters
entitle "Keep A Going" Please have
your secretary to copy it and send
to me I meant to have do so my
self before leaving.
                    Jane

BETHUNE-COOKMAN COLLEGE

Daytona Beach, Florida

OFFICE OF THE PRESIDENT   January 10, 1935

My dear, dear Jane,

It does give me a thrill to know that you are in your beautiful home. How I wish I could have entered it withou and spent the first night to enjoy its comfort and to ad - mire it. You are so worthy of it. You have done a good day's work, old girl. God is doing to stand by you. You will not fail.

I have laughred myself fat on my gift not having reached you. I am putting it in the mail before I mail this letter to you. It is just one of the things - many things - that escaped me. I hope it will add just a little more beauty to your cultured home. I am looking forward with much delight to my return to Cleveland and my visit to you.

Now, Jane, please promise this: We are having the dedication of our new buildings March 8-9-10. I do want you with me. Just take that little rest and drive down. Spend a week with me. Come the week before so that you have help me to plan. I need you! I want to talk some very close matters over with you regarding the work. I think we both need to begin thinking carefully of what is to take place tomorrow in regards to our efforts now.

I am very happy you had a fine vacation. I had a quiet and pleasant time here. Hattie Feger, Atlanta University, came down and spent the holidays with me. I think she enjoyed it very much.

Blessings upon you! Just keep telling the Father about us and pray that our needs of the morrow be supplied. Love to Ethel and all the staff and a great deal for yourself and for my friends in Cleveland.

Devotedly yours,

Mary McLeod Bethune

MMB:idb

ABOVE: MARY MCLEOD BETHUNE TO JANE. Phillis Wheatley Association Papers, Phillis Wheatley Association, Cleveland. Used by permission of the Phillis Wheatley Association of Cleveland, Ohio.

MARY McLEOD BETHUNE TO JANE E. HUNTER
January 10, 1935

My dear, dear Jane,

It does give me a thrill to know that you are in your beautiful home. How I wish I could have entered it without and spent the first night to enjoy its comfort and to admire it. You are so worthy of it. You have done a good day's work, old girl. God is [going] to stand by you. You will not fail.

I have laughed myself fat on my gift not having reached you. I am putting it in the mail before I mail this letter to you. It is just one of the things—many things—that escaped me. I hope it will add just a little more beauty to your cultured home. I am looking forward with much delight to my return to Cleveland and my visit to you.

Now, Jane, please promise this: We are having the dedication of our new buildings March 8-9-10. I do want you with me. Just take that little rest and drive down. Spend a week with me. Come the week before so that you can help me to plan. I need you! I want to talk some very close matters over with you regarding the work. I think we both need to begin thinking carefully of what is to take place tomorrow in regards to our efforts now.

I am very happy you had a fine vacation. I had a quiet and pleasant time here. Hattie Feger, Atlanta University, came down and spent the holidays with me. I think she enjoyed it very much.

Blessings upon you! Just keep telling the Father about us and pray that our needs of the morrow be supplied. Love to Ethel and all the staff and a great deal for yourself and for my friends in Cleveland.

Devotedly yours,

Mary McLeod Bethune

APPENDIX G

By the mid-1940s, city agencies and black Clevelanders were becoming increasingly vocal regarding their wish for a different type of leadership at the Phillis Wheatley Association. While Hunter continued to emphasize the viability of a segregated facility and domestic service to address the needs of the African American community, particularly women and girls, Clevelanders desired the development of integrated agencies and more progressive programs. On September 30, 1947, as she neared her sixty-fifth birthday, Hunter reluctantly submitted her resignation letter to the PWA to avoid losing retirement benefits from Cleveland's Welfare Federation, which managed her pension. She officially retired in December of 1948.

JANE E. HUNTER TO MRS. MORRIS
September 30, 1947
Mrs. C. T. Morris, Chairman
Personnel Committee
15616 Edgewater Drive
Cleveland, Ohio

Dear Mrs. Morris:

For some time I have been greatly depressed over the impending necessity of giving up the work at Phillis Wheatley due to the requirement of the Pension Plan under which we operate, namely, that I retire upon reaching the age of 65. This condition will occur for me on my next birthday, December 13, 1947.

I had so wanted to accomplish three major and important things at Phillis Wheatley before withdrawing from active service, namely, (1) the securing of a well-

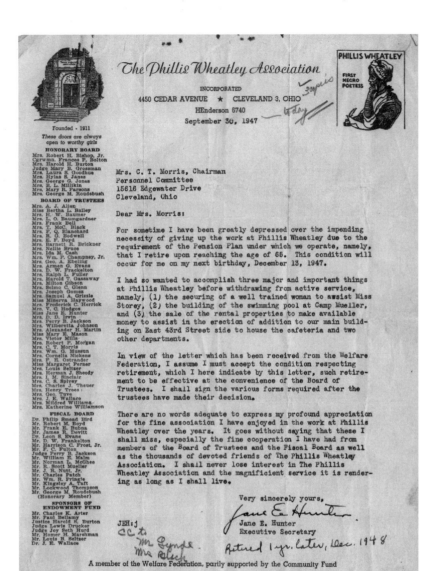

The Phillis Wheatley Association

PHILLIS WHEATLEY
FIRST NEGRO POETESS

INCORPORATED
4450 CEDAR AVENUE ★ CLEVELAND 3, OHIO
HEnderson 6740
September 30, 1947

Founded - 1911

These doors are always open to worthy girls

HONORARY BOARD
Mrs. Robert H. Bishop, Jr.
Cgrwmn. Frances P. Bolton
Mrs. Harold H. Burton
Judge Mary B. Grossman
Mrs. Laura S. Goodhue
Mrs. Hylas S. Janes
Mrs. George G. Jones
Mrs. B. L. Millikin
Mrs. Mary H. Parsons
Mrs. George M. Roudebush

BOARD OF TRUSTEES
Mrs. A. J. Allen
Miss Bertha L. Bailey
Mrs. H. W. Baumer
Mrs. L. O. Baumgardner
Mrs. Frank Bell
Mrs. T. McC. Black
Mrs. F. Q. Blanchard
Mrs. R. O. Bodwell
Mrs. E. F. Boyd
Mrs. Barnett R. Brickner
Mrs. Nellie Bruce
Mrs. Ida M. Cash
Mrs. Wm. P. Champney, Jr.
Mrs. Geo. A. Ebeling
Mrs. Armen G. Evans
Mrs. D. W. Frackelton
Mrs. Ralph L. Fuller
Mrs. Harold T. Gassaway
Mrs. Milton Gibson
Mrs. Selmo C. Glenn
Mrs. Joseph Gomes
Mrs. Samuel A. Grizzle
Miss Minerva Haywood
Mrs. Frederick C. Herrick
Mrs. V. G. Hodges
Miss Jane E. Hunter
Mrs. D. D. Irwin
Mrs. Perry B. Jackson
Mrs. Wilberetta Johnson
Mrs. Alexander H. Martin
Miss Mary E. Mason
Mrs. Victor Mills
Mrs. Robert P. Morgan
Mrs. C. T. Morris
Mrs. Wm. G. Mussun
Mrs. Cornelia Nickens
Miss F. E. Ostrander
Miss Margaret Perner
Mrs. Louis Seltzer
Mrs. Herman J. Sheedy
Mrs. I. M. Sinclair
Mrs. C. S. Spivey
Mrs. Charles J. Theuer
Mrs. Henry Trees
Mrs. Geo. Tuve
Mrs. J. E. Wallace
Mrs. Mildred Williams
Mrs. Katherine Williamson

FISCAL BOARD
Dr. Philip Smead Bird
Mr. Robert M. Boyd
Mr. Frank E. Bubna
Mr. James R. Davitt
Dr. Leon S. Evans
Mr. D. W. Frankelton
Mr. Harrison C. Frost, Jr.
Mr. F. C. Fulton
Judge Perry B. Jackson
Mr. William E. Malm
Mr. Norman L. McGhee
Mr. R. Scott Mueller
Mr. J. R. Nutt, Jr.
Mr. Charles Patch
Mr. Wm. R. Pringle
Mr. Kingsley A. Taft
Mr. Lockwood Thompson
Mr. George M. Roudebush
   (Honorary Member)

SPONSORS OF
ENDOWMENT FUND
Mr. Charles K. Arter
Mr. Paul Bellamy
Justice Harold H. Burton
Judge Lewis Drucker
Judge Joy Seth Hurd
Mr. Homer H. Marshman
Mr. Louis B. Seltzer
Dr. J. E. Wallace

Mrs. C. T. Morris, Chairman
Personnel Committee
15616 Edgewater Drive
Cleveland, Ohio

Dear Mrs. Morris:

For sometime I have been greatly depressed over the impending
necessity of giving up the work at Phillis Wheatley due to the
requirement of the Pension Plan under which we operate, namely,
that I retire upon reaching the age of 65. This condition will
occur for me on my next birthday, December 13, 1947.

I had so wanted to accomplish three major and important things
at Phillis Wheatley before withdrawing from active service,
namely, (1) the securing of a well trained woman to assist Miss
Storey, (2) the building of the swimming pool at Camp Mueller,
and (3) the sale of the rental properties to make available
money to assist in the erection of addition to our main building on East 43rd Street side to house the cafeteria and two
other departments.

In view of the letter which has been received from the Welfare
Federation, I assume I must accept the condition respecting
retirement, which I here indicate by this letter, such retirement to be effective at the convenience of the Board of
Trustees. I shall sign the various forms required after the
trustees have made their decision.

There are no words adequate to express my profound appreciation
for the fine association I have enjoyed in the work at Phillis
Wheatley over the years. It goes without saying that these I
shall miss, especially the fine cooperation I have had from
members of the Board of Trustees and the Fiscal Board as well
as the thousands of devoted friends of The Phillis Wheatley
Association. I shall never lose interest in The Phillis
Wheatley Association and the magnificent service it is rendering as long as I shall live.

Very sincerely yours,

Jane E. Hunter

Jane E. Hunter
Executive Secretary

JEH:j
CC to

A member of the Welfare Federation, partly supported by the Community Fund

ABOVE: JANE E. HUNTER TO MRS. MORRIS. Phillis Wheatley Association Papers,
Phillis Wheatley Association, Cleveland. Used by permission of the Phillis Wheatley Association of Cleveland, Ohio

trained woman to assist Miss Storey, (2) the building of the swimming pool at Camp Mueller, and (3) the sale of the rental properties to make available money to assist in the erection of [an] addition to our main building on East 43rd Street side to house the cafeteria and two other departments.

In view of the letter which has been received from the Welfare Federation, I assume I must accept the condition respecting retirement, which I here indicate by this letter, such retirement to be effective at the convenience of the Board of Trustees. I shall sign the various forms required after the trustees have made their decision.

There are no words adequate to express my profound appreciation for the fine association I have enjoyed in the work at Phillis Wheatley over the years. It goes without saying that these I shall miss, especially the fine cooperation I have had from members of the Board of Trustees and the Fiscal Board as well as the thousands of devoted friends of The Phillis Wheatley Association. I shall never lose interest in The Phillis Wheatley Association and the magnificent service it is rendering as long as I shall live.

Very sincerely yours,

Jane E. Hunter
Executive Secretary

NOTES

Epigraph

1 "Others" was Hunter's favorite poem. She included it in many PWA's publications and described it as her "creed."

Foreword

1 Joanne M. Braxton, "Symbolic Geography and Psychic Landscapes: A Conversation with Maya Angelou," in *Maya Angelou's I Know Why the Caged Bird Sings: A Casebook*, ed. Joanne M. Braxton (NY: Oxford University Press, 1999), 4.

Introduction

1 Jane E. Hunter to Booker T. Washington, June 17, 1914, Booker T. Washington Papers, Container 883J, Manuscript Division, Library of Congress, Washington, DC (hereafter cited in text as BTWP). David A. Gerber cites this incident in *Black Ohio and the Color Line, 1860–1915* (Urbana: University of Illinois Press, 1976), 457.

2 George A. Myers to Booker T. Washington, July 20, 1914, Box 16, Folder 5, George A. Myers Papers, Ohio Historical Center, Columbus, OH (hereafter cited in text as GAMP).

3 Booker T. Washington to Jane Hunter, Aug. 4, 1914, BTWP and Booker T. Washington to George A. Meyers, Aug. 4, 1914, GAMP. Several years later, Mrs. Booker T. Washington (Margaret James Murray) provided assistance to the PWA by recommending a cooking teacher for its after-school program for girls. Jane E. Hunter, "A Vacation Camp," *Southern Workman* (Jan.–Dec. 1921): 75-79.

4 "Wings Over Jordan," *Open Door* (Jul. 1938).

5 Jane E. Hunter to George A. Myers, March 28, 1921, Box 17, Folder 5, GAMP.

6 Jane E. Hunter to George A. Myers, Feb. 18, 1925, Box, 18, Folder 1, Ibid.

7 Jane E. Hunter to D. W. E. B. DuBois, Oct. 11, 1935, Phillis Wheatley Association Papers, Phillis Wheatly Association, Cleveland (hereafter cited in the text as PWAP).

8 "Colored Girls in Cleveland," *Crisis* 36 (Dec. 1929): 411–12.

9 "Miss Jane E. Hunter," Editorial, *Journal of the American Medical Association* 18.2 (Apr.–Jun. 1926): 85.

10 Adrienne Jones, *Jane Edna Hunter: A Case Study of Black Leadership, 1910–1950* (Brooklyn: Carlson, 1990), 123-124.

11 Hunter, "The Story of the Phillis Wheatley," *Open Door*

12 Hunter, "Story of the Phillis Wheatley Association," Ibid. (Mar. 1927).

13 Charles W. Chesnutt, "The Negro in Cleveland," *The Clevelander* 5.7 (Nov. 1930): 24.

14 Jane E. Hunter to Charles W. Chesnutt, Oct. 3, 1922, Charles Chesnutt Papers, Microfilm, Western Reserve Historical Society Library, Cleveland.

15 "Phillis Wheatley Celebrates, Dr. Moton is Dedication Speaker," *Open Door* (Apr. 1928).

16 Jane E. Hunter to Alice Dunbar Nelson, Oct. 16, 1933, and Telegram from Alice Dunbar Nelson to Jane Hunter, Oct. 17, 1933, Western Union, PWAP.

17 "Mother's Club," *Open Door* (Apr. 1929) and "Activities of the Educational Department: Dr. Carter G. Woodson Visits The Phillis Wheatley Association," *Open Door* (May 1929).

18 Hunter, "The Story of the Phillis Wheatley Association," *Open Door* (May 1927).

19 Robert H. Bishop, Jr. to Mrs. B. A. Spanye, Jan. 9, 1925, Phillis Wheatley Association Papers.

20 Carrie W. Clifford, ed., *Sowing for Others to Reap* (Cleveland/Boston: Charles W. Alexander, 1900), 3.

21 Warren R. Van Tine and Michael Dale, *Builders of Ohio: A Biographical History* (Columbus: Ohio State University Press, 2003), 239.

22 "The Phillis Wheatley Department of the National Association of Colored Women," Oct. 21, 1936, "H" Miscellaneous 1933–41, n.d., Box 21, Folder 3, National Association of Colored Women, Jennie D. Moton Papers, Moton Family Papers, Manuscript Division, Library of Congress.

23 Mary McLeod Bethune to Jane E. Hunter, Mar. 10, 1938, PWAP; "White House Conference," *Open Door* (Feb. 1940); and Jones, *Jane Edna Hunter*, 124.

24 Jane E. Hunter to Nannie Burroughs, Nov. 2, 1929, "Hunter, Jane E.," Box 13, Folder 22, Nannie Helen Burroughs Papers, Manuscript Division, Library of Congress (hereafter cited in text as NHBP). Used by permission of the Nannie Burroughs School, Inc.

25 Jane E. Hunter to Nannie Burroughs, Dec. 24, 1937, Ibid.

26 Nannie H. Burroughs to Jane E. Hunter, Apr. 1, 1955, Ibid.

27 Jane E. Hunter to Mary McLeod Bethune, Jan. 3, 1934, PWAP.

28 Jane Edna Hunter to John Bennett, Jan. 10, 1939, "Hunter, Jane E." folder, John Bennett Papers, South Carolina Historical Society, Charleston (hereinafter cited in text as JBP).

29 Joanne M. Braxton, *Black Women Writing Autobiography: A Tradition within a Tradition* (Philadelphia: Temple University Press, 1989), 9.

30 Ibid., 142.

31 Jones, *Jane Edna Hunter*

32 Virginia Boyton, "Contested Terrain: The Struggle over Gender Norms for Black Working-

Class Women in Cleveland's Phillis Wheatley Association, 1920–1950," *Ohio History* (1998): 5–22.

33 Hazel Carby, "Policing the Black Woman's Body in an Urban Context," *Critical Inquiry* 18.4 (1992): 739.

34 Ibid., 741–46.

35 Daphne Spain, "Safe Havens for Cleveland's Virtuous Women, 1868-1928," *Journal of Planning History* 3.4 (2004): 267–91.

36 A fiery monster that vainly attempts to lure Christian from the path to heaven.

37 Harriet Jacobs, *Incidents in the Life of a Slave Girl*, ed. Lydia Maria Child (Boston: Author, 1860), 44, 84.

38 Daniel wrote profiles on Janie Porter Barrett, Mary McLeod Bethune, Charlotte Hawkins Brown, Nannie Helen Burroughs, Lucy Craft Laney, Jane Edna Hunter, and Maggie Lena Walker.

39 "Jane Edna Hunter," Sadie Iola Daniel, *Women Builders* (Washington, DC: Associated Publishers, 1931), 164–87.

40 Jane Edna Hunter to Dr. G. Lake Imes, Apr. 1, 1937, PWAP.

41 Dr. G. Lake Imes to Jane Edna Hunter, May 25, 1937, Ibid.

42 Jane E. Hunter to Mr. A. T. Smythe, Jan. 3, 1939, "Jane Edna Hunter" folder, JBP.

43 Jane Edna Hunter to John Bennett, Jan 10, 1939, JBP.

44 Jane E. Hunter to John Bennett, Apr. 11, 1939, Ibid.

45 Frances Phillips, William Morrow & Company, Inc. to Jane E. Hunter, Apr. 28, 1938, Ibid.

46 Jane E. Hunter to John Bennett, Apr. 20, 1939, Ibid.

47 John Bennett to Jane E. Hunter, Apr. 26, 1939, Ibid.

48 Ibid.

49 "Hunter, Jane Edna of U.S.," *A Nickel and a Prayer*, Nov. 27, 1940, Entry No. 146,910, Copyright Office of the United States of America, Library of Congress, Washington, DC.

50 "Miss Hunter Holds House Warming At Elle-Kani Sunday December 9th," Press Release, Dec. 9, 1935, PWAP.

51 The Ohio State Federation of Colored Women's Clubs Annual Meeting program, Jun. 23–26, 1946, Ibid.

52 Ronald L. Jackson and Sonja M. Brown, "Hallie Quinn Brown," *Black Pioneers in Communication Research* (Thousand Oaks, CA: Sage, 2006), 64–83.

53 John Bennett,, "S.C. Negro Woman's Life Is Welfare Drama," review of *A Nickel and a Prayer*, by Jande Edna Hunter, *News and Courier*, November 14, 1940, and "South Carolina Negro's Biography Is Remarkable And Inspiring Testament," review of *A Nickel and a Prayer*, by Jane Edna Hunter, *The State*, December 1, 1940.

54 Carter G. Woodson, "Review: *A Nickel and a Prayer*," *Journal of Negro History* 26.1 (Jan. 1941): 118–20.

55   Ibid.

56   *The Worker: A Missionary and Educational Quarterly* (Jan. Feb. March 1941): 5, and Nannie Burroughs to Jane E. Hunter, Jan. 11, 1943, NHBP.

57   "Books by Negro Authors, 1940," *Crisis* (Mar. 1941): 76.

58   "Mere Mention," *Phylon* 2.2 (2nd Qtr., 1941): 195–97.

59   Eugene F. Gleason, "Faith Wins Fight for Negro Girls: 'A Nickel and a Prayer' tells Phillis Wheatley Story," revew of *A Nickel and a Prayer*, by Jane Edna Hunter, *Cleveland Plain Dealer*, November 17, 1940.

60   Rhoda E. McCulloch to Jane E. Hunter, Dec. 24, 1940, Folder 19, Jane Edna Hunter Papers, Series II, 1909–1964 Westerm Reserve Historical Society Library, Cleveland (hereater cited in text as JHEP II).

61   Edna K. Wooley, "Modern Youngsters Expect Generosity," Book Review, *Cleveland News*, Dec. 15, 1940.

62   Everett C. Hughes, Book Review, *A Nickel and a Prayer*, *American Journal of Sociology* 48.1 (Jun. 1942): 156.

63   Invoice from The Parthenon Press, Nov. 17, 1941, PWAP.

64   Jane E. Hunter to Mrs. C. T. Morris, Sept. 30, 1947, Ibid.

65   An interfaith Christian movement started in the 1920s by Rev. Frank N. D. Buchman that was based on four ideals: honesty, purity, unselfishness, and love. Adherents were encouraged to be socially and politically active in their communities.

66   Doris O'Donnel, "Jane Hunter Recalls Wheatley Group's 42 Years," *Cleveland News*, May 10, 1955.

67   Last Will and Testament, April 20, 1957, Folder 3, Western Reserve Historical Society Library, Jane Edna Hunter Papers, 1930–1969, Cleveland, (hereafter cited in text as JEHP).

ORIGINAL TABLE OF CONTENTS

1   Hunter added Chapter 17, "Fireside Musings," to the second printing of the first edition of *A Nickel and a Prayer* but did not revise the table of contents to reflect this change.

ORIGINAL INTRODUCTION

1   *Phillis Wheatley Association*: In 1913, Jane Edna Hunter began operating the Phillis Wheatley Association (PWA), a residential, employment, and cultural center for unmarried black women and girls in Cleveland, Ohio. Two years earlier, she and several friends had founded the organization as the Working Girls' Home Association but renamed it to honor the first published African American woman poet and to distinguish it from a settlement house, the Colored Working Girls' Christian Home, which James Beason was seeking to establish.

SOURCE: Jones, *Jane Edna Hunter*, 55, 154; and Jane Edna Hunter, "Miscellaneous Writings," JEHP.

2   *Jane Addams*: In 1889, white social activists Jane Addams (1860–1935) and Ellen Gates Starr (1859–1940) cofounded Hull House, a settlement house in Chicago's nineteenth ward that provided civic, social, and educational services for European immigrants.

    SOURCE: Jane Addams, *Twenty Years at Hull House* (New York: MacMillan, 1910).

3   *Dr. Graham Taylor*: In 1894, white Chicago Theological Seminary professor Dr. Graham Taylor (1851–1938) founded the Chicago Commons Settlement House, which he modeled on Hull House, to provide various services for immigrants, including a kindergarten, and a variety of classes and clubs.

    SOURCE: Louise Carroll Wade, *Graham Taylor: Pioneer for Social Justice, 1851–1938* (Chicago: University of Chicago Press, 1964).

4   *two schools of thought*: Bellamy is likely referring to the debate between Booker T. Washington and W. E. B. Du Bois regarding the most effective means for racial uplift. While Washington advocated a "cast down your buckets where you are" strategy that required African Americans to engage in manual labor and domestic work before fighting for equality, Du Bois advocated liberal education for a "Talented Tenth" who would lift up the rest of black America while fighting for civil rights.

    SOURCE: Jacqueline Moore, *Booker T. Washington, W.E.B. Du Bois, and the Struggle for Racial Uplift* (Lanham, MD: Rowman & Littlefield, 2003).

5   *George A. Bellamy*: In 1897, white social activist George Albert Bellamy (1872–1960) and several classmates from Hiram College in Hiram, Ohio founded Hiram House, the first settlement house in Ohio, for European immigrants. Bellamy was Hiram House's first director, serving from 1897–1946.

    SOURCE: Case Western Reserve University and the Western Reserve Historical Society, *Encyclopedia of Cleveland History*, 2002, http://ech.case.edu/index.html, s.v. "Bellamy, George Albert" (hereafter cited in text as *ECH*).

ORIGINAL PREFACE

1   *publisher*: Although Hunter cites Elli Kani as her publisher, evidence suggests that she likely self-published her autobiography. She described her private home in Cleveland as "Elle Kani," an African tribal term that means 'house of faith'" when she invited friends to a housewarming party in 1935. When she filed the copyright for the 1941 edition of *A Nickel and a Prayer*, she left the "Place, Publisher, Date" section blank but listed Elli Kani Publishing Company with the PWA's address as the copyright's claimant. Thus, she may be referencing the feedback she received from Harcourt, Brace & Company, Farrar & Rinehart, and William Morrow & Company who rejected her manuscript either because it did not "come within the scope of their publications" or because they believed it needed to be more of a personal narrative about her life and career.

    SOURCE: "Miss Hunter Holds House Warming At Elle-Kani Sunday December 9th," Press Release, Dec. 9, 1935, PWAP; Jane E. Hunter to John Bennett, Apr. 11, 1939, "Hunter, Jane E." folder, JBP; and "Hunter, Jane Edna of U.S.," *A Nickel and a Prayer*, Nov. 27, 1940, Entry No. 146,910, Copyright Office of the United States of America, Library of Congress, Washington, DC.

2   *Mrs. Robert H. Bishop*: White social and civic activist and club woman Constance Mather
    Bishop (1889–1969) served as PWA trustee and as chairman of the Preliminary Gifts Com-
    mittee for the PWA capital campaign and the PWA Committee on Community Activities.
    Her father, industrialist and philanthropist Samuel Mather (1851–1931), was a descendant
    of Rev. Richard Mather, patriarch of the prominent Puritan New England Mather family and
    grandfather of Cotton Mather, writer and Congregational minister. Her husband, Dr. Robert
    H. Bishop Jr. (1879–1955), was a leader in hospital administration and public health initiatives,
    and chairman of the PWA capital campaign.

    SOURCE: "Minutes of the Meeting of the Phillis Wheatley Board of Trustees," May 11, 1937
    and Jun. 8, 1937, Container 1, Phillis Wheatley Association Records, 1914–1960, Western
    Reserve Historical Society Library, Cleveland (hereafter cited in text as PWAR); R. Y. Mc-
    Cray, ed., *Representative Clevelanders: A Biographical Directory of Leading Men and Women
    in Present-Day Cleveland Community* (Cleveland: Cleveland Topics, 1926), "Bishop, Robert
    H.," 33 (hereafter cited in text as *RC*); *ECH*, s.v. "Bishop, Robert H., Jr.;" and Elroy McKendree
    Avery, vol. 6 of *A History of Cleveland and its Environs: the Heart of New Connecticut* (Chicago:
    Lewis, 1918), 1–3.

3   *Mr. and Mrs. D. W. Frackelton*: white Clevelanders David Waddell Frackelton (1871–1959) and
    Fannie Pitcairn Frackelton (1886–1983) were both active in civic affairs. David Frakelton, press
    manufacturer and banker, was a PWA trustee, while Fannie Frackelton served as president
    of the PWA Board of Trustees from 1923–27 and as building committee member and team
    captain for the 1926 PWA capital campaign.

    SOURCE: William Ganson Rose, *Cleveland: the Making of a City* (Kent, OH: Kent State Uni-
    versity Press, 1990), 474; National Foreign Trade Council, *Official Report of the Second National
    Foreign Trade Convention* (Cambridge, MA: Harvard University, 1922), 276; and Jones, *Jane
    Edna Hunter*, 80, 82.

4   *Mr. W. S. Richardson*: Willard S. Richardson (1866–1952), white pastor of Cleveland's Fifth
    Avenue Baptist Church, served as secretary of the Rockefeller Foundation and as director of
    the Laura Spelman Rockefeller Memorial, which made substantial contributions to African
    American institutions, including Spelman College, a historically black college for women in
    Atlanta, Georgia.

    SOURCE: Albrecht Gerber, *Deissmann the Philologist* (Berlin: Walter de Gruyter, 2010).

5   *Mrs. Levi. T. Scofield*: In 1913, white civic leader Elizabeth Clark Wright Scofield (1845?–1914)
    was elected president of the PWA Board of Trustees, a position she held while also serving as
    president of the board of Cleveland's YWCA, which preferred a predominately white clientele.
    Her husband, Levi T. Scofield (1842–1917), was a prominent Cleveland architect and friend of
    John D. Rockefeller Sr.

    SOURCE: *ECH*, s.v. "Scofield, Levi. T." and George Frederick Wright, *Representative Citizens of
    Ohio: Memorial-Genealogical* (Cleveland: Memorial, 1913), s.v. "Mrs. Elizabeth Clark Scofield,"
    87–96.

6   *Miss Zuleime Garrett: Zuleime Garrett* (1888–1976), white writer, editor, and English teacher
    from Chillicothe, Ohio, eventually taught at East Technical High School in Cleveland.

    SOURCE: Jane E. Hunter to John Bennett, Jan. 10, 1939, JBP; and *English Journal* 19.2 (Feb.
    1930): 154, 171.

7   *Mr. John Bennett*: John Briscoe Bennett (1865–1956), white writer, editor, and artist, provided editorial assistance for the first edition and second printing of *A Nickel and a Prayer*. Hunter had met Bennett at Woodburn Farm in the late 1800s when he was conducting research on Negro spirituals.

SOURCE: Jane E. Hunter to John Bennett, Jan.10, 1939, and Jane E. Hunter to John Bennett, Mar. 10, 1941, JBP; and Harlan Greene, *Mr. Skylark: John Bennett and the Charleston Renaissance* (Athens: University of Georgia Press, 2001), 239.

8   *Miss Rhoda E. McCullough*: Hunter is referring to white pacifist and women's rights activist Rhoda Elizabeth McCulloch (1884–1978), a longtime employee of the national office of the YWCA in New York City. Her tenure included twenty-one years as editor-in-chief of the YWCA's publications department and monthly magazine *The Woman's Press*.

SOURCE: Rhoda E. McCulloch to Jane E. Hunter, Dec. 24, 1940, Folder 19, JEHP II.

CHAPTER 1

1   "*Old Times are Not Forgotten*": In the title of Chapter 1, Hunter alludes to "Dixie," a nostalgic song about the Old South published by composer and minstrel performer Daniel Decatur Emmett in 1859. Emmett had originally titled the song "Dixie's Land" and written it for Bryant's Minstrels, a group of white performers in blackface, but the tune quickly became known simply as "Dixie." After the Confederacy adopted the song as its anthem during the Civil War, Abraham Lincoln accused the South of misappropriating the tune for its cause. By introducing her recollections of childhood through the lens of "Dixie," Hunter encourages her readers to adopt a romanticized view of the South, particularly of relationships between masters and slaves.

SOURCE: Roy P. Basler, ed., vol. 8 of *Collected Works of Abraham Lincoln* (Piscataway, NJ: Rutgers University Press, 1953, 1990), 393; and Gilbert Chase, *America's Music, from the Pilgrims to the Present*, 3rd ed. (Champaign: University of Illinois Press, 1992).

2   *Woodburn Farm*: In 1830, Charles Cotesworth Pinckney (1789–1865), a white Harvard-trained lawyer who preferred the life of affluence associated with being a rice planter, built Woodburn Plantation as a summer home for his family. Eighteen years later, Pinckney sold the plantation to David Taylor, who managed Woodburn for six years before selling it to the Adgers, a prominent Charleston white slaveholding family that included missionaries and businessmen. After the Civil War, Woodburn became a farm that specialized in breeding race horses and hogs.

SOURCE: Paul M. Franklin and Nancy Mikula, *South Carolina's Plantations and Historic Homes* (Osceola, WI: Voyageur Press, 2006); and Beth Ann Wiles, "Pinckney Home Built Soon After Revolutionary War is Still Standing," *Anderson Daily Mail*, Mar. 11, 1932.

3   *Erskine Caldwell*: Twentieth-century white American writer and editor Erskine Caldwell (1903–1987) published popular works that explored race, class, politics, and gender, particularly in the South, but he was also criticized for his depictions of rural poverty.

SOURCE: James Korges, *Erskine Caldwell: American Writers 78, University of Minnesota Pamphlets on American Writers* (Minneapolis: University of Minnesota Press, 2009).

4   *Margaret Bourke-White*: Internationally renowned white photojournalist Margaret Bourke-

White (1904–1971) toured the South with Erskine Caldwell in 1936 to take photographs for their book *You Have Seen Their Faces* (1937), a photo-essay about poor, rural Southerners during the Great Depression.

SOURCE: Vicki Goldberg, *Margaret Bourke-White: A Biography* (New York: Harper Collins, 1986).

5   *Edward Harris*: Edward Harris (1858–1892) was about twenty years old when he married Harriet Milliner.

6   *English plantation overseer*: Not yet identified.

7   *Full-blooded Negro woman*: Rose Harris (1830–?) had at least five other children, Clara (1854–?), Charlott (1864–?), Thadius (1866–?), Elizabeth (1869–?), and Henry (1871–?).

8   *Winston, Jane, Rosa, and Rebecca*: Winston Harris (1882?–1944), Rosa Harris (?–1907), and Rebecca Harris (1893–?).

9   *he had a violent temper*: Hunter presents a dramatically different recollection of her parents' temperaments in an undated draft of her manuscript: "Mother had a temper, but it was controlled equally as it was aroused, when the sense of reasoning came to her." Rather than focus on her father's temper, she writes affectionately of an "energetic" man who found happiness in working hard to care for his family and serve the Methodist Episcopal Church.

SOURCE: Hunter, "My Childhood Days," Folder 7, JEHP.

10   *mother*: Harriet Milliner (1865–1910) was about fifteen years old when she married Edward Harris.

11   *Grandfather Milliner*: In an undated draft of her manuscript, Hunter presents a different account of William Milliner's (ca. 1840–?) attitude toward the marriage of his daughters: "Mother often told me that her father, Lanky Milliner, was insanely and cruelly strict with his children even to the extent that all of the girls in her family had to run away to be married." Hunter also added the racial marker, "native-born African," in the second printing of her autobiography.

SOURCE: Hunter, "My Childhood Days," Folder 7, JEHP.

12   *Hanckel Place*: Hunter is likely referring to William H. Hanckel's 382-acre property that adjoined Woodburn Farm.

SOURCE: Clerk of Court, Register of Deeds, Anderson County, South Carolina. Anderson County Public Library, Anderson, SC. Microform, Vol. R2, 247 (hereafter cited in text as Register of Deeds). microfilm, 247.

13   *first child, Winston*: Hunter may have been the firstborn child in the family. She cites her birth date as December 13, 1882; census, death, and military records present Winston Harris's birth date as December 16, 1882 or 1884.

SOURCE: "Mrs. Jane Hunter," Container 9, Folder 3, PWAR; Social Security Death Index, s.v. "Winston Harris;" "Winston Edward Harris," U.S. World War I Draft Registration Card; and "Winston Edward Harris," U.S. World War II Draft Registration Card.

14   *Jane McCrary*: Not yet identified.

15   *house leaks*: Hunter is referring to houseleeks, a medicinal plant that folk doctors often used to treat sprains, bee stings, and warts.

Source: J. K. Crellin, Jane Philpott and A. L. Tommie Bass, *Herbal Medicine Past and Present: A Reference Guide to Medicinal Plants* (Durham: Duke University Press, 1990).

16 *four o'clocks*: Flowers that gained their name because their trumpet-shaped blossoms open in the late afternoon.

17 *camp meeting*: White Methodist minister John McGee initiated the first camp meeting in 1799 when his powerful sermon delivered at a religious gathering on the Red River in Kentucky led to a series of meetings where attendees enjoyed listening to child and adult preachers and exhorters. Baptists, Methodists, Presbyterians, and Episcopalians flocked to the area and formed an encampment so they could attend all of the services. During the nineteenth century, some denominations, particularly the Methodists, continued to hold camp meetings that featured fervent preaching, singing, and praying over several days.

Source: Barlow Weed Gorham and John Bray, *Camp Meeting Manual, a Practical Book for the Camp Ground; in Two Parts* (Boston: H. V. Degen, 1854).

18 *Grandma Milliner was part Cherokee Indian*: Hunter added these details about her grandmother Pauline "Polly" Milliner's (1835–1910) Native American heritage in the second printing of her autobiography on the advice of Hannah Smythe Wright, John Bennett's sister-in-law, whom Hunter had known when she and Hannah lived at Woodburn. Wright recalls, "Was not Polly part Cherokee Indian? She was tall, straight, red-brown and carried herself well…. As you know there were and still are not few, both white and dark who have that strain of Indian blood, and are rather proud of it."

Source: John Bennett to Jane E. Hunter, Apr. 1, 1941, JBP.

19 *snowballs*: Another name for a hydrangea, a plant that produces large, flowering blooms that resemble snowballs.

20 *morning glories*: Saucer-shaped flowers that open in the morning.

21 *mulatto*: The definition of "mulatto" has varied by historical period and context. The term initially referred to a person of African American and white American descent; it has also been used to describe racially mixed African Americans, Native Americans, and admixtures thereof. Although the U.S. Federal Census Bureau included "mulatto" as a multiracial designator on its survey forms from 1850 to 1920 (with the exception of 1910), it did not always offer its field agents clear guidance as to how to determine a respondent's multiracial status. The word is widely considered an epithet.

Source: Jack D. Forbes, *Africans and Native Americans: The Language of Race and the Evolution of Red-Black Peoples*, 2nd ed. (Urbana: University of Illinois Press, 1993); and Ann Morning, "New Faces, Old Faces: Counting the Multiracial Population Past and Present," in *New Faces in a Changing America: Multiracial Identity in the 21st Century*, eds. Loretta I. Winters and Herman L. De Bose (Thousand Oaks, CA: Sage Publications, 2003), 41–67.

22 *Dr. Thomas Pickens*: Thomas Jones Pickens Jr. (1842–1894), son of Colonel Thomas Jones (1808–1894) and Keziah Miles Pickens (1810–1889), was a prominent physician in Pendleton, South Carolina, and a descendent of Revolutionary War hero General Andrew Pickens (1739–1817).

Source: Cecil B. Hartley, *Heroes and Patriots of the South, Comprising the Lives of General*

Francis Marion, General William Moultrie, General Andrew Pickens, and Governor John Rutledge, (Philadelphia: G. G. Evans, 1860).

23 *"I wonder were my mother has gone" with the refrain, "Oh, you must have that pure religion":* Hunter is conflating lines from two Negro spirituals, "I Wonder Where My Mother Has Gone" and "Oh, You Must Have that True Religion," that enslaved African Americans created to express their faith in God to provide freedom from sin and slavery on earth and entry into heaven where they would be reunited with loved ones.

24 *Great-grandmother Cumber:* Cumber Hamilton (1813–?).

25 *corn pone:* A biscuit much like corn bread, made of white corn meal, butter, salt, milk, and eggs.

26 *hug-me-tight buggy:* A horse-drawn buggy designed for two people and often favored by couples who were courting.

27 *revival:* An intense religious awakening in a church or community characterized by public confession of sin and recommitment to God.

28 *Methodist Church:* The King's Chapel African Methodist Episcopal Church in Pendleton, South Carolina, was founded in 1865 when land was purchased to build the Pendleton Colored Methodist Church. In 1870, the church affiliated itself with the AME denomination.

Source: W. J. Megginson, *African American Life in South Carolina's Upper Piedmont,* 1780–1900 (Columbia: University of South Carolina Press, 2006), 295–96.

29 *mercy bench:* A kneeling area in front of the church pulpit where the penitent gather to confess their sins and pray that God will grant them mercy and pardon.

30 *"Sing":* Nickname given to Hunter by her father.

31 *In the happier circumstances of slavery:* Hunter is referencing the idealized view of slavery as a paternalistic institution in which masters treated enslaved African Americans as members of an "extended family" to mitigate charges that bondage was dehumanizing and oppressive.

Source: Jeffrey Robert Young, *Domesticating Slavery: The Master Class in Georgia and South Carolina,* 1670–1837 (Chapel Hill: University of North Carolina Press, 1999).

32 *Pendleton:* The region of South Carolina that in 1894 comprised Anderson, Pickens, and Oconee counties became known as Pendleton after the Cherokees, Chickasaws, Choctaws, and Creeks ceded the land in the 1785 signing of the Treaty of Hopewell. Scots-Irish immigrants and affluent planters and politicians from the South Carolina Lowcountry were the town's first residents. Pendleton is named for Judge Henry Pendleton of Culpepper, Virginia, organizer of the Culpepper Minute Men who fought in the Revolutionary War.

Source: Hurley E. Badders, *Remembering South Carolina's Old Pendleton District* (Charleston, SC: History Press, 2006); and D. E. Frierson, "Old Stone Church and Cemetery, Address of Rev. D. E. Frierson, of Anderson, S.C., Delivered before the Old Stone church and Cemetery Association on October 11, 1894," in *The Old Stone Church of Oconee County, South Carolina,* ed. Richard Newman Brackett (Columbia, SC: R. L. Bryan, 1905), 110–26.

33 *seventy-five cents a rod:* Edward Hunter's purchasing power for every five and one half yards of ditches that he dug is equivalent to approximately US$(2010)17.00.

34 *school*: The Silver Spring Baptist Church congregation opened a school for African American children in the first church building they had erected on their property. By 1870, seventy-six students and one teacher were meeting in the one-room school.

SOURCE: State Historic Preservation Office, *African American Historic Places in South Carolina* (Columbia: South Carolina Department of Archives and History, 2007), 2.

35 *Silver Spring Baptist Church*: During the 1860s, African American Baptists in Pendleton desired their own church. Initially, they worshiped with the Abel Baptist Church in Clemson. Seven deacons from the Abel church soon decided to build a Baptist church in Pendleton, however, and purchased a tree-filled site that included a spring, hence the name Silver Spring.

SOURCE: Megginson, *African American Life*, 296 and 306.

36 *Mr. Richardson's*: Not yet identified.

37 *Miss Ruby Sands*: Not yet identified. In an undated draft of her manuscript, however, Hunter identifies her benefactor as Miss Ruby Sharp.

SOURCE: Hunter, "My Childhood Days," Folder 7, JEHP.

38 *Werner Place*: Not yet identified.

39 *Fant plantation*: Fant plantation was located in part of the current day Fant's Grove area in Anderson and Pickens Counties, South Carolina. The old 1837 plantation house is now incorporated into the Victorian farmhouse that stands directly across Hwy 187 from the Pendleton High School.

SOURCE: Timothy Drake, e-mail message to the editor, November 29, 2010.

40 *"Oh Lawd, Won't You Hear Me Pray?"*: a Negro spiritual also known as "Oh, Lord, Won't You Hear Me Pray."

41 *"Swing Low, Sweet Chariot"*: Negro spiritual that draws on the imagery from the biblical narrative of the prophet Elijah being transported to heaven in a fiery chariot at the end of his earthly ministry. "And it came to pass, as they still went on, and talked, that, behold, there appeared a chariot of fire, and horses of fire, and parted them both asunder; and Elijah went up by a whirlwind into heaven" (2 Kings 2:11).

42 *"Walk Together, Children, Don't You Get Weary"*: Negro spiritual that reflects the Israelites' journey from slavery in Egypt to freedom in the Promised Land, but the slaves identified the destination of their sojourn as a fervent religious revival in an earthly land of liberty and in heaven.

43 *Aunt Neat*: Neat Milliner (?–?) was a midwife and the sister of Hunter's mother.

44 *"We Are Climbing Jacob's Ladder"*: Negro spiritual based on the biblical story of Jacob, who dreamed of angels ascending and descending upon a ladder between earth and heaven while he was fleeing from home after stealing his twin brother Esau's birthright (Gen. 28:12–13).

45 *reels*: Popular late nineteenth-century dance tunes. White composer Stephen C. Foster (1826–1864) wrote many reels, including "Swanee River" and "Old Black Joe." Foster's lyrics often featured stereotypical African American characters who expressed nostalgia for the pre-Civil War South.

SOURCE: William Austin, *"Susanna," "Jeanie," and "The Old Folks at Home": The Music of Stephen C. Foster from His Time to Ours* (New York: MacMillan, 1975).

46 *St. John's Baptist Church*: Not yet identified.

47 *hod-carrier*: Laborer who carried supplies for bricklayers, stonemasons, cement finishers, or plasterers.

48 *Clemson College*: Land-grant public college established by a bequest in Thomas Green Clemson's (1807–1888) will for South Carolina young people to study scientific agriculture and mechanical arts. In 1889, South Carolina Governor John Peter Richardson signed the bill that created the Clemson Agricultural College on Fort Hill Plantation. The college opened as a military school for white males in 1893, became coeducational in 1955, was integrated in 1963, and renamed Clemson University in 1964.

Source: Alma Bennett, ed., *Thomas Green Clemson* (Clemson, SC: ClemsonPrints, 2009).

49 *Carey Farm*: Hunter is likely referring to J. W. Carey's 159-acre farm located in Anderson and Oconee Counties northwest of Woodburn Farm.

Source: Register of Deeds, Microform, Vol. P2, 149.

50 *yellow homespun tick*: Coarse, homemade linen fabric used as a covering for mattresses that were filled with feathers, straw, or wild grass.

51 *brass-tipped brogan shoes*: Thick, heavy, straight-footed shoes made of rough leather that were often worn by farm workers and soldiers.

52 *Blue Back Speller, The Little Red Hen*, and *First Reader*: In 1783, the Hartford firm Hudson & Goodwin published Noah Webster's *A Grammatical Institute of the English Language: Comprising, an Easy, Concise, and Systematic Method of Education*. This title was changed to *The American Spelling Book* and, later, to *The Elementary Spelling Book*, but the text was commonly known as the "Blue-Back Speller" for its familiar blue cover. In the late nineteenth century, the popular folk tale "The Little Red Hen" was adapted as a children's story to teach moral lessons to beginning readers. Lewis Baxter Monroe's *The First Reader* (1873) was a primary school textbook.

Source: Joseph Ellis, *After the Revolution* (New York: Norton, 2002), 172; Lewis Baxter Monroe, *The First Reader* (Philadelphia: Cowperthwait, 1873); and Richard L. Venezky, *The American Way of Spelling: The Structure and Origins of American English Orthography* (New York: Guilford, 1999).

53 *"setting-up"*: *Settin' up* was a funeral ritual similar to a wake in which the body of the deceased was prepared ("set up") for viewing and mourners gathered to sing, pray, and reminisce. Among African Americans in the late nineteenth century, the settin' up took place in the home of the departed on the eve of the funeral and sometimes included an all-night vigil.

Source: Suzanne E. Smith, *To Serve the Living: Funeral Directors and the African American Way of Death* (Cambridge, MA: Belknap Press of Harvard University Press, 2010), 84.

54 *"I'm Going Home to Die No More"*: William Hunter (1811–77) wrote the words and William Miller (1801–1878) wrote the music for this hymn, "The Heavenly Home," first published in William Hunter's *Sacred Melodies* (1838).

CHAPTER 2

1   *Aunt Flora*: Flora Milliner (1862–?) was the sister of Hunter's mother.

2   *Calhoun Family*: The Calhouns were descendants of John C. Calhoun (1782–1850), the seventh vice president of the United States who resigned from office to become a U.S. senator so that he could more effectively champion states' rights. John Calhoun's daughter, Anna Calhoun (1817–1875), married Thomas Green Clemson (1807–1888), founder of Clemson College (now Clemson University).

Source: Bennett, *Thomas Green Clemson*.

3   *Anderson*: Anderson County was formed when the US government deeded Cherokee land in the South Carolina Piedmont to the state in 1777. The town, named in honor of Revolutionary War hero General Robert Anderson (1741–1813), developed because it was located on a major trading route between Georgia and North Carolina. The city of Anderson was incorporated in 1882.

Source: Anderson Chamber of Commerce, *History of Anderson County, South Carolina* (Anderson: Anderson Area Chamber, 1981).

4   *James Wilson Family*: Not yet identified. In an undated draft of her manuscript, however, Hunter identifies the family as the Watkinses.

Source: Hunter, "Miscellaneous Writings," Folder 7, JEHP.

5   *Mother had remarried*: Hunter's step-father has not yet been identified.

6   *Aunt Anna*: Anna Milliner (1871–?) was one of Hunter's mother's younger sisters.

7   *perambulator*: A stroller, or baby buggy.

8   *King St.*: The affluent business and residential main street of historical downtown Charleston.

9   *50 cents a week*: Hunter's purchasing power for a week's wages is equivalent to approximately US$(2010)12.00.

10   *Aunt Caroline*: Caroline Milliner (1855–?) was married to Hunter's mother's brother Abe Milliner.

11   *Captain Joseph Ellison Adger*: Joseph Ellison Adger (1824–1889), who served in the Confederate army, owned Woodburn Plantation from 1859 to 1881.

Source: Yates Snowden, ed., vol. 3 of *History of South Carolina* (Chicago: Lewis, 1920), s.v. "John Bailey Adger," 105.

12   *Augustine T. Smythe*: Augustine Thomas Smythe (1842–1914), lawyer, South Carolina state senator, and former Confederate army major, owned Woodburn during the time Hunter's family lived and worked there. In 1865, he married Louisa Rebecca McCord (1845–1928) of Columbia, South Carolina.

Source: William J. Cooper, *The Conservative Regime: South Carolina, 1877–1890* (Columbia: University of South Carolina Press, 2005).

13   *overseer's*: Benjamin Bonneau Harris Jr. (1851–1925?).

14   *Miss Orpha*: Orpha G. Harris (1876–1969).

15 *buck-dancer*: A nineteenth-century performer of dance routines that involved intricate shuffle and tap movements. Buck-dancers in minstrel or vaudeville shows often performed routines that exaggerated and derided African American dance, however.

16 *Charleston*: A folk dance rooted in African dance traditions of stomping and clapping that was popularized by African Americans in the South, particularly in Charleston, South Carolina, and evolved into a dance featuring fast swaying arm and foot movements performed to ragtime music in the early twentieth century.

17 *Uncle Abe*: Abe Milliner (1853–1946) was the older brother of Hunter's mother.

18 *stripping fodder*: Harvesting corn, wheat, or grass for livestock.

19 *Misses "Susy" and "Hannah" and the Major's two sons*: Augustine and Louisa Smythe's children Susan Dunlap Smythe (1878–?), who married John Bennett, one of the editors Hunter consulted for *A Nickel and a Prayer*; Hannah McCord Smythe Wright (1874–1955), who provided editorial commentary for the second printing of the autobiography; Langdon Cheves McCord Smythe (1883–1941); and Augustine Thomas Smythe III (1885–1962). The Smythes had two other children: a son, Augustine Thomas Smythe II (1877–1884), who died when he was seven years old, and a daughter, Louisa Cheves Smythe Stoney (1868–1939).

SOURCE: John Bennett to Jane E. Hunter, Jan. 12, 1939 and John Bennett to Jane E. Hunter, Apr. 1, 1941, JBP.

20 *"jiner"*: A fair weather convert.

CHAPTER 3

1 *Pendleton County School*: Hunter is likely referring to the Pendleton County Negro School.

2 *Two Presbyterian missionaries*: In 1883, the Presbyterian Board of Missions for Freedmen sent Rev. Emory W. (?–1910) and Mrs. Ella V. Chase Williams (1852 or 1854–?) to Abbeville, South Carolina, to build a church and school. When the local white Presbyterians refused to support their work, the Williamses successfully petitioned the Presbyterian General Assembly to allow them to establish a separate synod for black churches, which led to the founding of the Colored Presbyterian Church in 1898.

SOURCE: Daniel, *Women Builders*, 168; Linda Spencer, vol. 8 of *African American National Biography*, eds. Henry Louis Gates Jr. and Evelyn Brooks Higginbotham (New York: Oxford University Press, 2008), s.v. "Williams, Ella V.," 314–16 (hereafter cited in text as AANB); and Lowry Ware, *Old Abbeville: Scenes of the Past of a Town Where Old Times are not Forgotten* (Columbia, SC: SCMAR, 1992).

3 *Ferguson and Williams College*: The Williamses established Ferguson College in 1885 to provide industrial training and religious, musical, and literary education for African American children. They named the school in honor of Presbyterian minister Rev. James Alexander Ferguson (1843–?), a major northern donor. Ella Williams, a Howard University trained educator, served as administrator and teacher, and Emory Williams raised funds and garnered support for the college from Southern blacks. In 1894, the Williamses founded Ferguson and Williams College after they were forced out of Ferguson College by white Southerners, who were envious of their success, and by the Presbyterian Board of Missions for Freedmen, who sought to control the school.

SOURCE: Ibid and Nagueyalti Warren, vol. 2 of *Notable Black American Women*, ed. Jessie Carney Smith (Detroit: Gale Research, 1996), s.v. "Williams, Ella V. Chase," 714–16.

4 *Bringing in the Sheaves*: In 1874, Knowles Shaw (1834–1878) wrote the lyrics, and in 1880, George A. Minor, a Civil War veteran, wrote the music for the hymn "Bringing in the Sheaves."

5 *liveried butler*: Head servant or slave in a household, often the footman who cared for horses and carriages, who wore a colorful, ornate uniform that clearly identified his occupation but also signified his lower status as a domestic.

6 *Little Sally Walker*: Hunter was likely alluding to a sweetheart song enjoyed by southern children. There are many different adaptations of this song based on the following rhyme: "Little Sally Walker, sitting in a saucer, / Crying and sighing for some young man to come. / Rise, Sally, rise and wipe your weeping eyes; / fly to the East and fly to the West, / And kiss the one you love the best."

SOURCE: Paul G. Brewster, *Children's Games and Rhymes* (Manchester, NH: Ayer Publishing, 1976), 130–31.

7 *beef-lights*: The lungs of cows or sheep that were also used as fish bait.

SOURCE: Fred Mather, *Modern Fish Culture in Fresh and Salt Water* (New York: Forest and Stream, 1900), 130.

8 *"Blessed are those who hunger and thirst, for they shall be fed."*: Hunter is appropriating a scripture from the Beatitudes to reiterate the students' hunger and dissatisfaction with their meal: "Blessed are they which do hunger and thirst after righteousness: for they shall be filled" (Matt. 5:6).

9 *Tennyson's "Queen of the May"*: "The May Queen" is an early poem by Alfred Lord Tennyson that focuses on a young girl, the "May Queen," who tells her mother what she will accomplish in her new role. The celebrations date back to Elizabethan times when a teenage girl, selected as the May Queen, wore a white gown and crown, gave a speech, and led a parade to initiate the spring festival.

SOURCE: Alfred Tennyson, *The May Queen* (London: Sampson Low, 1861).

10 *Presbyterian ladies in the North*: White Northern women, often affiliated with the Presbyterian Board of Missions for Freedmen, who raised funds for the religious, civic, and academic education of African Americans in the South after the Civil War.

SOURCE: Lois A. Boyd and R. Douglas Brackenridge, *Presbyterian Women in American: Two Centuries of a Quest for Status* (Santa Barbara, CA: Greenwood, 1996), 23–50.

11 *orphan girl*: In the first edition of *A Nickel and a Prayer*, Hunter uses the word "pickaninny" to describe herself. She may have decided to change the word to "orphan girl" because her mother never reunited the family after her husband's death, although the word "orphan" was also used to describe children who only had one living parent.

CHAPTER 4

1 *"I Feel Like a Motherless Child"*: Hunter is quoting lyrics from the Negro spiritual, "Sometimes I Feel Like a Motherless Child."

2   *cartwhips*: Given the pastoral setting, Hunter is probably referring to the eastern coachwhip snake, which derives its name from the resemblance of its scale pattern to a braided leather whip, similar to the cart-whips overseers used to punish slaves. The eastern coachwhip is present in the South Carolina Upstate.

3   *snake doctors*: Southern term for dragonfly.

4   *biblical injunction*: "In the sweat of thy face shalt thou eat bread, till thou return unto the ground; for out of it wast thou taken: for dust thou art, and unto dust shalt thou return" (Gen. 3:19).

5   *"still small voice"*: After the prophet Elijah won a victory for God on Mt. Carmel, he fled to the wilderness when Queen Jezebel threatened to kill him. Instead of manifesting himself through a powerful force of nature, God communicated with Elijah in a "still small voice": "And after the earthquake a fire; but the LORD was not in the fire; and after the fire a still small voice" (2 Kings 9:11–12).

6   *"When the mist is rolled away and the morning comes"*: Hunter may be referencing the hymn "By and By" (1906) by African American Methodist minister Charles Robert Tinley (1851–1933).

7   *"I'm almost home"*: Lyrics are from the old plantation hymn "Dem Charming Bells."

8   *"Walk together children"*: Lyrics are from the Negro spiritual "Walk Together Children."

9   *"Weep no more, my lady/weep no more today"*: Not yet identified.

10   *Uncle John*: Likely a reference to Parris John Milliner (1860–1941), an older brother of Hunter's mother.

11   *Pullman car cleaning*: The Pullman Palace Car Company was a railroad corporation that offered porter jobs, one of the few steady forms of employment for African American men in the late-nineteenth- and early- to mid-twentieth century. Pullman car cleaning was an extensive cleaning and disinfecting of a railcar after its journey.

   SOURCE: Joseph Husband, *Story of the Pullman Car* (Chicago: A. C. McClurg, 1917).

12   *marriage*: Hunter provides conflicting information about her marriage. In a biographical sketch about Hunter published in *Women Builders* (1931), Sadie Iola Daniel writes, "When Jane's mother learned that her daughter planned to stay in Abbeville where she could earn five dollars a month, she ordered Jane to come home and marry a rich old man. To escape marrying she went to her uncle in Florida, where she attended Harlen [*sic*] Academy one year." In an undated draft of her manuscript, Hunter writes that after completing her education at Ferguson and Williams College, her mother "came and took me home where I was supposed to marry an old man whom I did not love, but who was very rich. I went from home to keep from marrying, and went with my Uncle John to his home in Florida where I attended the Harlem Academy for one year. Upon my return to mother (I was then quite seventeen years old) I persuaded Aunt Caroline and my mother to permit me to go to Charleston S.C. to work in the home of a very wealthy family whose ancestors were the slave owners of my grand parents [*sic*] on my mother's side."

   SOURCE: Daniel, *Women Builders*, 168; and Hunter, typed manuscript page number 6, Folder 7, JEHP.

13   *Edward Hunter*: Not yet identified.

1   *Major & Mrs. Benjamin Rutledge*: Benjamin Huger Rutledge (1860–1925) was born in Charleston to the prominent Rutledge family, descendants of John Rutledge (1739–1800), the first governor of South Carolina. Benjamin Rutledge served in the Confederate army and then practiced law for many years. He was also a member of the South Carolina General Assembly. In 1882, he married Emma Craig Blake (1865–1935) of Fletcher, North Carolina.

SOURCE: Snowden and Cutler, vol. 5 of *History of South Carolina*, 116.

2   *Like Paul the apostle*: Ironically, Hunter may be comparing herself to the Apostle Paul who rented a home where he could receive guests and preach the gospel, instead of being housed with the other prisoners: "And Paul dwelt two whole years in his own hired house, and received all that came in unto him" (Acts 28:30).

3   *Mrs. Ella Hunt*: Ella Hunt (?–?) was chairman of the African American Ladies' Auxiliary of the Cannon Street Hospital and Training School for Nurses in Charleston, South Carolina.

SOURCE: Daniel, *Women Builders*, 169.

4   *Cannon Street Hospital and Training School for Nurses*: In 1896, African American physician Alonzo C. McClellan established this institution in Charleston for the training of African American nurses.

SOURCE: Edmund L. Drago, *Charleston's Avery Center: From Education and Civil Rights to Preserving the African American Experience* (Charleston: History Press, 2006), 99.

5   *Squeers School*: A reference to Mr. Wackford Squeers's academy, Dotheboys Hall, in Charles Dickens's *Nicholas Nickelby*. The "Squeers School" is synonymous with an absence of sympathy and an abundance of difficult labor.

SOURCE: Frank Louis Soldan, *The Century and the School and Other Educational Essays* (New York: MacMillan, 1912), 118.

6   *whipped [blood], as I went along, to separate the fibrin from the serum*: Hunter was employing a crude method to separate fibrin, a blood clotting agent, from the serum, blood plasma.

SOURCE: Ruth E. McCall and Cathee M. Tankersley, *Phlebotomy Essentials* (Philadelphia: Lippincott Williams & Wilkins, 2007), 205–06.

7   *caste system based upon color*: During slavery, lighter-skinned African Americans were often preferred over darker-skinned African Americans, within both white and black communities. Bi-racial and light-skinned African Americans frequently formed separate residential communities, such as the Blue Vein Society, and even separate churches, and were favored for jobs and educational opportunities.

SOURCE: Trina Jones, "Shades of Brown: The Law of Skin Color," *Duke Law Journal* 49. 6 (2000): 1487–1557.

8   *Dr. T. Grange Simons*: White physician Thomas Grange Simons Jr. (1843–1927) attended Charleston College and served in the Confederate Army. After the war, he studied medicine and worked at the Charleston City Hospital, and later opened a private practice. Simons also served on numerous medical boards and was well-known and respected in the city for his service.

SOURCE: Snowden, vol. 5 of *History of South Carolina*, 164–65.

9   *Dr. McClellan*: Hunter is referring to African American physician Alonzo Clifton McClellan (1855–1912) who received his medical training at Howard University. He founded the Cannon Street Hospital and Training School for Nurses and the People's Pharmacy in Charleston and established the Palmetto Medical, Dental, and Pharmaceutical Association for black physicians in South Carolina who were denied admission to the American Medical Association. He also established and edited the *Hospital Herald*, a monthly newsletter that provided information for medical professionals, mothers, and the sick.

Source: Edward H. Beardsley, vol. 5 of *AANB*, s.v. "McClellan, Alonzo Clifton," 475–76; Evangeline Banks Harrison, "Address," Evangeline Banks Harrison Papers, Avery Research Center for African American History and Culture, Charleston; and G. F. Richings, *Evidences of Progress Among Colored People* (Philadelphia: Geo. S. Ferguson, 1905), 550.

10   *Charleston City Hospital*: Hunter likely refers to two hospitals founded in 1865. One was located in the Bischoff mansion in Hampstead and treated whites; the second was located in a work house and treated African Americans. Along with the Marine Hospital, they were called the City Hospitals of Charleston.

Source: Records of the Commissioners of the City Hospital, 1879–1907, Charleston Archives, Special Collections, Charleston County Public Library, Charleston, SC.

11   *Nicodemus*: Hunter compares her evening visit with Dr. Simons to that of the wealthy Pharisee Nicodemus's late night conference with Jesus when the member of the Jewish Sanhedrin secretly sought to understand the Kingdom of God. Hunter was likely seeking to conceal her intentions from Dr. McClellan and other mentors who may have been disappointed that she did not accept the equally prestigious head nurse position at Cannon Hospital. She chooses instead to work for one of Charleston's prominent white physicians, whom she transforms into a miracle-working Jesus-figure (John 3:1–21).

12   *Swedish massage:* A massage style developed in Sweden in the 1830s that relied on a mixture of long strokes and kneading and was designed to increase circulation in the surface tissues.

Source: Mary Beth Braun, et al., *Introduction to Massage Therapy* (Philadelphia: Lippincott Williams & Wilkins, 2007), 15–18.

13   *Wagner family, Wagner Sleeping Car Company*: In 1858, white businessman Webster Wagner (1817–1882) founded the second-largest sleeping car company in America. He was a protégé of railroad magnate Cornelius Vanderbilt and headed the management of the Vanderbilt sleeping car system, later renaming it the Wagner Palace Car Company. Wagner served in the New York State Assembly and the state senate.

Source: John H. White Jr., *The American Railroad Passenger Car* (Baltimore: Johns Hopkins University Press, 1985), 655; and H. M. Harter, *World Railways of the Nineteenth Century* (Baltimore: Johns Hopkins University Press, 2005), 250.

14   *Dr. Charles U. Shepard, owner of Shepard Tea Farm*: Charles Upham Shepard (ca. 1804–1886), white professor of chemistry, botany, and mineralogy, taught at the South Carolina Medical College in Charleston. He established a tea plantation in Pinehurst, near Summerville, South Carolina, just prior to the Civil War. His tea pickers consisted entirely of African Americans, mostly children, who were paid twenty to fifty cents a day.

Source: United States Industrial Commission, "Testimony of Mr. Charles U. Shephard," vol.

10 of *Report of the U.S. Industrial Commission on Agriculture and Agricultural Labor* (Washington: Government Printing Office, 1901), 441; James D. Dana and Edward S. Dana, eds., vol. 31 of *The American Journal of Science*, Nos. 181–186 (New Haven, CT: J. D. and E. S. Dana, 1986), 483; and "Sketch of Charles Upham Shepherd," *Popular Science* 47. 35 (Aug. 1895): 548–53.

15   *Legare Walker, Attorney-at-Law*: Legare Walker Jr. (1905–1973), a member of a prominent white South Carolina family, began practicing law in 1898 in Charleston and Summerville and also became a leading Democrat in the state.

   SOURCE: Snowden, vol. 5 of *History of South Carolina*, 246; and Herbert Ravenel Sass, *History of the South Carolina Lowcountry* (West Columbia, SC: J. F. Heyer, 1956).

16   *horrible slums of historic Charleston*: Although Charleston was one of the most racially integrated US cities from the Civil War through the first half of the twentieth century, certain streets and neighborhoods were almost entirely inhabited by poor African Americans. These streets often lay directly beside wealthy, white residential areas. Perhaps the most famous of these tenement slums was Cabbage Row on Church Street, fictionalized as "Catfish Row" in the novel and Broadway musical *Porgy and Bess*.

   SOURCE: Sidney Bland, *Preserving Charleston Past, Shaping Its Future: the Life and Times of Susan Pringle Frost* (Columbia: University of South Carolina Press, 1999), 48–49; and Timothy J. Nelson, *Every Time I Feel the Spirit: Religious Experience and Ritual in an African American Church* (New York: New York University Press, 2004), 16.

17   *Dixie Hospital and Training School for Nurses*: In 1892, the Hampton Nurse Training School and Dixie Hospital were established for the teaching and training of African American nurses.

   SOURCE: Faustine C. Jones-Wilson, et al., eds., *Encyclopedia of African American Education* (Westport, CT: Greenwood, 1996), s.v. "Nursing Education, African Americans, And," 336.

18   *Hampton Institute*: Educational institution founded by the American Missionary Association in 1870 and further developed by former Union general Samuel Chapman Armstrong to train black teachers for rural schools. Hampton provided the model for the Tuskegee Institute.

   SOURCE: Frances Greenwood Peabody, *Education for Life: The Story of Hampton Institution* (Garden City, NJ: Doubleday, 1918), 95–126.

19   *Miss Mollie Williamson*: Not yet identified.

20   *Mr. and Mrs. William Coleman*: Not yet identified.

CHAPTER 6

1   *Central Avenue*: African American residents and businesses clustered along Central Avenue in Cleveland during the early twentieth century, because racial and economic discrimination prevented the majority of them from settling in other areas of the city.

   SOURCE: Kenneth Kusmer, *A Ghetto Takes Shape* (Urbana: University of Illinois Press), 41–42.

2   *Woodluff Hall*: A dance hall for African Americans in Cleveland owned by Albert D. "Starlight" Boyd.

   SOURCE: Katrina Hazzard-Gordon, *Jookin: The Rise of Social Dance Clubs in African-Ameri-*

can Culture (Philadelphia: Temple University Press, 1990), 127–31.

3   *"Starlight"*: Influential mixed-race business owner, real estate speculator, hustler, and community leader Albert D. "Starlight" Boyd (1872–1921) who helped finance Thomas W. Fleming's successful campaign to become Cleveland's first black city councilman and ingratiated himself to the African American community by providing assistance to needy families.

    Source: Ibid., 744-75; Russell H. Davis, *Black Americans in Cleveland: George Peake, to Carl B. Stokes, 1796–1969*, (Washington, DC: Associated Publishers, 1972), 144; and Jones, *Jane Edna Hunter*, 74–75.

4   *Dr. Christian LaTrobe Mottley*: Barbadian Christian LaTrobe Mottley (1858–1915) graduated from Cleveland Homeopathic Medical College in 1891 and founded the Cleveland Training School for Colored Nurses in 1898, which he incorporated as Bethesda Hospital and Training School for Nurses in 1899.

    Source: Davis, *Black Americans in Cleveland*, 174, 176; and Jacqueline Jones Roster, *Profiles of Ohio Women 1803–2003* (Athens: Ohio University Press, 2003), 188.

5   *Dr. Sieglestein*: Dr. L. E. Sieglestein (?–?) was the Cuyahoga County coroner.

    Source: · Jones, *Jane Edna Hunter*, 40 and *Open Door*, (Dec. 1926).

6   *Mrs. John T. Kepke*: Not yet identified.

7   *Bolton Presbyterian Church*: In the late 1870s, Reverend Hiram C. Hayden (1831–1913) established the Bolton Mission as a branch of the First Presbyterian Church. In 1896, the Mission was reorganized as the Bolton Presbyterian Church with Reverend John S. Zelie as pastor.

    Source: Edward A. Roberts, *Official Report of the Centennial Celebration of the Founding of the City of Cleveland and the Settlement of the Western Reserve* (Cleveland: Cleveland Printing and Publishing, 1896), 212.

8   *Mrs. Cornelia F. Nickens*: Cornelia F. Nickens (1871–1965) was president of the Board of Trustees for the Cleveland Home for Aged Colored People.

    Source: G.A. Bellamy et al., eds, *Social Year Book: The Human Problems and Resources of Cleveland* (Cleveland: Cleveland Federation for Charity and Philanthropy, 1913), 47.

9   *St. John's AME Church*: In 1836, the African Methodist Episcopal Society became the first African American church founded in Cleveland prior to the Civil War. The congregation was initially known as the Bolivar Street AME Church before adopting its current name in 1878.

    Source: *ECH*, s.v. "St. John's AME Church."

10   *Dr. H. F. Biggar Sr.*: Canadian born Hamilton Fisk Biggar Sr. (1839–1926) was a homeopathic physician, professor, author, and researcher in Cleveland.

    Source: Cleveland Necrology File, Cleveland Public Library, s.v. "Biggar, Hamilton Fisk" (hereafter cited as CNF); and *RC*, s.v. "Biggar, Hamilton Fisk," 32.

11   *John D. Rockefeller*: John Davison Rockefeller Sr. (1839–1937), founder of Standard Oil Company, was well known for his philanthropic endeavors throughout the United States, which included generous donations to colleges, medical institutions, historical societies, and social organizations.

    Source: Ron Chernow, *Titan: the Life of John D. Rockefeller, Sr.* (New York: Random, 2006).

12   *Mrs. Marie Taylor Gates*: Not yet identified.

13   *Mrs. W. S. Gilkey*: Mary Virginia King Gilkey (1875?–1953), wife of William Sanborn Gilkey (1869?–1922), founder of the W. S. Gilkey Printing Company in Cleveland.

    Source: *RC*, s.v. "Gilkey, Ellery Frederick," 141, and *CNF*, s.v.v. "Gilkey, William S." and "Gilkey, Virginia King."

14   *Dr. Harlan Pomeroy*: Harlan Pomeroy (1853–1911) was a prominent white homeopathic physician and educator who specialized in internal medicine and obstetrics in Cleveland.

    Source: William Harvey King, *History of Homeopathy and its Institutions in America* (New York: Lewis, 1905), 65.

15   *Dr. Lawrence A. Pomeroy*: Lawrence Alson Pomeroy (1883–1955), son of Harlan Pomeroy, was the consulting surgeon at Cleveland's maternity hospital, visiting radium therapist at Cleveland's City Hospital, and a trustee for the Cleveland Academy of Medicine and the Cleveland Medical Library Association.

    Source: *RC*, s.v. "Pomeroy, Lawrence A.," 290.

16   *Huron Road Hospital*: In 1869, a group of homeopathic physicians founded the Cleveland Homeopathic Hospital College and then purchased property a year later to establish the Huron Road Hospital.

    Source: *ECH*, s.v. "Meridian Huron Hospital."

17   *Dr. James H. Dillard*: James Hardy Dillard (1856–1940), after whom private, historically black Dillard University was named, was a white educator and active proponent of African American education. Dillard directed the Negro Rural School Fund from 1908 to 1931, served in various capacities on the Slater Fund, the Anna T. Jeanes Fund, the Phelps-Stokes Fund, and the Southern Education Board, and as a trustee for several black colleges.

    Source: Beth L. Savage, et al., *African American Historic Places* (Hoboken, NJ: John Wiley and Sons, 1994), 262.

18   *Dr. Beatrice Gaines Adams*: Not yet identified.

19   *progressive whist*: A game in which participants play one hand of cards at a series of tables where the winners stay seated and the losers find new partners until a specified number of rounds are played and prizes awarded for points earned.

    Source: Edmond Hoyle, *Hoyle's Games* (New York: McClure, 1938), 387.

20   *Popular Lady Contest*: Fundraising contest sponsored by organizations that awarded prizes to the woman who raised the most money for an institution or cause.

21   *The Home for Aged Colored People*: Founded in 1896 by mixed-race community activist Eliza Bryant (1827–1907), the organization was the first secular welfare institution sponsored by African Americans in Cleveland.

    Source: Davis, *Black Americans in Cleveland*, 193 and *ECH*, s.v. "Bryant, Eliza."

22   *"I need Thee every hour; stay Thou near by [sic]. . ."*: Hunter is quoting the second verse of the hymn "I Need Thee Every Hour" (1872) with lyrics written by Annie S. Hawks (1835–1918) and music composed by Hawks's pastor, Dr. Robert Lowry (1826–1899).

1   *"Toiling, rejoicing, sorrowing"*: Hunter is quoting key words from Henry Wadsworth Longfellow's poem "The Village Blacksmith" (1842): "Toiling,—rejoicing,—sorrowing/ Onward through life he goes." The poem summarizes the titular character's day-to-day routine of working, attending church, and mourning his wife's untimely death. Hunter, who similarly immersed herself in work and faith after her mother died, likely sought to draw a parallel between herself and the blacksmith.

SOURCE: Henry Wadsworth Longfellow, "The Village Blacksmith," in *Ballads and Other Poems* (Cambridge, MA: J. Owen, 1842).

2   *"Old, unhappy, far-off things"*: Hunter alludes to William Wordsworth's ballad "The Solitary Reaper" (1807) in which the narrator observes from a distance an unidentified woman who sings as she works in a field of grain. Hunter seems to intimate that both time and distance had eased memories of the difficulties she had experienced in her relationship with her mother during her formative years.

SOURCE: William Wordsworth, "The Solitary Reaper," *The Poetical Works of Wordsworth* (New York: John Wurtele Lovell, 1881), 257.

3   *Virginia Reel or the Quadrille*: The Virginia Reel was a folk dance introduced by English colonists who settled in Virginia; it involved columns of dancers facing each other while performing lively steps and turns given by a caller. The Quadrille was a formal square dance particularly suited for balls.

SOURCE: Allen Dodworth, *Dancing and Its Relation to Education and Social Life, With a New Method of Instruction* (New York: Harper, 1885), 136–37 and 79–99.

4   *"hot suppers"*: Outdoor social gatherings organized by African Americans in the antebellum and postbellum periods that included refreshments, dancing, gambling, and singing.

SOURCE: Fox Butterfield, *All God's Children: the Bosket Family and the American Tradition of Violence* (New York: Harper, 1996), 62.

5   *okra purloe*: "Purloe" is one of several spellings and pronunciations of the Southern rice dish pilau, of which Hoppin' John is the most well-known. A 1901 South Carolina recipe for okra pilau calls for cut-up okra and sliced bacon to be fried together and then cooked with long-grain rice until the rice has absorbed most of the liquid.

SOURCE: Harriet Ross Colquitt, ed., *The Savannah Cookbook: A Collection of the Old Fashioned Recipes from Colonial Kitchens* (Charleston, SC: Colonial, 1933), xiii, xviii, 82; and Karen Hess and Samuel G. Stoney, T*he Carolina Rice Kitchen: The African Connection* (Columbia: University of South Carolina Press, 1992), 43–52, 56.

6   *mallata rice*: Hunter is likely using a dialect spelling of mulatto rice, a Southern dish named for the color the rice acquires from being cooked with browned onions, crisp-fried bacon, and chopped tomatoes. Mulatto rice is also known as red rice and as tomato pilau.

SOURCE: Ibid.

7   *Uncle Tenus*: Tenus Winston (?–?)

8   *harmonious music*: In the PWA newsletter *The Open Door* and her profile in *Women Builders*,

Hunter provides a different recollection of the event that inspired her commitment to race work. She states that while grieving her mother's unexpected death, she shut herself in the doctor's office where she was employed and pleaded with God to reveal her life work. She was impressed to offer shelter, employment assistance, and guidance to African American females who were migrating to Cleveland.

Source: Hunter, "The Story of the Phillis Wheatley Association," *Open Door* (Jan. 1927) and Daniel, *Women Builders*, 171–72.

Chapter 8

1   *"To fisherman and tax gatherers"*: Jesus called fishermen Simon Peter, James, John, and Phillip, and tax collector Matthew to be his disciples. "And Jesus, walking by the sea of Galilee, saw two brethren, Simon called Peter, and Andrew his brother, casting a net into the sea: for they were fishers. And he saith unto them, Follow me, and I will make you fishers of men. And they straightway left their nets, and followed him. And going on from thence, he saw other two brethren, James the son of Zebedee, and John his brother, in a ship with Zebedee their father, mending their nets; and he called them. And they immediately left the ship and their father, and followed him" (Matt. 4:18–22). "The day following Jesus would go forth into Galilee, and findeth Philip, and saith unto him, Follow me" (John 1:43). "And as Jesus passed forth from thence, he saw a man, named Matthew, sitting at the receipt of custom: and he saith unto him, Follow me. And he arose, and followed him" (Matt. 9:9).

2   *Hattie Harper*: Not yet identified.

3   *Florence Evans*: Not yet identified.

4   *Ruth Strickland*: Not yet identified.

5   *Lincoln Hospital*: The Lincoln Hospital Training School for Nurses was founded in 1899 at the Lincoln Hospital and Home in New York.

Source: Thomas Jesse Jones, ed., vol. 2, no. 39 of "Negro Education: A Study of the Private and Higher Schools for Colored People in the United States," *Bulletin 1916* (Washington, DC: Government Printing Office, 1917), 698.

6   Amy Cohen: Not yet identified.

7   *Jeanette Tubbs*: Not yet identified.

8   *Rebecca Haynes*: Not yet identified.

9   *Rose Harris*: Not yet identified.

10   *Euclid Beach*: A popular destination for bathers and picnickers located on the southern shore of Lake Erie that was considered the "Coney Island of Cleveland." African Americans were given access on a few "Jim Crow" days during the summer.

Source: Kusmer, *A Ghetto Takes Shape*, 58, 180; and Dale Samuelson and Wendy Yegoiants, *The American Amusement Park* (St. Paul: MBI, 2001), 118.

11   Hunter uses the first name "Janet" here, rather than Jeanette Tubbs whom she identifies in the second paragraph of this chapter.

12   *hundreds and hundreds of girls here in Cleveland*: Prior to the great migration, Cleveland's

African American population was less than 10,000. After 1920, that number rose to more than 30,000, giving Cleveland the largest African American urban population in the state.

Source: William W. Giffin, *African Americans and the Color Line in Ohio: 1950–1930* (Columbus: Ohio State University Press, 2005), 220.

13 *Y.W.C.A.s*: In 1866, the constitution for the first American Young Women's Christian Association (YWCA) was drafted in Boston. Early YWCAs began as non-denominational prayer-groups for young women and later offered housing for working women. The Cleveland YWCA was founded on November 21, 1868, as the Women's Christian Association of Cleveland.

Source: *ECH*, s.v. "The Young Women's Christian Assn. (YWCA);" and Mary S. Sims, *The Natural History of a Social Institution: the Young Women's Christian Association* (New York: Woman's Press, 1936).

14 *settlement houses*: Between 1896 and 1898, three settlement houses were established in Cleveland: Goodrich Social Settlement helped German and Irish immigrants; Hiram House initially served Jews from Europe; and the Alta House assisted Italians.

Source: Laura Tuennerman-Kaplan, *Helping Others, Helping Ourselves: Power, Giving and Community Identity in Cleveland, Ohio, 1880–1930* (Kent, OH: Kent State University Press, 2001), 50.

15 *twenty-five cents a week; I suggested a nickel*: Twenty-five cents is approximately US$(2010)5.84; a nickel is worth about US$(2010)1.17.

16 *let our light shine before men*: "Let your light so shine before men, that they may see your good works and glorify your Father which is in heaven" (Matt. 5:16).

17 *And all these other things will be added unto you*: Hunter is appropriating the scripture, "Seek ye first the kingdom of God, and all these things shall be added unto you" (Matt. 6:33). In adding the word "other," she seems to intimate that God will not only provide what is needful when believers keep him foremost in their lives but will also fulfill the dreams of those who desire to work for the good of others.

18 *club women*: These women were likely members of the Ohio Federation of Colored Women's Clubs and the National Association of Colored Women. The Black Women's Club Movement began in the United States in the late nineteenth century when African American women, particularly from middle class families in New York, Boston, and Washington, D.C., founded organizations to support the development and advancement of their communities, as well as to protect the character and celebrate the achievements of black women.

Source: Darlene Clarke Hine, *Hine Sight: Black Women and the Reconstruction of Black History* (Bloomington: Indiana University Press, 1997), 69–70.

19 *for they knew not what they were doing*: Hunter is alluding to the scripture that records Jesus's prayer for his tormentors during His crucifixion: "Father forgive them, for they know not what they do" (Luke 23:34).

20 *Booker T. Washington, "I have made it a rule," he said, "never to answer my critics"*: In 1881, African American activist and educator Booker T. Washington (1856–1915) established the Tuskegee Institute, a school for African Americans in Alabama. Quote not yet identified.

Source: Robert J. Norrell, *Up from History: The Life of Booker T. Washington* (Cambridge, MA: Belknap of Harvard University Press, 2009).

21 *Interdenominational Ministerial Alliance*: An organization for black ministers in Cleveland that Hunter also described as the "Ministerial Alliance."

SOURCE: Hunter, "Story of the Phillis Wheatley Association," *Open Door* (Feb, 1927).

22 *Rev. Charles Bundy*: Charles Bundy (1855–1927) was pastor of the African Methodist Episcopal Church and St. John's AME Church in Cleveland, member of the Federal Council of Churches of Christ in America, and trustee of Wilberforce University.

SOURCE: *Annual Reports of the Federal Council of the Churches of Christ in America* (New York: n.p, 1913); Elliot M. Rudwick, *Race Riot at East St. Louis: July 2, 1917* (Champaign: University of Illinois Press, 1982), 120–21; and R. S. Dills, *History of Fayette County, Together with Historic Notes on the Northwest, and the State of Ohio* (Dayton, OH: Odell & Mayer, 1881), 493; *Open Door* (May 1927).

23 *Cleveland Gazette*: Established in 1883 as the first post-bellum African American newspaper published in Cleveland, the *Cleveland Gazette* earned national acclaim for its stances against racism and discrimination. African American Harry Clay Smith (1863–1941), the *Gazette*'s first editor, publicly criticized Hunter for seeking to establish a segregated facility.

SOURCE: *ECH*, s.v.v "Cleveland Gazette" and "Smith, Henry Clay;" Giffin, *African Americans and the Color Line*, 69; and Irvin Garland Penn, *The Afro-American Press and Its Editors* (New York: Arno and The New York Times, 1969), 280–85.

CHAPTER 9

1 *"Walk Together Children"*: Hunter is referring to the Negro spiritual "Walk Together Children."

2 *Sarah C. Hills Training School*: Established in 1937 and named for Sarah C. Hills, the PWA's third president, this auxiliary of the PWA offered scientific domestic training in hygiene, cooking, laundry, housekeeping, and sewing for women to improve their skills as homemakers and domestic servants.

SOURCE: Warren Van Tine and Michael Pierce, *Builders of Ohio: A Biographical History* (Columbus: Ohio State University Press, 2003), 237; and "Sarah C. Hills Training School," *Open Door* (Sept. 1937).

3 *Women's Missionary Board of the Second Presbyterian Church*: An auxiliary of the Woman's Presbyterial Home Missionary Society founded by representatives from Cleveland area churches in 1881 to support local projects as well as those sponsored by the Woman's Executive Committee of Home Missions located in New York. In the late nineteenth century, Presbyterian women had organized a home mission society to provide opportunities for members to broaden their influence outside the domestic sphere through projects that addressed the needs of African Americans, Native Americans, immigrants, and Americans who lived in rural areas.

SOURCE: *ECH*, s.v. "Presbyterian Women;" and "Introduction;" and Boyd and Brackenridge, *Presbyterian Women in American*.

4 *Presbyterian Missionary Society of Cuyahoga County*: An affiliate of the Woman's Presbyterial Home Missionary Society that provided services for Cuyahoga County, where the PWA was located.

5 *Boulevard Presbyterian Church*: Founded in Cleveland in 1897.

Source: Foster Armstrong, Richard Klein, and Cara Armstrong, *A Guide to Cleveland's Sacred Landmarks* (Kent, OH: Kent State University Press, 1992), 94–95.

6   *Antioch Baptist Church*: Organized in 1893 at the home of Henry Meyers, Antioch Baptist was the second African American church established in Cleveland. By 1915, under the leadership of Reverend Horace C. Bailey, Antioch had become the largest and most influential church in the city.

Source: Eric Arnesen, Julie Greene, and Bruce Laurie, *Labor Histories: Class, Politics and the Working Class Experience* (Champaign: University of Illinois Press, 1998), 236; Kusmer, *A Ghetto Takes Shape*, 95; and Davis, *Black Americans in Cleveland*, 185.

7   *Dr. A. B. Meldrum, minister of the Old Stone Church*: Scottish-born theologian Andrew Barclay Meldrum (1857–1928) served as pastor of the First Presbyterian Church, known as Old Stone Church, from 1902 to 1924 and as pastor emeritus until 1928.

Source: *RC*, s.v. "Meldrum, Andrew Barclay," 248.

8   *Patrick Stephens*: Hunter identifies her counselor as P. H. Stevens, a former employee of Henry A. Sherwin whom she met and talked with about the PWA while waiting for a train in Cleveland's Public Square.

Source: Hunter, "The Story of the Phillis Wheatley Association," *Open Door* (Mar. 1927).

9   *Mr. Henry A. Sherwin*: In 1866, businessman, paint pioneer, and philanthropist Henry Alden Sherwin (1842–1916) and businessman Edward Porter Williams (1843–1903) established the Sherwin-Williams Company in Cleveland. By the 1920s, it had become the largest paint company in the United States.

Source: Kathleen McDermolt and Davis Dyer, *America's Paint Company: A History of Sherwin-Williams* (Cambridge, MA: Winthrop Group, 1991); and *ECH*, s.v. "Sherwin Williams Co."

10   *Director of Public Welfare / Welfare Director*: Not yet identified.

11   *Secretary of State*: Charles H. Graves (1872–1940), who served from 1911 to 1915.

Source: Nevin Otto Winter, vol. 2 of *A History of Northwest Ohio: A Narrative Account of Its Historical Progress and Development from the First European Exploration of the Maumee and Sandusky Valleys and the Adjacent Shores of Lake Erie, down to the Present Time* (Chicago: Lewis, 1917), 678–79.

12   *He and his wife*: Likely Mr. and Mrs. James Beason.

Source: Daniel, *Women Builders*, 172.

13   *Phillis Wheatley*: Phillis Wheatley (ca. 1754–1784) was born in Africa, captured, and brought to Boston as a slave around 1760. Prominent white tailor John Wheatley purchased her as a maid for his wife Susannah. The Wheatleys taught Phillis to read and write, and helped publish her poetry and letters. In 1773, she became the first person of African descent to publish a collection of poems in the colonies.

Source: John C. Shields, vol. 8 of *AANB*, s.v. "Phillis Wheatley," 224–26.

14   *National Association of Colored Women*: In 1896, black club women organized a national convention in Washington, DC, where they merged the Colored Women's League of Washing-

ton and the National Federation of Afro-American Women into the National Association of Colored Women to combat white Americans' characterizations of black women as immoral and black men as rapists following Ida B. Wells's anti-lynching campaign. Mary Church Terrell (1863–1954) served as the NACW's first president.

SOURCE: Dorothy Salem, vol. 2 of *Black Women in America*, 2nd ed., ed. Darlene Clark Hine (New York: Oxford University Press, 2005), s.v. "National Association of Colored Women," 428–36.

15 *Phillis Wheatley Department*: In 1930, the Phillis Wheatley Department became an auxiliary of the NACW that provided homes, social services, and meeting facilities throughout the nation for African American girls and women. By 1939, ten Phillis Wheatley Houses were operating in Chicago; Greenville, South Carolina; Minneapolis; Winston-Salem, North Carolina; Toledo, Ohio; Canton, Ohio; New Haven, Connecticut; Steubenville, Ohio; Oberlin, Ohio; and Cleveland.

SOURCE: *The Phillis Wheatley Department of the National Association of Colored Women*, n. p., July 1939, PWAP.

16 *Mrs. Elmer F. Boyd*: School teacher and member of the Federation of Colored Women's Clubs Cora Stuart (1875–1960) was married to Elmer F. Boyd (1878–1944), owner of a funeral home in Cleveland eventually known as E. F. Boyd & Son.

SOURCE: *ECH*, s.v. "Boyd, Elmer F.;" and Davis, *Black Americans in Cleveland*, 165.

17 *Negro minister*: Reverend Horace Charles Bailey (1860–1942), pastor of the Antioch Baptist Church from 1903 to 1942.

SOURCE: Jones, *Jane Edna Hunter*, 55; and *ECH*, s.v. "Bailey, Rev. Dr. Horace Charles."

18 *Mrs. Adin T. Hills*: White civic leader Sarah C. Tucker Hills (1858?–1936) was president of the PWA from 1914 to 1915 and 1918 to 1919. Her husband, prominent white Cleveland attorney Adin T. Hills (1854–1928), wrote the constitution for the PWA.

SOURCE: *Open Door* (Mar. 1927); and *Men of Ohio in Nineteen Hundred* (Cleveland: Benesch Art, 1901), s.v. "Adin T. Hills," 19.

19 *J. R. Wylie*: J. R. Wylie (?–?), a white businessman affiliated with the Cleveland Trust Company, was treasurer of the PWA Board of Trustees from 1913 to 1931.

SOURCE: *Open Door* (Feb. 1929) and (Jun. 1931).

20 *Mrs. Laura S. Goodhue*: White civic leader and club woman Laura Singletary Goodhue (1871–1962) was a member of the PWA Advisory Board and affiliated with the Daughters of the American Revolution, United States Daughters of 1812, Daughters of American Colonists, Daughters of Founders and Patriots, and Women's City Club.

SOURCE: *RC*, s.v. "Goodhue, Laura S.," 144.

21 *John P. Green*: In 1873, John P. Green (1845–1940) became the first African American public official in Cuyahoga County, Ohio, when he was elected justice of the peace. He was Cleveland's first black member of the bar and later served as Ohio State Representative and Senator.

SOURCE: Davis, *Black Americans in Cleveland*, 90; and *History Central*, s.v. "John P. Green."

22 *Robert E. Lewis*: White businessman Robert Ellsworth Lewis (1869–1969) was a member of the

PWA Advisory Board, general secretary of the Cleveland YMCA from 1909 to 1929, and advisor to the Chinese minister of foreign affairs from 1930 to 1935.

SOURCE: *ECH*, s.v. "Lewis, Robert Ellsworth;" and *RC*, s.v. "Lewis, Robert Ellsworth," 223–24.

23   *Emma Henderson*: Not yet identified.

24   *The May Company*: In 1888, David May and Louis, Joseph, and Moses Schoenberg founded this department store company in Denver, Colorado and then opened a store in downtown Cleveland a year later that became the largest department store in the state of Ohio by 1931.

SOURCE: *ECH*, s.v. "May Co. of Cleveland."

25   *Charles Blue*: Not yet identified.

26   *Dr. and Mrs. Paul F. Sutphen*: White minister Paul Frederick Sutphen (1856–1929) was pastor of the Woodland Avenue Presbyterian Church and the Second Presbyterian Church, as well as associate pastor of the Church of the Covenant in Cleveland. He also participated in the Liberty Loans campaign, helped establish Cleveland's Karamu House, a settlement house that supported interracial theater and arts, and served as a trustee for Hiram House, Western Reserve University, and Wooster College. His wife Bertha B. Davies Sutphen (ca. 1860–1932) was a PWA trustee.

SOURCE: *RC*, s.v. "Sutphen, Paul F.," 359; and *ECH*, s.v. "Sutphen, Rev. Paul Frederick."

27   *Cleveland Trust Company*: Organized in 1894, the Cleveland Trust Company was the first bank to advertise nationally for savings deposits through the mail system and the first bank in Cleveland to develop a separate department for women.

SOURCE: Edward Tin Broeck Perine, *The Stories of Trust Companies* (New York: G. P. Putnam's Sons, 1916).

28   *one Negro man*: Hunter is referring to African American writer and activist Charles Waddell Chesnutt (1858–1932) who served on the PWA board during its early years.

29   *Mrs. Stevenson Burke*: White civic leader Ella M. Southworth Burke (ca. 1842–1931), the second wife of Judge Stevenson Burke (1826–1904), was a trustee for the Cleveland School of Art and the PWA, and a member of the Daughters of the Revolution.

SOURCE: Avery, vol. 3 of *A History of Cleveland*, 419.

30   *Meaning of Prayer*: The influential book *The Meaning of Prayer* (1915), published by popular white liberal Protestant minister Harry Emerson Fosdick (1878–1969), features ten week-long lessons about prayer for personal or group study. Fosdick and his brother, Raymond Blaine Fosdick (1883–1972), were longtime public servants and associates of John D. Rockefeller Jr.

SOURCE: Robert Moats Miller, *Harry Emerson Fosdick: Preacher, Pastor, Prophet* (New York: Oxford University Press, 1985).

31   *Aunt Daisy*: Not yet identified.

32   *three-story apartment building on East Fortieth Street and Central Avenue*: After raising $1,500, Hunter established the PWA's second home for seventy-five boarders in a building that was adjacent to St. John's AME Church.

SOURCE: Daphne Spain, *How Women Saved the City* (Minneapolis: University of Minnesota Press, 2000).

33   *Two-story building*: In 1929, a group of African Americans launched a successful campaign to purchase a building that provided activity and meeting rooms for their community.

SOURCE: Jones, *Jane Edna Hunter*, 71.

34   *Girl Reserves*: In the early twentieth century, the Girl Reserve Movement established clubs in many American cities to teach young women how to be model Christians in their homes, churches, and communities. The PWA club offered leadership training, as well as entertainment and recreation, for twelve- to eighteen-year-old girls.

SOURCE: Daniel, *Women Builders*. 184; Mrs. Margaret Francis, "The Girl Reserve Movement," *Open Door* (Oct. 1926); and "Girl Reserves 'Facing life squarely' and 'Find and give the best,'" Ibid, (Nov. 1928).

CHAPTER 10

1   *Our New Home*: The new nine-story PWA building with two lower levels provided private rooms for 135 residents. The education department, club rooms, and parlors were on the third floor, while the cafeteria featuring three dining rooms and private rooms operated on the second floor. Laundry facilities and a beauty parlor were located on the ground floor.

SOURCE: *Open Door* (Dec. 1927) and (Jan. 1928).

2   *music department*: In 1926, the PWA began operating the Institute of Music and Dramatic Arts. The music department offered a variety of private voice and instrument lessons, membership in the glee club, in orchestras, and in various choruses. In 1929, the two-story building adjacent to the PWA was purchased to house the preschool and music school. In 1937, the PWA Board of Trustees named the music school for Dr. and Mrs. Paul Sutphen in recognition of their contributions to the PWA and Cleveland's African American community.

SOURCE: David, *Black Americans in Cleveland*, 348; and *Open Door* (Feb. 1926) and (Oct.1937).

3   *We knew that if we asked we should receive*: Hunter is alluding to the scripture, "Ask, and it shall be given you; seek, and ye shall find; knock, and it shall be opened unto you: For every one that asketh receiveth; and he that seeketh findeth; and to him that knocketh it shall be opened" (Matt. 7:7–8).

4   *"Mother Rich"*: Not yet identified.

5   *Ellen Jackson*: Not yet identified.

6   *Rockefeller Foundation*: Inspired to become more involved in philanthropy by Andrew Carnegie's essay "The Gospel of Wealth," John D. Rockefeller Sr. founded and incorporated this private foundation in 1913 to distribute millions of dollars for education, medical, social service, cultural, and research projects throughout the world.

SOURCE: Raymond Blaine Fosdick, *Story of the Rockefeller Foundation* (New York: Harper, 1952).

7   *Mrs. Edwin Burke*: Not yet identified.

8   *Laura Spelman Foundation*: The Laura Spelman Rockefeller Memorial was established in memory of Laura Celestia Spelman Rockefeller (1839–1915), wife of John D. Rockefeller Sr., in

1918 as one of the philanthropic boards under the broader umbrella of the Rockefeller Foundation. The Laura Spelman Rockefeller Memorial focused primarily on the social sciences from 1923 until it merged with the Rockefeller Foundation in 1928.

SOURCE: Fosdick, *Story of the Rockefeller Foundation*, 136–37.

9   *John D. Rockefeller Jr.*: John Davison Rockefeller Jr. (1874–1960) financed the construction of the Rockefeller Center in New York City during the Great Depression and was the first president of the Rockefeller Foundation, which his father John D. Rockefeller Sr. founded in 1913.

SOURCE: Fosdick, *John D. Rockefeller, Jr.: A Portrait* (New York: Harper, 1956).

10 *Negro undertaker*: Jay Walter Wills Sr. (1874–1971), the founder of Ohio's largest African American-owned funeral home, was an early supporter of Hunter and a member of the PWA advisory board. In 1925, Wills bought a home in the Van Sweringen Allotment of Shaker Heights, a predominately white Cleveland suburb.

SOURCE: Jones, *Jane Edna Hunter*, 50, 86.

11 *white real estate broker*: Not yet identified.

12 *The Heights*: Hunter is likely referring to three Cleveland neighborhoods, Shaker Heights, Garfield Heights, and Cleveland Heights, where middle-and upper-class whites moved as Cleveland's African American urban population increased during the early twentieth century.

SOURCE: Kusmer, *A Ghetto Takes Shape*, 165.

13 *Mr. Charles Adams*: White manufacturer and philanthropist Charles Edgar Adams (1859–1933) was president and general manager of the Cleveland Hardware Company; director of Commonwealth Savings and Loan Company, Cleveland Trust Company, and Cleveland Life Insurance Company; and trustee of the Cleveland Community Fund, YMCA, YWCA, and Welfare Federation.

SOURCE: *RC*, s.v. "Charles Adams," 2; and Alan Horvath, ed., *Book of Clevelanders: A Biographical Dictionary of Living Men in the City of Cleveland* (Cleveland: Burrows Brothers, 1923), s.v. "Adams, Charles E.," 8 (hereafter cited in text as *BOC*).

14 *Charles K. Arter*: Harvard educated white attorney, businessman, and civic leader Charles Kingsley Arter (1875–1957) was a PWA trustee and member of the PWA Building Committee.

SOURCE: *RC*, "Arter, Charles Kingsley," 11; and *Open Door* (Oct. 1928).

15 *Arthur D. Baldwin*: Yale and Harvard educated white attorney and civic leader Arthur Douglas Baldwin (1876–1955) was a World War I veteran, president of the Babies Dispensary and Hospital, and trustee of the Cleveland Welfare Federation and Legal Aid Society.

SOURCE: *BOC*, s.v. "Baldwin, Arthur Douglas," 21–22.

16 *Mrs. Arthur D. Baldwin*: White civic leader Reba Williams Baldwin (1876–1941) was a trustee of the PWA, the Visiting Nurse Association, Anti-Tuberculosis League, Babies' Hospital, St. Barnabas Guild of Nurses, and the Cleveland institute of Music, and member of the PWA Building Committee.

SOURCE: *RC*, s.v. "Baldwin, Reba Williams," 19.

17 *That His will might be done upon the earth*: Hunter is appropriating a verse from the Lord's

Prayer: "Thy kingdom come, Thy will be done in earth, as it is in heaven" (Matt. 6:10).

18   *cornerstone*: Included were the names of 3,689 individuals who had paid on their pledges; the names of every PWA trustee who had served on the board; the names of the Cooperative and Advisory Committee; a copy of a letter from Elizabeth Clark Scofield; the endorsement from the Colored Ministerial Alliance; a copy of materials that had been used in the 1925 building campaign; pamphlets signed by Dr. Robert H. Bishop, chairman of the building campaign; papers signed by Reba Williams Baldwin who was appointed chairman after Dr. Bishop became ill; the history of the PWA; a picture of Reba Williams Baldwin; and a copy of the program for the laying of the cornerstone.

   Source: *Open Door* (Jul. 1927).

19   *Mrs. Solon Severance*: White civic leader Emily C. Allen Severance (1840–1921), wife of banker Solon L. Severance (1834–1915) who established Cleveland's Euclid Avenue National Bank (eventually renamed the First National Bank).

   Source: *BOC*, s.v. "Severance, Solon L.," 236–37.

20   *Mr. David E. Green*: David Edward Green (1874–1940), prominent white Cleveland businessman and attorney who served as a trustee for the PWA, Cleveland Welfare Federation, and Dennison University, counsel for the Attorney General of Ohio and Cleveland's Community Fund, and chairman of the PWA Building Committee.

   Source: *RC*, s.v. "Green, David Edward," 148.

21   *Dr. Robert R. Moton*: African American educator, writer, and civil rights activist Robert Russa Moton (1867–1940), a graduate and administrator of the Hampton Institute, was elected principal of the Tuskegee Institute in 1915 after the death of the school's founder, Booker T. Washington. Moton published an autobiography, *Finding a Way Out* (1920), and a political treatise, "What the Negro Thinks" (1928); served as an advisor to US Presidents Howard Taft and Woodrow Wilson; and chaired the Campaign Committee on Interracial Cooperation in 1930.

   Source: Maceo Crenshaw Dailey Jr., vol. 6 of *AANB*, s.v. "Moton, Robert Russa," 71–73.

22   *Frank Radke*: Not yet identified.

23   *Mrs. Kaney Radke*: Not yet identified.

24   *"the whole world must be cleansed, or not a man or woman of us all can be clean."*: Hunter is likely appropriating a quote from Nathaniel Hawthorne's Our *Old Home: A Series of English Sketches* (1863), "Let the whole world be cleansed, or not a man or woman of us can be clean." Hawthorne is recalling a trip to an English laundry at an almshouse. The experience reminded him of the artificiality of class structures, as the scents from the laundry wafted outside and mingled with air that even the queen might breathe. Hunter intimates that PWA supporters have abided by this motto through the development of interracial alliances involving men and women from all classes who have addressed the needs of African American migrant women in Cleveland.

   Source: Nathaniel Hawthorne, *Our Old Home: A Series of English Sketches* (Boston: Houghton, Mifflin, 1863), 340.

Chapter 11

1   *Apollyon*: In John Bunyan's *The Pilgrim's Progress* (1678), the protagonist Christian encounters the foul beast Apollyon, representative of Satan, immediately after he receives assurance of salvation. Also see Revelation 9 for more insights into the Apollyon figure.

    SOURCE: John Bunyan, *The Pilgrim's Progress from this World to that which is to Come* (London: E. P. Dutton, 1918), 65.

2   *"Out of its belly came fire and smoke, and its mouth was as the mouth of a lion"*: Hunter is quoting from the description of Apollyon in *The Pilgrim's Progress*: "Now the monster was hideous to behold; he was clothed with scales like a fish (and they are his pride), he had wings like a dragon, feet like a bear, and out of his belly came fire and smoke, and his mouth was as the mouth of a lion."

    SOURCE: Ibid.

3   *and its wages are death*: Hunter is quoting Christian's response to Apollyon's assertion that he must die for his sins: "I was born indeed in your dominion, but your service was hard and your wages such as a man could not live on, for 'the wages of sin is death' (Rom. vi. 23)." "For the wages of sin is death; but the gift of God is eternal life through Jesus Christ our Lord" (Rom. 6:23).

    SOURCE: Ibid., 66.

4   *we know that we shall be more than conquerors through Him that loved us*: As Christian is losing his fight against Apollyon, he recovers his sword and wounds the monster: "Christian perceiving that, made at him again, saying, 'Nay, in all these things we are more than conquerors through him that loved us' (Rom. viii. 37). And with that Apollyon spread forth his dragon's wings, and sped him away, that Christian for a season saw him no more (Jam. iv. 7)." By characterizing "commercialized vice" as "Apollyon" and herself and Cleveland's black community as "Christian," Hunter transforms their struggle into an allegorical battle between good and evil that they are destined, despite difficulties, to win.

    SOURCE: Ibid., 69.

5   *three hundred percent*: Cleveland's African American population grew 307.8% between 1910 and 1920, increasing from 8,448 (1.5% of the total population) to 34,451 (4.3% of the total population).

    SOURCE: United States Department of Commerce Bureau of the Census, *Negroes in the United States, 1920-1932* (Washington, DC: Government Printing Office, 1935), 55; and Kimberley L. Phillips, "'But It Is a Fine Place to Make Money': Migration and African-American Families in Cleveland," *Journal of Social History* 30 (1996): 393–413.

6   *"black belts"*: Hunter identifies Cleveland's "black belt" as the area "north of Cedar Avenue and south of Quincy Avenue, between East 55th and 105th Streets" that was filled with clubs, smoking saloons, and restaurants and characterized by "vice, crime and filth." She urged residents to exercise their voting rights to transform their neighborhood into a safe, prosperous community.

    SOURCE: "It's Our Problem: Voters in the Black Belt," *Open Door* (Oct. 1938).

7   *Dr. A—*: Not yet identified. One prominent Cleveland "Dr. A—" of the period, however, is Dud-

ley Peter Allen (1852–1915) who was connected to the Severances, Cleveland's homeopathic doctors, the Medical Library Association, and the Cleveland Museum of Art.

SOURCE: Ohio Medical Society, "Dudley P. Allen," in *Transactions of the Forty-Eighth Annual Meeting Held at Put-in Bay, June 28, 29, and 30, 1893*, (Cincinnati: Earhart & Richardson, 1893), 23–45.

8 *Osie, Starlight's wife*: Boyd's first wife, Olive Azaler Boyd (1881–1920).

9 *a house of prostitution*: Starlight Dance Hall, owned by Albert "Starlight" Boyd, included a barbershop, pool hall, and dance floor, and served as the unofficial Republican party headquarters of the Cuyahoga 11th Ward.

SOURCE: Jones, *Jane Edna Hunter*, 74–75; and *ECH*, s.v. "Boyd, Albert Duncan 'Starlight.'"

10 *Mrs. Mary Rathburn Judd*: White civic leader Mary Rathburn Judd (?–?) was a speaker at one of the open meetings held for the community at the PWA. Starting with Judd in 1913, the general secretary of the Cleveland YWCA automatically received membership status on the Cooperative Board of the PWA.

SOURCE: Jones, *Jane Edna Hunter*, 62, 69.

11 *Indian clubs*: Heavy wooden pins shaped like bowling pins that were swung around one's body in an exercise routine.

SOURCE: Morris Bornstein, *Manual of Instruction in the Use of Dumb Bells, Indian Clubs, and Other Exercises* (New York: Excelsior, 1889).

12 *"Roaring Third"*: The predominately African American "red light district" under the jurisdiction of the third police precinct in Cleveland. Black activists criticized the police for arresting patrons rather than proprietors in the unsavory business district.

SOURCE: Giffin, *African Americans and the Color Line*, 21–22.

13 *Street Railway Company*: Hunter is likely referring to the Cleveland Railway Company, which held exclusive rights to Cleveland's public railway franchise from 1910 to 1942.

SOURCE: *ECH*, s.v. "Cleveland Railway Co."

14 *Negro vote was still overwhelmingly Republican*: The vast majority of African Americans voted for Republican candidates following the Civil War because of Republican President Lincoln's Emancipation Proclamation and the party's support of civil rights. The Great Depression and President Franklin D. Roosevelt's New Deal, coupled with the Democratic Party's active pursuit of African American voters migrating into Northern cities during the Progressive Era, caused the shift to the Democratic Party being the party of choice for most African Americans.

SOURCE: Daniel Scroop, *Mr. Democrat: Jim Farley, the New Deal, and the Making of Modern American Politics* (Ann Arbor: University of Michigan Press, 2006), 122.

15 *Tim Flagman*: Hunter is referring to African American Thomas W. Fleming (1874–1948) who was involved in the Republican Party Club in his neighborhood, held various positions in local and state organizations, and soon earned the status as alternate delegate to the 1904 Republican National Convention in Chicago. In 1903, he helped establish the *Cleveland Journal*, a weekly African American newspaper. In 1906, he completed law school and was admitted to the bar. Fleming was elected to city council in 1909, but lost his re-election bid in 1911. He won

re-election to the city council in 1916, and held the office until he resigned in 1929 after being indicted on corruption and illegal soliciting charges. Fleming acquired the PWA's charter from the Secretary of State in 1912. Like Hunter, he admired Booker T. Washington, and he was an early PWA supporter because of his belief in all-black institutions.

SOURCE: Davis, *Black American in Cleveland*, 143–44; *ECH*, s.v. "Fleming, Thomas W;" Giffin, *African Americans and the Color Line*; and *Open Door* (Feb. 1927); and David A. Geber, *Black Ohio and the Color Line*, 1860–1915 (Urbana: University of Illinois Press, 1976), 404–06.

16   *Councilmanic Chamber*: The specific place in the city council meeting room where a politician elected from a particular district sits.

17   *ward-heeler*: Elected official who carries out more influential politicians' orders like a dog obeys his master.

SOURCE: William Safire, *Safire's Political Dictionary* (New York: Oxford University Press, 2008), 56.

18   *cheated out of a hard-earned victory*: In 1921, Cleveland adopted a "City Manager Plan" of electing twenty-five councilmen from four districts who then chose a city manager to be the city's chief executive.

SOURCE: Chester C. Maxey, "The Cleveland Election and the New Charter," *American Political Science Review* 16 (1922): 83–86.

19   *Dora*: Not yet identified.

20   *switchboard*: Shared telephones lines that were connected to a switchboard, also known as a telephone exchange, where operators redirected calls to subscribers using distinct rings. The PWA telephone operator could eavesdrop on a resident's conversation by staying on the line after she patched a call through to a subscriber.

SOURCE: Sharon McMaster, *The Telecommunications Industry* (Westport, CT: Greenwood, 2002), 53–55.

21   *Howard E. Murrell*: In 1926, black businessman Howard E. Murrell (?–1926) became manager of the African American owned Empire Savings and Loan Bank that had been established in 1911 to serve Cleveland's African American community. Murrell was a PWA trustee for 12 years.

SOURCE: Davis, *Black Americans in Cleveland*, 243–44; *ECH*, s.v. "The Empire Savings and Loan;" and *Open Door* (Oct. 1923).

22   *St. Louis voodoo blues*: Blues music that includes dream imagery, charms, and curses in the lyrics and which may also posit musicians as conjurers whose music casts a spell over their listeners.

SOURCE: William Ferris, *Blues from the Delta*, rev. ed. (New York: Da Capo, 1984), 77–78; and Phil Pastras, *Dead Man Blues: Jelly Roll Morton Way out West* (Berkeley: University of California Press, 2001), 61.

CHAPTER 12

1   *Central High*: Established on July 13, 1846, Central was the first high school in Cleveland that provided free education through public funding.

SOURCE: *ECH*, s.v. "Central High School."

2   *Western Reserve University*: Case Western Reserve University began as the Western Reserve College founded by David Hudson (1824–1897) in Hudson, Ohio, in 1826. The college relocated to Cleveland in 1882 and adopted the name Case Western University. In 1887, Leonard Chase Jr. (1820–1880) initiated the development of the Case School of Applied Science in Cleveland. In 1967, the two institutions combined to form the Case Western Reserve University.

    Source: *ECH*, s.v. "Cramer, C. H."

3   *Greater Cleveland Federation of Women*: The Federation of Women's Clubs of Greater Cleveland was a non-profit, nonsectarian organization founded in 1901 by U. and I. Literary Society President Sarah Porter (?–?) to foster collaboration between white women's clubs and serve the varied needs of the Cleveland community.

    Source: *ECH*, s.v. "The Federation of Women's Clubs of Greater Cleveland."

4   *Harlem Hospital*: Founded in 1887 as a municipal hospital in which white doctors treated mostly lower-income white patients, Harlem Hospital and its gradually integrated staff served the increasingly African American population of New York's Harlem vicinity. In 1923, the Harlem Hospital School of Nursing opened to train young African American women for careers as nurses.

    Source: A. Peter Bailey, *The Harlem Hospital Story: 100 Years of Struggle Against Illness, Racism, and Genocide* (Richmond, VA: Native Sun, 1991).

5   *Camp Merrimam*: Hunter is referring to Camp Merriam, which the PWA opened in 1925 on Lake Erie for young girls after a flood demolished its first camp in Rocky River Valley. The program focused on the campers' "physical, mental, and spiritual" development. Activities included tennis, hiking, basketball, dramatics, fishing, handicrafts, baseball, boating, and swimming. Walter H. Merriam (1868–1916), a Cleveland physician, purchased the land for Hunter, because African Americans were forbidden from conducting such business transactions.

    Source: *Open Door* (Mar. 1925), (Apr. 1925), and (Jun. 1925).

6   *Miss Edna M. Studebaker*: Edna M. Studebaker (1891–1985).

7   *Cleveland Foundation*: Established in 1914 by Frederick H. Goff (1853–1923), the Cleveland Foundation was the world's first community charity where wealthy individuals could leave funds and other assets to support humanitarian projects.

    Source: *ECH*, s.v. "Cleveland Foundation."

8   *"farmed them out"*: To farm out children is to place them in the care of families or other guardians who required them to work for a specified time in exchange for room, board, and clothing.

9   *Sabbath Schools*: Bible classes held on Sundays for children and youth to provide training for work in the home, community, and nation.

    Source: Richard Gay Pardee, *The Sabbath School Index: Pointing Out the History and Progress of Sunday-Schools* (Philadelphia: J. C. Garrigues, 1868).

10 *Mrs. Walter H. Merriam*: Cliffe Updegraff Johnson Merriam (1867–1943), a homeopathic physician and graduate of Oberlin College, served as president of Cleveland's YWCA, and as vice president and president of the PWA Board of Trustees.

    Source: Harriet Taylor Upton, vol. 2 of the *History of the Western Reserve* (Chicago: Lewis,

1910), 958–59; and *Open Door* (Feb. 1923) and (Feb. 1928).

11 *Ohio State University*: In 1862, the Ohio State legislature passed the Morrill Act that established the Ohio State Agricultural and Mechanical College in 1870 as a land-grant university in Columbus. The college was renamed The Ohio State University in 1878.

SOURCE: Ed. Thomas C. Mendenhall, *Addresses and Proceedings of the Semicentennial Celebration October 13–16 1920*, vol. 3 of *History of the Ohio State University* (Columbus: Ohio State University Press, 1922), 211–13.

12 *Traveler's Aid*: In 1920, Cleveland began operating a Traveler's Aid Society that dispatched agents to meet white migrants and European immigrants, especially young women, at train depots, boat docks, and urban centers, and helped them find housing and employment. Brian Mullanphy, mayor of St. Louis, had established the first Traveler's Aid Society in America in 1851 to assist immigrants in accessing local resources.

SOURCE: *ECH*, s.v. "Traveler's Aid Society."

13 *retarded girls*: In the early twentieth century, the word "retarded" was used to describe individuals with cognitive disabilities. More recently the phrase "intellectual disability" has become the preferred term to describe people who have severe mental challenges.

SOURCE: Licia Carson, *Faces of Intellectual Disability: Philosophical Reflections* (Bloomington: Indiana University Press, 2009).

14 *Seed had not fallen upon barren ground*: Hunter is alluding to Jesus's Parable of the Sower in which seed falls upon the wayside, and thorny, stony, and good ground (Matt. 13:3–23, Mark 4:2–20, and Luke 8:4–15).

15 *Josephine Kohler Pre-School*: PWA auxiliary named in honor of white civic leader Josephine (Josie) Modroch Kohler (1864?–1948), the wife of prominent Cleveland police officer and Republican politician Frederick Kohler (1864–1934) who funded the purchase of equipment and supplies for the school.

SOURCE: *ECH*, s.v. "Kohler, Frederick" and *Open Door* (Apr. 1935).

16 *Junior Mothers' Club*: PWA organization that offered classes and activities to teach young mothers how to care for their children and homes.

SOURCE: *Open Door* (Nov. 1933) and (Dec. 1933).

17 *Promised Land for which we must "work together, children"*: Hunter is appropriating the Negro spiritual "Walk Together Children," but changing the line "walk together children" to "work together children."

CHAPTER 13

1 *Ella Ford Finishing House*: PWA auxiliary named for white civic leader Ella Almira White Ford (1883–1952), daughter of Thomas H. White (1836–1914), founder of the White Sewing Machine Company, who was educated at several finishing schools in New England and Simmons College in Boston. Her husband, Horatio Ford (1881–1952), was the son of Horatio Clark Ford (1853–1915), founder of Cleveland Trust Company.

SOURCE: *RC*, s.v. "Ford, Ella White," 126.

2 *normal schools*: Educational institutions founded in the early nineteenth century to train school teachers, primarily white women. Normal schools specifically for African Americans were established after the Civil War.

> Source: Janet Alsup. *Teacher Identity Discourses: Negotiating Personal and Professional Spaces* (New York: Routledge, 2006), 27–33.

3 *library schools*: College and university training programs that offered degrees in library science. In 1929, Hampton College received a grant from the Carnegie Corporation to establish the first school to train African Americans librarians. Library Schools for African Americans were also established at the North Carolina College for Negroes (now the North Carolina Central University) in 1939 and at the Atlanta University (now the Clark Atlanta University) in 1941.

> Source: Jones-Wilson, *Encyclopedia of African American Education*, s.v. "Libraries and Librarians, African-American," 259.

4 Hunter is referencing the scriptures, "And there are differences of administrations, but the same Lord" (1 Cor. 12:5) and "But all these worketh that one and the selfsame Spirit, dividing to every man severally as he will" (1 Cor. 12:11).

5 *Continuation schools*: Established in the early twentieth century to teach homemaking skills to teenage girls.

> Source: Guy Montrose Whipple, "Communications and Discussions: Continuation Schools for Girls," *Journal of Educational Psychology* 3.3 (1912): 158–59.

6 *Jane Addams School*: Originally named the "Girls Opportunity School" when it opened in 1924, this educational institution offered vocational and special education classes for girls until 1927 when it became a trade school for boys.

> Source: *ECH*, s.v. "Cleveland Public Schools."

7 *Longwood School*: Offered special education courses for students who needed to increase their grade point averages so they could transfer back into regular classes. By 1929, Cleveland's black community had begun to complain that Longwood's student population had become disproportionately African American youth who had few opportunities to return to traditional classrooms.

> Source: Ibid.

8 *Unemployment Sewing Circle*: Arose from an early twentieth-century movement that encouraged young women to meet and learn to sew and perform other household chores.

> Source: *American Legion Monthly*, 11–12 (1931).

9 *Mrs. Alexander H. McGaffin*: White civic leader Anna DeYoe McGaffin (1876–1966) was a member of the YWCA and Women's City Club as well as the employment department chairman and a trustee for the PWA. Her husband, Alexander McGaffin (1870–1929), served as pastor of several Presbyterian churches and the Church of the Covenant in Cleveland.

> Source: *RC*, s.vv. "McGaffin, Anna DeYoe" and "McGaffin, Alexander," 235; and *Open Door* (Oct. 1925).

10 *Mrs. McC.Black*: Mrs. McC.Black (?–?) was president of the PWA board of trustees from 1947 to 1949.

Source: "The Phillis Wheatley Association Board Presidents, 1911-1976," n.d., PWAP.

11   *Church of the Covenant*: Founded in 1920 after the merger of three prominent Presbyterian Churches in Cleveland.

Source: *ECH*, s.v. "Church of the Covenant."

12   *green Indian Head*: A sturdy, versatile cotton fabric introduced in 1831 by the Indian Head factory in Nashua, New Hampshire. By the early 1900s, Indian Head cloth was one of the most popular fabrics in America.

Source: Norma R. Hollen and Jane Saddler, *Textiles*, 3rd ed. (New York: MacMillan, 1955), 121.

13   *compensation that would permit the right sort of living*: In the 1930s, wages for African American domestic workers in the North averaged $433.50 or US$(2010)6,885.37 annually.

Source: Jacqueline Jones, *Labor of Love, Labor of Sorrow: Black Women, Work, and the Family from Slavery to the Present* (New York: Basic Books, 1985), 206–08.

14   *Thomas H. White Trust Fund*: Massachusetts native and inventor of the New England sewing machine Thomas Howard White (1836–1914) moved to Cleveland in 1866 and founded the White Sewing Machine Corporation in 1876. In 1913 he established the Thomas H. White Charitable Trust, which funded education and community service projects.

Source: *ECH*, s.v. "Thomas H. White Foundation."

CHAPTER 14

1   *Mrs. Frank A. Arter*: white civic leader Eliza Kingsley Arter (1851–1927) was a member of the PWA's Board of Trustees.

Source: *RC*, s.v. "Arter, Frank A.," 12.

2   *Mr. Arter*: white businessman Frank Asbury Arter (1843–1928) retired from a career in the petroleum oil industry in 1907 and remained active in the community, maintaining club memberships and acting as director of various business interests, including the First National Bank, St. Luke's Hospital, and the Cleveland Life Insurance Company.

Source: Ibid, and *BOC*, s.v. "Arter, Frank A.," 16.

3   *John Brown*: Born in Connecticut and raised in Ohio, white abolitionist John Brown (1800–1859) led an unsuccessful raid on a federal armory at Harpers Ferry in 1859 to secure weapons for a slave rebellion in what is now West Virginia. Brown was subsequently tried, convicted, and executed.

Source: David S. Reynolds, *John Brown Abolitionist: the Man who Killed Slavery, Sparked the Civil War, and Seeded Civil Rights* (New York: Knopf, 2005).

4   *Kingsley-Arter Center*: Located at 2314 East 100th Street, this branch of the Phillis Wheatley Association named after Eliza Kingsley Arter and Frank A. Arter offered a pre-school and programs and clubs for children and adults.

Source: *Open Door* (Sep. 1935) and (Aug. 1936).

5   *Stereopticon lecture*: A popular diversion from the seventeenth century until the early twentieth

century, stereopticon lectures were entertaining and/or informative slide shows in which the speaker employed a stereopticon (frequently referred to as a "magic lantern") to enlarge and illuminate images from gelatin-coated glass slides and project them onto a wall or a screen.

SOURCE: Anna Verona Dorris, *Visual Instruction in the Public Schools* (Boston: Ginn, 1928), 153–56.

6   *Mrs. Benjamin L. Milliken*: Hunter is referring to white editor and musician Julia W. Severance Millikin (1862–1950), daughter of Solon L. and Emily C. Severance, who married Cleveland doctor Benjamin L. Millikin (1851–1916).

SOURCE: Emilius O. Randall and Daniel Joseph Ryan, vol. 6 of *History of Ohio: The Rise and Progress of an American State* (New York: Century History, 1912), 194; and *BOC*, s.v. "Severance, Solon L.," 236–37.

7   *Mr. Raymond Clapp*: White associate director of the Welfare Federation Raymond Clapp (1880–1845) later served, from 1924 to 1941, as principal of the Schauffler Missionary Training School, which was dedicated to the education of young women for Christian missionary work.

SOURCE: Mildred Chadsey, ed., *The Cleveland Yearbook 1922* (Cleveland: Cleveland Foundation, 1922) 203–04; and William Ganson Rose, *Cleveland: The Making of a City* (Cleveland: World, 1950), 750.

8   *Community Fund and the Welfare Federation of Cleveland*: The Federation for Charity and Philanthropy was founded in 1913 to meet Cleveland's health and human services needs through coordinated fundraising efforts. The Federation merged with the Cleveland Welfare Council in 1917, and the eighty-eight federated agencies of the two organizations became the Welfare Federation of Cleveland. In 1919, the Federation established the Community Fund, coordinated campaigns to raise funds for the Community Chest.

SOURCE: Ibid. and *ECH*, s.v. "United Way Services."

9   *Mr. M. A. Bradley*: White civic leader Morris A. Bradley (1859–1926) was founder and president of the Cleveland and Buffalo Transit Company, president of the United States Coal Company, as well as a prominent Cleveland banker and real estate investor.

SOURCE: Avery, *A History of Cleveland and its Environs*, 427–28; and *RC*, s.v. "Bradley, Morris A.," 43.

10   *Unitarian Church*: Early American Unitarianism emerged in Puritan New England as a liberal and rational response to the revivalism of the Great Awakening of the 1740s. The early Unitarian movement rejected Calvinist doctrine and emphasized human dignity, free will, and God's benevolence. The Unitarian Church organized as a denomination in the early nineteenth century.

SOURCE: David Robinson, *The Unitarians and the Universalists* (Westport, CT: Greenwood, 1985).

11   *Mrs. Bradley*: Anna A. Leiminger Bradley (1864?–1952).

12   *Honorable Maurice Maschke*: Harvard-educated white attorney Maurice Maschke (1868–1936) led the Cuyahoga County Republican Party as a political boss for thirty-five years. An ally of Hunter's nemesis Albert Duncan "Starlight" Boyd, Maschke was instrumental in placing a number of African Americans in public service positions.

Source: *ECH*, s.v. "Maurice Maschke;" Philip W. Porter, *Cleveland: Confused City on a See-saw* (Columbus: Ohio State University Press, 1976), 8; and *RC*, s.v. "Maschke, Maurice," 244.

13   *Mrs. Maschke*: Minnie Rice Maschke (ca. 1877–1972).

14   *Mrs. Josephine B. Kohler*: In 1940, Josephine B. Modroch Kohler donated $100,000, US$(2010)1,560,000, toward the renovation of a dormitory that had stood since 1866 on the campus of Baldwin-Wallace College, located about ten miles from Cleveland in Berea, Ohio.

Source: *ECH*, s.v.s. "Berea" and "Kohler, Frederick;" and Rose, *Cleveland: The Making of a City*.

15   *Frances P. Bolton*: Frances Payne Bingham Bolton (1885–1977) was a politically active white Ohio Republican who worked to promote nursing as a profession, served on the board of the National Organization of Public Health Nurses, and helped found the Army School of Nursing. After her husband Chester Castle Bolton (1882–1939) died, Frances Bolton completed his term representing Ohio's 22nd District in the US Congress and was elected to successive terms in Congress from February 27, 1940 to January 3, 1969.

Source: David Loth, *A Long Way Forward: The Biography of Congresswoman Frances P. Bolton* (New York: Longmans, Green, 1957).

16   *"Lord, make me a light. . ."*: Hunter modified the first lines of verse from "A Child's Prayer," by M. (Matilda) Betham-Edwards (1836–1919): "God make my life a little light / Within the world to glow; / A little flame that burneth bright, / Where ever I may go."

Source: Betham-Edwards, Matilda. "A Child's Prayer," in *The Child's Song Garden*, ed. by Mary Bartholomew Ehrmann, illus. by Dixie Selden (Cincinnati, OH: W. H. Willis, 1908), 58–9; and Ibid., "Hymn for a Little Child," *Little's Living Age* 117 (1873): 770.

17   *Miss Bertha L. Bailey*: White civic leader Bertha Louise Bailey (1877–1955) was a trustee and president of the PWA and a member of the Western Reserve Chapter of the Daughters of the American Revolution.

Source: *RC*, s.v. "Bailey, Bertha Louise," 16.

18   *Oberlin College*: In 1833, white Presbyterian ministers John J. Shipherd and Philo P. Stewart established the Oberlin Collegiate Institute, which was renamed Oberlin College in 1850. In 1835, the private liberal arts institution in Oberlin, Ohio, became the first US college to admit African American students and, in 1837, the first to offer a co-educational baccalaureate program.

Source: James H. Fairchild, *Oberlin, Its Origin, Progress and Results: An Address, Prepared for the Alumni of Oberlin College*, Assembled August 22, 1860 (Oberlin, OH: Shankland and Harmon, 1871).

19   *Mrs. F. W. Stecher*: white civic leader Lue Morgan Stecher (1866–1940) was married to Frederick William Stecher (1866–1916), a pharmacist and purveyor of wholesale barber supplies. In 1901, Frederick Stecher created Pompeian Massage Cream, a face cream that was sold in drugstores and barbershops around the world.

Source: "Beauty and Printer's Ink," *The Independent* 79.3422 (July 6, 1914): 144; William R. Coates, vol. 2 of *A History of Cuyahoga County and the City of Cleveland* (Chicago: American Historical Society, 1924), 32–35; and *RC*, s.v. "Stecher, Frederick William," 351.

20   *J. E. Cutler*: white sociologist James Elbert Cutler (1876–1959), a charter member of the American Sociological Association, helped establish and served from 1916 to 1941 as the first dean of the School of Applied Social Sciences and later a trustee at Western Reserve University and the Welfare Federation.

Source: *ECH*, s.v. "Cutler, James Elbert."

21   *Phillis Wheatley Association of Greenville, SC*: Hunter's friend African American Hattie Logan Duckett (1885–1956) founded the PWA of Greenville, South Carolina in 1919 after having paid a visit to the Cleveland PWA. Three white businessmen contributed $50,000 and African Americans donated the remainder of the $75,000 needed to construct the building in Greenville's business district.

Source: Archie Vernon Huff Jr., *Greenville: the History of the City and in the South Carolina Piedmont* (Columbia: University of South Carolina Press, 1995), 313–14; *Open Door* (Sep. 1925).

22   *Thomas F. Parker*: The Greenville PWA reorganized with a biracial board of trustees in 1922, and white South Carolina businessman Thomas Fleming Parker (1860–1926) became its first president in 1923.

Source: Ibid.

Chapter 15

1   *Mrs. Viola Smith Buell*: In 1876, white Ohio native Viola Smith Buell (1854–1931) became the first woman to graduate from Western Reserve College. She completed graduate work at Cornell University and taught in the Cleveland public school system for forty years.

Source: "Obituaries, Mrs. Viola Smith Buell '80," *Cornell Alumni News*, 33.24 (April 16, 1931): 293.

2   *Miss Florence Simms*: White elocutionist and workplace reformer Daisy Florence Simms (1873–1923) served as national secretary of the YWCA college department before being appointed director of the new industrial department established in 1909. She created industrial clubs that offered religious, employment, and leisure programs in a various workplaces throughout the United States. During World War I, she led the War Work Council's Industrial Commission. She also traveled abroad to explore opportunities for developing international work standards for women.

Source: Anne Commire, ed., vol. 2 of *Dictionary of Women Worldwide: 25,000 Women through the Ages* (Detroit: Thomson, Gale, 2007); James T. Edwards, ed., vol. 3 of *Notable American Women, 1607–1950* (Cambridge, MA: Belknap Press of Harvard University Press, 1971), 293; and Richard Roberts, *Florence Simms, A Biography* (New York: Women's Press, 1925).

3   *Girls' Industrial Conference*: Summer meetings organized in the early nineteenth century by industrial members of the YWCA to address the concerns of working women.

Source: "Religious Mission and Politics," *Journal of Women's History* 19.2 (Summer 2007): 85–110.

4   *Mrs. W. P. Champney Sr.*: Clara P. Champney (1855–1933).

5   *Baldwin-Wallace Law School*: Baldwin-Wallace Law School was affiliated with Baldwin-Wallace College in Berea, Ohio.

    SOURCE: Jane E. Hunter, Distinguished Alumni Award, Baldwin-Wallace Law School, PWAP.

6   *Judge Florence E. Allen*: White Democrat Florence Ellinwood Allen (1884–1966) rose from assistant Cuyahoga County prosecutor in 1919 to state Supreme Court justice in 1923.

    SOURCE: *RC*, s.v. "Allen, Florence Ellinwood," 6; *Open Door* (Aug. 1927).

7   *Wilberforce University*: A private, historically black liberal arts university in Wilberforce, Ohio, established in 1843 as Ohio African University. In 1863, the university's name was changed to memorialize the eighteenth-century British abolitionist William Wilberforce.

    SOURCE: Julian B. Roebuck and Komanduri S. Murty, *Historically Black Colleges and Universities: Their Place in American Higher Education* (Westport, CT: Praeger, 1993).

8   *Dr. Frederick D. Patterson*: African American educator Frederick Douglass Patterson (1901–1988), a doctor of veterinary medicine who married Catherine Elizabeth Moton (1909–1999), daughter of Tuskegee's second principal Robert Russa Moton, served as the institute's first president from 1935 to 1953 and established its School of Veterinary Medicine. In 1944, Patterson founded the United Negro College Fund.

    SOURCE: Frederick D. Patterson, *Chronicles of Faith: the Autobiography of Frederick D. Patterson*, (Tuscaloosa: University of Alabama Press, 1991).

9   *Mrs. Ralph L. Fuller*: Thalia Maude Reese Fuller (1881–1962), white civic activist and Republican Party operative, was married to politician Ralph Lathrop Fuller (1865–1932), who helped to incorporate the village of Euclid and served as mayor and councilman.

    SOURCE: *RC*, s.v.v. "Fuller, Ralph Lanthrop" and "Fuller, Thalin Reese Fuller," 133–34.

10   *Willoughby Methodist Church*: Located in Willoughby, Ohio, northeast of Cleveland, Willoughby United Methodist Church originated as a class for religious instruction taught by Reverend Ira Eddy in 1818.

    SOURCE: J. N. Fradenburgh, *History of Erie Conference* (Oil City, PA: Derick, 1907), 335–59.

11   *American Association of Social Workers*: Established by social workers in 1921 to develop a common identity and training practices for a diverse group of professionals.

    SOURCE: John Middlemist Herrick and Paul H. Stuart, eds., *Encyclopedia of Social Welfare History in North America* (Newbury Park, CA: Sage, 2005), s.v. "National Association of Social Workers," 252.

12   *National Conference of Social Work*: Founded in 1873 as the National Conference of Charities and Corrections, this organization for philanthropic groups was reorganized and renamed the National Conference of Social Workers at the 1917 conference.

    SOURCE: "Communication: New Name Wanted," *The Survey* 37 (Dec. 16, 1916): 316.

13   *"Survey"*: Progressive publication dedicated to social work and social reform published from 1909 to 1952, ran as two national journals with slightly different emphases from 1922 to 1948: *Survey Graphic* was written for socially conscious members of the general public, while *Survey Midmonthly* was intended for professionals in the field of public welfare.

Source: Herrick and Stuart, eds., *Encyclopedia of Social Welfare History*, s.v. "*The Survey* (United States)," 403–04.

14 *first colored woman*: Mary B. Martin (1877–1939), a former school teacher who had migrated to Cleveland from Raleigh, North Carolina in 1886 and graduated from Central High School, was appointed to an unexpired term on the board in May of 1929. In November of that year, she was elected to the board of education. She served two successive four-year terms but declined the nomination in 1937. Two years later, the Citizens School Board Committee convinced her to run again. With endorsements from the *Cleveland Plain Dealer* and the Citizens League, she won the election but died of a brain hemorrhage before being sworn into office.

Source: Davis, *Black Americans in Cleveland*, 291; *Cleveland Gazette*, June 29, 1929, Nov. 16, 1929, Nov. 18, 1929, Aug. 28, 1937, Aug. 12, 1939, and Nov. 25, 1939; *Cleveland Press*, Nov. 3, 1937; and Marion J. Morgan, *Women in Cleveland: An Illustrated History* (Bloomington: Indiana University Press, 1995), 203.

15 *Ohio State School at Delaware*: In 1869, the State Reform and Industrial School for Girls was founded in Concord Township near Delaware, Ohio, as a correctional facility for female juvenile offenders. In 1872, the Ohio state legislature changed the institution's name to the Girls' Industrial School.

Source: W. H. Perrin and J. H. Battle, *History of Delaware County and Ohio* (Chicago: O. L. Baskin, 1880), 247.

16 *Ohio Federation of Colored Women's Clubs*: Carrie Williams Clifford (1862–1934) helped organize the Ohio Federation of Colored Women's Clubs to address racial issues throughout the state and nation.

Source: Davis, *Black Americans in Cleveland*, 208.

17 *Charles H. Garvin*: Howard University-educated African American physician, medical school professor and researcher, and World War II veteran Charles H. Garvin (1890–1968) was appointed to the Cleveland Library Board and later elected its president.

Source: Ibid., 179.

Chapter 16

1 *Mr. Henry C. Richman and Mr. Charles L. Richman*: In 1904, white businessman Henry (1876–1934) and Charles Richman (1874?–1936), along with their brother Nathan (ca. 1868–1941), became owners of the Richman Brothers Company, a prominent men's clothing manufacturer and retailer.

Source: *ECH*, s.v. "Richman Brothers Co."

2 *Fiscal Board of Trustees*: About 1927, the PWA Board of Directors became all female, with the exception of treasurer J. R. Wylie, and a group of prominent Cleveland leaders was soon appointed to a Fiscal Board of Trustees to provide business and legal advice.

Source: *Open Door* (Apr. 1927) and (Feb. 1929).

3 *Richman Brothers Company*: In 1853, white businessman Henry Richman (ca. 1837–1906) founded Richman Brothers Company, a men's clothing and manufacturing business, in Ports-

mouth, Ohio. In 1879, he moved the firm to Cleveland where his sons took over the business in 1904. The company became a subsidiary of the F.W. Woolworth Company in 1969, moved its corporate headquarters to Massachusetts in 1986, closed its manufacturing plant in 1990, and went out of business by 1992.

Source: *ECH*, s.v. "Richman Brothers Co."

4   *$2,000*: US$(2010)31,424.00.

5   *Housewives*: The term *housewife* derives from the Old English term *hūswīf*, a word for *housewife* or *hussy*. Until the 1700s, both words referred to females who were heads of their households, but the term *housewife* was also used to describe a married woman. By the mid-1700s, however, as definitions for femininity and womanhood dramatically shifted, *hussy* was associated with "sordid" women, while *housewife* represented domesticity. With the advent of the industrial revolution and the emergence of capitalism, housewives sought new means to wield their collective power to incite social change and demand civil rights.

Source: Jane Mills, *Womanwords: A Dictionary of Words About Women* (New York: MacMillan, Free Press, 1992), 120–23.

6   *National Housewives' League*: Also known as the National Negro Housewives' League of America, the National Housewives' League (NHL) was comprised of local groups dedicated to promoting African American businesses within their communities. It had its origins in the Housewives' League of Detroit, the success of which led African American women in other cities to form similar leagues. In 1933, those leagues united to form the NHL.

Source: Darlene Clark Hine, vol. 1 of *Black Women in America*, 2nd ed. (New York: Oxford University Press, 2005), 354.

7   *Fannie B. Peck*: Fannie B. Peck (1879–1970) founded the Detroit Housewives' League on June 10, 1930 at Bethel AME Church in Detroit. As president, Peck urged African American housewives to use their collective purchasing power to support Detroit's African American businesses. She also served as president of the National Negro Housewives' League.

Source: Hine, *Hine-Sight*, 78–79.

8   *Rev. Mr. Peck*: Reverend William H. Peck (1878–1944), husband of Fannie B. Peck and pastor of the Bethel AME Church in Detroit, established the Booker T. Washington Business Association in Detroit in 1930. It was one of many such associations that were modeled on the Negro Business League, which Washington founded in Boston, Massachusetts, in 1900.

Source: Jessie Carney Smith, vol. 1 of *Encyclopedia of African American Business* (Santa Barbara, CA: Greenwood, 1999), s.v. "Booker T. Washington Business Association," 99–101.

9   *George Carver*: African American scientist Dr. George Washington Carver (1864–1943) earned national acclaim for his research in agriculture and practical small-scale farm technology. In 1896, Booker T. Washington appointed him agriculture director at the Tuskegee Institute.

Source: Rackham Holt, *George Washington Carver* (Garden City, NY: Doubleday, Doran, 1943).

10   "Where there is no vision, the people perish: but he that keepeth the law, happy is he" (Prov. 29:18).

11   *gerrymandering districts*: Congressional districts established with boundaries that influence the outcome of an election by giving one political party or group a majority of registered voters.

12   *"black belt"*: A demographic term that refers to jurisdictions in which the African American population significantly outnumbers the white population.

SOURCE: Boyd Childress, vol. 2 of *Slavery in the United States: A Social, Political and Historical Encyclopedia*, ed. Junius P. Rodriguez (Santa Barbara, CA: ABC-CLIO, 2007), s.v. "Black Belt," 190.

13   *Richard Allen*: Richard Allen (1760–1831), the Methodist Church's first African American deacon, was one of the founders and the first bishop of the African Methodist Episcopal Church.

SOURCE: Richard S. Newman, *Freedom's Prophet: Bishop Richard Allen, the AME Church, and the Black Founding Fathers* (New York: New York University Press, 2008).

14   *African Methodist Episcopal Church*: In the November 1787 incident to which Hunter refers, African Americans were first relegated to the back of the gallery for Sunday services and finally forced from their knees during prayer at the St. George Methodist Episcopal Church in Philadelphia. The event motivated Allen to found his own congregation, the Bethel African Methodist Episcopal (AME) Church in 1794. Its success and that of other African American Methodist congregations ultimately led to the organization of a new denomination, the AME Church in 1816.

SOURCE: Ibid.

15   *Black Belt of Alabama*: Geologically, the term refers to the layer of rich, dark soil that characterized an area which in the early twentieth century cut across south central Alabama from the Mississippi border in the west to Montgomery in the east and encompassed twenty-one counties within 4,300 square miles. Culturally, the term represents the region's predominately African American population who struggled with difficult socioeconomic challenges stemming from the legacy of slavery's plantation system in the region.

SOURCE: Herdman F. Cleland, "The Black Belt of Alabama," *Geographical Review* 10 (1920): 375–87; and Rodriguez, vol. 2 of *Slavery in the United States*, s.v. "Black Belt," 190.

16   *Tuskegee Institute*: In 1881, Alabama governor Rufus Willis Cobb (1829–1913) signed into law a bill passed by the Alabama State Legislature that called for the establishment of a school for African Americans. On July 4, 1881, Booker T. Washington founded the Tuskegee Normal School in Tuskegee to train African Americans for careers as teachers.

SOURCE: Max Bennett Thrasher, intro., Booker T. Washington, *Tuskegee: Its Story and Its Work* (Boston: Small, Maynard, 1900).

17   *But between us and this goal . . .* : Hunter is appropriating the scripture, "Every valley shall be exalted, and every mountain and hill shall be made low: and the crooked shall be made straight, and the rough places plain" (Isa. 40:4), that prophesies the coming of a forerunner who would prepare the way for the Messiah. Hunter draws a parallel between the work of the leaders of the early twentieth-century civil rights struggle and that of John the Baptist who proclaimed the advent of the Jesus's ministry in the wilderness to indicate her faith in the ultimate success of race work for African Americans.

Chapter 17

1 *My sister, the battle is so hard*: Not yet identified.

2 *George A. Brown*: Not yet identified.

3 *Julius Rosenwald*: Jewish businessman, civic leader, and philanthropist Julius Rosenwald (1862–1932) was president of the Sears, Roebuck and Company from 1909 to 1924 and became known for, among numerous other charitable enterprises, spearheading the construction of over 5,000 public school buildings and "Rosenwald Schools" for African Americans in the South between 1917 and 1932.

   Source: Edwin Rogers Embree and Julia Waxman, *Investment in People: The Story of the Julius Rosenwald Fund* (New York: Harper, 1949).

4 *Rosenwald Fund*: In 1917, Rosenwald created the Julius Rosenwald Fund to coordinate his charitable giving with the stipulation that the foundation expend its funds within twenty-five years of his death rather than become a perpetual endowment. The Fund's expenditures at the time of its dissolution in 1948 totaled $22,249,624 or US$(2010)200,892,870.64.

   Source: Ibid.

5 *Mr. Samuel H. Halle*: In 1891, white Cleveland businessman Samuel Horatio Halle (1869?–1954) and his brother Salmon Portland Chase Halle (1866–1949) founded the high-end department store Halle Brothers Company.

   Source: *ECH*, s.v.v. "Halle, Salmon Portland" and "Halle Brothers Co."

6 *Young Men's Christian Association*: In 1844, Englishman George Williams and several friends established the Young Men's Christian Association (YMCA) in London to provide religious activities for and address the social needs of male workers who were moving to the city during the Industrial Revolution. The organization served constituents from diverse nationalities, races, age groups, and denominations. In 1851, the first YMCA began operating in the United States in Boston. Cleveland's first YMCA opened in 1854.

   Source: Charles Howard Hopkins, *History of the Y.M.C.A. in North America* (New York: Association Press, 1951) and *ECH*, s.v. "Young Men's Christian Assn."

7 *Aunt Nan*: Nancy Milliner English (1868–?) was the sister of Hunter's mother.

   Source: Jane E. Hunter to Mrs. Nan English, Dec. 31, 1935, Personal Correspondence, PWAP.

8 *Soon-a will be don-a with the troubles of the world . . .* : Hunter is referencing the refrain of the Negro spiritual, "Soon-a will be don-a with the troubles of the World."

9 *Wendell Phillips High School*: Named for prominent abolitionist and social activist Wendell Phillips (1811–1884), the school was established in 1904 for the children of affluent white Chicago residents. By the 1920s, however, the student population had become African American after the great migration drew thousands of blacks to Chicago among other major cities beyond the South seeking to escape racism and sparse employment opportunities in the South.

   Source: Meyer Weinburg, *A Chance to Learn: The History of Education and Race in the United States*, 2nd ed. (Long Beach: California State University Press, 1995), 69.

10 *Josephine St. Pierre Ruffin*: African American journalist, suffragist, and civil rights leader

Josephine St. Pierre Ruffin (1842–1924) established *Woman's Era*, a magazine devoted to racial uplift in 1890, and later the Woman's Era Club, which eventually became the National Association of Colored Women.

SOURCE: Roger A. Schuppert, vol. 7 of *AANB*, s.v. "Ruffin, Josephine St. Pierre," 30–31.

11 *Hallie Q. Brown*: Educator, elocutionist, author, and black women's club movement pioneer Hallie Quinn Brown (ca. 1845–1949) was a member of the Women's Missionary Society of the AME Conference, the Colored Women's League of Washington, D.C, and the NACW; and she published collections of her writings and speeches, the most popular being *Homespun Heroines and Other Women of Distinction* (1926).

SOURCE: Lisa E. Rivo, vol. 1 of *AANB*, s.v. "Brown, Hallie Q.," 609–11.

12 *Emma Miller*: Not yet identified.

13 *Lucy C. Jefferson*: Entrepreneur, philanthropist, and black club woman Lucy Crump Jefferson (1866–1953) was co-owner of the prosperous W. H. Jefferson Funeral Home established in 1894, one of the first black-owned businesses in Mississippi.

SOURCE: George A. Sewell and Margaret L. Dwight, *Mississippi Black History Makers*, rev. and enl. ed. (Jackson: University Press of Mississippi, 1984), 341–42, s.v. "Lucy C. Jefferson, Business, Club and Religious Leader."

14 *Rebecca Styles Taylor*: Hunter is likely referring to educator and black club woman Rebecca Stiles Taylor (1880–1970) who served as the first executive secretary of the NACW and was a civic activist in Savannah, Georgia.

SOURCE: Jessie Carney Smith, vol. 2 of *Notable Black American Women*, 631–32, s.v. "Taylor, Rebecca Stiles."

15 *Mary McLeod Bethune*: Women's and civil rights activist and black club woman Mary Jane McLeod Bethune (1875–1955) founded the Daytona Educational and Training School in 1904, which merged with the Cookman School, an educational institution for males, and eventually attained junior college status as Bethune-Cookman College in 1931. Bethune was also a member of the National Urban League, founder and president of the National Council of Negro Women, and president of the NACW and the Association for the Study of Negro Life and History, and served in various capacities within the presidential administrations of Calvin Coolidge, Herbert Hoover, and Franklin D. Roosevelt.

SOURCE: Darlene Clark Hine, vol. 1 of *AANB*, s.v. "Bethune, Mary McLeod," 388–90, and Rackham Holt, *Mary McLeod Bethune: A Biography* (Garden City, NY: Doubleday, 1964).

16 *Sallie W. Stewart*: Black club woman, educator, and community activist Sallie W. Stewart (1881–1951) spearheaded interracial initiatives to provide economic, health, recreational, and educational programs, and was involved with the NACW, including serving as president from 1928 to 1933.

SOURCE: Shennette Garrett, vol. 7 of *AANB*, s.v. "Stewart, Sallie W.," 407–09.

17 *Dr. Mary F. Waring*: African American physician, educator, and club woman Mary Fitzbutler Waring (c. 1870–1958) organized and became active in clubs that focused on the civic, economic, and social needs of the community. Her activism led to opportunities with organizations such as the National Council of Women, comprised mostly of white women; the NACW,

where she served as president from 1933 to 1937; and the International Council of Women. She also regularly contributed columns to black publications such as *National Notes*, the main organ of the NACW.

Source: Nadya J. Lawson, vol. 2 of *Notable Black American Women*, s.v. "Waring, Mary Fitzbutler," 680–83.

18   *Mrs. Robert R. Moton*: African American club woman and community activist Jennie Dee Booth Moton (1879–1942), Tuskegee principal Robert Russa Moton's second wife, served as director of Women's Industries at Tuskegee Institute; and president of the Tuskegee's Women's Club, the Alabama Association of Women's Clubs, and the NACW. She was also appointed field officer for the Southern Division of the Agricultural Adjustment Administration, a US Department of Agriculture agency that supported American farmers.

Source: Janet Sims-Woods, Ibid, s.v. "Moton, Jennie Dee Booth," 486–89.

19   *Alpha Kappa Alpha Sorority*: Founded in 1908 at Howard University as the first Greek-lettered sorority established and incorporated by African American college women. In 1928, Hunter became an honorary member of this sorority.

Source: Lawrence C. Ross Jr., *The Divine Nine: The History of African American Fraternities and Sororities* (New York: Kensington, 2000), 165.

20   *Delta Sigma Theta Sorority*: Founded in 1913 at Howard University and became the largest African-American Greek-lettered sorority in the world.

Source: Ibid., 215–16 and Jones, *Jane Edna Hunter*, 124.

21   *Zeta Phi Beta Sorority*: Founded in 1920 at Howard University as the first African American sister organization to the Phi Beta Sigma Fraternity, Inc.

Source: Ibid., 244.

22   *Iota Phi Lambda Sorority*: Founded in 1929 by Lola Mercedes Parker (1900–1987) and six African American women in Chicago to promote African American women's business interests.

Source: Robert E. Weems and Lewis A. Randolph, *Business in Black and White: American Presidents and Black Entrepreneurs in the Twentieth Century* (New York: New York University Press, 2009), 51–52, and Nancy Jean Rose, *Organizing Black America: An Encyclopedia of African American Associations*, Nina Mjagkij, ed. (Florence, KY: Routledge, Taylor and Francis, 2001), 285, s.v. "Iota Phi Lambda."

23   *Let us march on til victory is won*: Hunter is referencing "The Negro National Anthem," adopted by the National Association of Colored People in 1915. The song originated as a poem by James Weldon Johnson that was recited by school children to introduce Booker T. Washington at a celebration for the anniversary of Abraham Lincoln's birthday on February 12, 1900. John Johnson, James Johnson's brother, wrote music for the poem in 1905.

Source: Mary Loving Blanchard and Cara Falcetti, *Poets for Young Adults: Their Lives and Works* (Santa Barbara, CA: Greenwood, 2006), 131.

24   *Southernaires*: An African American vocal quartet that formed in 1929 and performed on live National Broadcasting Company (NBC) radio broadcasts and at the PWA.

Source: Maud Cuney Hare, *Negro Musicians and Their Music* (New York: Da Capo Press, 1974).

25 *Wings Over Jordan Singers*: In 1935, Glenn T. Settle (1895–1952), pastor of Gethsemane Baptist Church in Cleveland, founded the Wings Over Jordan Singers, an African American *a cappella* choir that became famous for its live Sunday morning radio broadcasts of Negro spirituals and gospel music on the Columbia Broadcasting Company (CBS) from 1937 to 1947.

SOURCE: *ECH*, s.v. "Wings Over Jordan Choir (WOJC)."

26 *Lord I couldn' hear nobody pray*: Hunter is alluding to the Negro Spiritual "Couldn't Hear Nobody Pray."

27 *the College farm*: Hunter is likely referencing the Clemson College farm that was located a few miles from Woodburn Farm, her childhood home.

28 *Old Stone Church*: The Hopewell-Keowee Presbyterian congregation was named Hopewell, after General Andrew Pickens's residence on the Seneca River nearby, and Keowee, after the river that feeds into the Seneca. Built in 1797 on land donated by newspaperman John Miller, the original log church was destroyed by a fire in 1796 and replaced by a stone structure in 1802.

SOURCE: Frederick C. Holder, *Historic Sites of Oconee County, South Carolina*, 2nd ed. (Oconee, SC: Oconee County Historical Society, 1991), 40–41, and Brackett, ed., *The Old Stone Church*.

29 *General Andrew Pickens*: Major General Andrew Pickens (1739–1817), son of a Virginia colonist who relocated his family to South Carolina, began his military career in the French and Cherokees wars and then later served with distinction in the Revolutionary War, particularly in the colonists' improbable victory over the British in the Battle of Cowpens, for which he earned a sword from Congress. The city of Pickens, South Carolina was named in his honor.

SOURCE: Hartley, *Heroes and Patriots of the South*, 269–76.

30 *Must Jesus bear the cross alone . . .*: The lyrics for this hymn, "Must Jesus Bear the Cross Alone," were written in 1693 by Church of England minister Thomas Shepherd (1665–1739), with additional lyrics by the Reverend Henry Ward Beecher (1813–1887), and music composed in 1846 by George Allen (1812–1877).

31 *Free at last, free at last*: Hunter is quoting from the Negro spiritual, "Free At Last." The song may have been first sung by African Americans when slavery was abolished after the Civil War. The spiritual has also been described as a shout that was included in Emancipation Day Celebrations.

SOURCE: William H. Wiggins, *"Free at Last": a Study of Afro-American Emancipation Day Celebrations*, unpublished Phd diss., University of Indiana, 1974, 175.

32 *loaves and fishes*: Hunter is referencing two of Jesus's miracles when he fed more than 5,000 people after blessing five loaves and two fishes (Matt. 14:13–21, Mark 6:31–44, Luke 9:10–17, and John 6:5–15), and on a second occasion more than 4,000 people after blessing seven loaves and some fishes (Matt. 15:39–39 and Mark 8:1–9).

33 *Benjamin Tillman*: Benjamin Ryan Tillman (1847–1918), often referred to as "Pitchfork Ben," was a white supremacist and Democrat who rose to power during the Reconstruction period and served as governor of South Carolina from 1890 to 1894 and in the US Senate from 1895 until his death. The South Carolina State Constitutional Convention he led in 1895 effectively disenfranchised African American men and codified what would become known as Jim Crow laws.

Source: Francis Butler Simkins, *Pitchfork Ben Tillman: South Carolinian* (Baton Rouge: Louisiana State University Press, 1944).

34   *library for Negroes*: In 1927, African American Susan Dart Butler initiated a fundraising drive to establish a reading room for black residents in the old print shop of Dart Hall, a building that had originally housed the Charleston Normal and Industrial Institute founded by her father, Reverend John L. Dart (1854–1915), who also published a newspaper, the *Southern Reporter*. Susan Butler stocked the shelves with books from her father's private library, texts donated by individuals and organizations, and those she purchased, and funded the library's operations. Within four years, the reading room became the Dart Hall Branch of the Charleston Free Library system with the assistance of grants from the Rosenwald and Carnegie Funds.

Source: Ethel Evangeline Martin Bolden, *Susan Dart Butler: Pioneer Librarian*, Thesis, Atlanta University, 1959; and George Brown Tindall, *South Carolina Negroes, 1877–1900* (Columbia: University of South Carolina Press, 1970, 2003), 205.

35   *Susie Butler, librarian*: African American community activist and educator Susan Dart Butler (1888–1959) was the first librarian for Charleston's library for African Americans.

Source: Bolden, *Susan Dart Butler* and Stephanie Jo Shaw, *What a Woman Ought to Be and to Do: Black Professional Women Workers during the Jim Crow Era* (Chicago: University of Chicago Press, 1996), 225.

36   *Avery Institute*: Established in 1865 by the American Missionary Association, the Avery Normal Institute offered normal, or teacher, training, as well as domestic service and manual labor courses to former slaves and free blacks. Reverend F. L. Cardoza organized the school at the end of the Civil War in 1865 with a $10,000 grant from the estate of Reverend Charles Avery of Pittsburgh, a philanthropic Methodist, for whom the school was named. The Freedman's Bureau and local merchants provided additional financial assistance.

Source: Drango, *Charleston's Avery Center*.

37   *Burke Industrial School for Negroes*: In 1894, African American activist Reverend John L. Dart founded the Charleston Normal and Industrial Institute to educate African American children. By 1911, Dart and other African American activists had convinced school board officials to assume responsibility for operating the school, which became known as the Charleston Colored Industrial School. Initially, white teachers provided industrial and elementary school instruction until an African American principal and African American teachers were hired in 1919. Two years later, the school was renamed Burke Industrial School for Negroes to memorialize James E. Burke, a member of the city board. By 1925, Burke offered industrial training, as well as elementary and high school education.

Source: Ibid.; and Sherman E. Pyatt, *Burke High School, 1894–2006* (Mt. Pleasant, SC: Arcadia Publishing, 2007).

38   *It makes me love everybody*: Hunter is quoting from the old revival hymn "Give Me that Old Time Religion."

39   *Mr. and Mrs. John Bennett*: In 1940 at Hunter's request, John and Susan Bennett offered extensive editorial advice for the revision of the manuscript for *A Nickel and A Prayer*. Bennett published a review of the autobiography in the Charleston *News and Courier* in November of 1940 that boosted sales. In 1941, John Bennett solicited the assistance of his sister-in-law to

provide further editorial commentary for the second printing of the first edition of *A Nickel and A Prayer*.

Source: Jane E. Hunter to John Bennett, Apr. 11, 1939, John Bennett to Jane E. Hunter, Apr. 28, 1939, and John Bennett to Jane E. Hunter, Apr. 1, 1941, JBP.

40   *St. Michael's Church*: The oldest church structure in Charleston began as a small wooden edifice built in the 1680s and named St. Philip's. In 1727, a larger brick building was built on Church Street. By 1751, the congregation had outgrown the facility and received permission to erect a new church on Market Street, which it renamed St. Michael's and completed in 1761.

Source: Moses Kimball Armstrong, *Early Empire Builders of the Great West* (Minnesota: E. W. Porter, 1901), 438; and Lee Davis Perry and J. Michael McLaughlin, *Insiders' Guide to Charleston: Including Mt. Pleasant, Summerville, Kiawah, and Other Islands, 11th ed.* (Guilford, CT: Globe Pequot Press, 2000), 161.

41   *St. Philip's Church*: Built in 1680 in Charleston on the corner of Market and Broad streets. In 1708, Gideon Johnston began serving as its first commissary. The church was rebuilt and relocated several times until it was established on its present site on Church Street in 1838.

Source: Perry and McLaughlin, *Insiders' Guide to Charleston*, 161–62.

42   *This love which passes all understanding*: Hunter is appropriating the scripture, substituting the word "love" for "peace": "And the peace of God, which passeth all understanding, shall keep your hearts and minds through Jesus Christ" (Phil. 4:6–7).

43   *shall "crown our good with brotherhood" and we shall hear America sing*: *Thank God I'm in-a this field*: By juxtaposing a line from "America the Beautiful" (1893) with a line from the Negro spiritual "Thank God I'm in-a This Field," Hunter ends her autobiography with an emphasis on her desire for interracial cooperation in the struggle for racial equality through allusions to two poems that assert an American identity for all citizens, Walt Whitman's "I hear American sing" (1855) and Langston Hughes' "I, too, sing America" (1925).

Appendix A

1   *George A. Myers*: In 1888, several wealthy white Clevelanders helped Myers purchase a barbershop in The Hollenden, the city's most luxurious hotel, which he transformed into a modern facility where white clients gathered to discuss business and politics. Beginning in 1892, he served as a delegate to several Republican National Conventions and remained active in politics until the early twentieth century, helping secure the black vote for Republican candidates and pressuring the party to enact civil rights legislation. He was a staunch opponent of segregated facilities in Cleveland. Myers supported Washington and kept him apprised of various attempts by black Clevelanders to obtain the influential activist's endorsement of their racial uplift initiatives or to stir up anti-Washington sentiments in the community.

Source: Davis, *Black Americans in Cleveland*, 136, 140–41.

Appendix B

1   Jane Edna Hunter, "The Campaign is On!!" *Open Door* (Jan. 1925); "List of Advance Subscribers of $100 and Over to the Phillis Wheatley Building Fund Campaign," Ibid.; and Hunter, "The Phillis Wheatley Building Campaign," Ibid., (Feb. 1925).

2   Moynelle "Monya" Katzenstein Spanye (1879–1945), wife of white businessman Bert Albert
    Spanye (1868–1941) who worked as a buyer for Bailey Company, a major department store in
    Cleveland.

    SOURCE: "Arrival of Buyers," *New York Times*, Business and Finance, Jul. 7, 1919, 22 and *ECH*,
    s.v. "Bailey Co."

APPENDIX C

1   "The Sarah C. Hills Training School of the Phillis Wheatley Association," PWAP.

APPENDIX D

1   John Bennett, "South Carolina Negro's Autobiography is Remarkable and Inspiring Testament,"
    review of *A Nickel and a Prayer*, by Jane Edna Hunter, *The State*, December 1, 1940.

BIBLIOGRAPHY

Collections

Booker T. Washington Papers. Manuscript Division, Library of Congress, Washington, DC.

Charles W. Chesnutt Papers. Western Reserve Historical Society Library, Cleveland.

Cleveland Necrology File. Cleveland Public Library, Cleveland.

Evangeline Banks Harrison Papers. Avery Research Center for African American History and Culture, Charleston, South Carolina.

George A. Myers Papers. Ohio Historical Society Library, Columbus.

Jane Edna Hunter Papers, 1930–1969. Western Reserve Historical Society Library, Cleveland.

Jane Edna Hunter Papers, Series II, 1909–1964. Western Reserve Historical Society Library, Cleveland.

Jane Edna Hunter Records. Phillis Wheatley Association, Cleveland.

John Bennett Papers. South Carolina Historical Society Library, Charleston.

Nannie Helen Burroughs Papers. Manuscript Division, Library of Congress, Washington, DC.

Phillis Wheatley Association Papers. Phillis Wheatley Association, Cleveland.

Phillis Wheatley Association Records, 1914–1960. Western Reserve Historical Society Library, Cleveland.

Records of the Commissioners of the City Hospital, 1879–1907. Charleston Archives, Special Collections, Charleston County Public Library, Charleston.

Published Works

Addams, Jane. *Twenty Years at Hull House*. New York: Macmillan, 1910.

Alsup, Janet. *Teacher Identity Discourses: Negotiating Personal and Professional Spaces*. New York: Routledge, 2006.

American Legion Monthly, nos. 11–12 (1931).

Armstrong, Foster, Richard Klein, and Cara Armstrong. *A Guide to Cleveland's Sacred Landmarks*. Kent, OH: Kent State University Press, 1992.

Armstrong, Moses Kimball. *Early Empire Builders of the Great West*. St. Paul: E. W. Porter, 1901.

Anderson Chamber of Commerce. *History of Anderson County, South Carolina*. Anderson: Anderson Area Chamber, 1981.

Anderson, Greta. *More than Petticoats: Remarkable Ohio Women*. Guilford, CT: TwoDot, 2005.

Arnesen, Eric, Julie Greene, and Bruce Laurie. *Labor Histories: Class, Politics and the Working Class Experience*. Champaign: University of Illinois Press, 1998.

Avery, Elroy McKendree. *A History of Cleveland and its Environs: The Heart of New Connecticut*. 3 vols. Chicago: Lewis, 1918.

Badders, Hurley E. *Remembering South Carolina's Old Pendleton District*. Charleston: History Press, 2006.

Bailey, A. Peter. *The Harlem Hospital Story: 100 Years of Struggle Against Illness, Racism, and Genocide*. Richmond, VA: Native Sun, 1991.

Basler, Roy P., ed. *Collected Works of Abraham Lincoln*. Vol. 8. Piscataway, NJ: Rutgers University Press, 1953.

Bellamy, G. A., C. Hubert LeBlond, R. H. Bishop Jr., Jeanette Bullis, and Myrta L. Jones, eds. *The Social Year Book: The Human Problems and Resources of Cleveland*. Cleveland: The Cleveland Federation for Charity and Philanthropy, 1913.

Bennett, Alma, ed. *Thomas Green Clemson*. Clemson, SC: ClemsonPrints, 2009.

Betham-Edwards, Matilda. "A Child's Prayer." In *The Child's Song Garden*, edited by Mary Bartholomew Ehrmann, 58, 59. Cincinnati: W. H. Willis, 1908.

———. "Hymn for a Little Child," *Little's Living Age* 117 (1873): 770.

Blanchard, Mary Loving, and Cara Falcetti. *Poets for Young Adults: Their Lives and Works*. Santa Barbara, CA: Greenwood, 2006.

Bland, Sidney. *Preserving Charleston Past, Shaping Its Future: the Life and Times of Susan Pringle Frost*. Columbia: University of South Carolina Press, 1999.

Bolden, Ethel Evangeline Martin. *Susan Dart Butler: Pioneer Librarian.* Master's thesis, Atlanta University, 1959.

The Book of Clevelanders: A Biographical Dictionary of Living Men of the City of Cleveland. Cleveland: Burrows Bros., 1914.

Booth, Stephane Elise. *Buckeye Women: The History of Ohio's Daughters*. Athens: Ohio University Press, 2001.

Bornstein, Morris. *Manual of Instruction in the Use of Dumb Bells, Indian Clubs, and Other Exercises*. New York: Excelsior, 1889.

Boyd, Lois A., and R. Douglas Brackenridge. *Presbyterian Women in American: Two Centuries of a Quest for Status.* Santa Barbara, CA: Greenwood, 1996.

Brackett, Richard Newman, ed. *The Old Stone Church, Oconee County, South Carolina*. Columbia, SC: R.L. Bryan Company, 1905.

Braun, Mary Beth, Stephanie J. Simonson, Debra C. Howard, and Marybetts Sinclair. *Introduction to Massage Therapy*. Philadelphia: Lippincott Williams & Wilkins, 2007.

Braxton, Joanne M. *Black Women Writing Autobiography: A Tradition within a Tradition.* Philadelphia: Temple University Press, 1989.

———. "Symbolic Geography and Psychic Landscapes: A Conversation with Maya Angelou." In *Maya Angelou's I Know Why the Caged Bird Sings: A Casebook*, edited by Joanne M. Braxton, 3-20. New York: Oxford University Press, 1999.

Brewster, Paul G. *Children's Games and Rhymes*. Manchester, NH: Ayer Publishing, 1976.

Bunyan, John. *The Pilgrim's Progress from this World to That which is to Come*. London: E. P. Dutton, 1918.

Butterfield, Fox. *All God's Children: the Bosket Family and the American Tradition of Violence*. New York: Harper, 1996.

Carby, Hazel V. "Policing the Black Woman's Body in an Urban Context." *Critical Inquiry* 18, no. 4 (1992): 738–55.

Carson, Licia. *Faces of Intellectual Disability: Philosophical Reflections*. Bloomington: Indiana University Press, 2009.

Chadsey, Mildred, ed. *The Cleveland Yearbook 1922*. Cleveland: Cleveland Foundation, 1922.

Chase, Gilbert. *America's Music, from the Pilgrims to the Present.* 3rd ed. Champaign: University of Illinois Press, 1992.

Chesnutt, Charles W. "The Negro in Cleveland." *The Clevelander* 5, no. 7 (1930): 3–4, 24, 26.

Chernow, Ron. *Titan: the Life of John D. Rockefeller, Sr.* New York: Random House, 2006.

Cleland, Herdman F. "The Black Belt of Alabama." *Geographical Review* 10, no. 6 (1920): 375–87.

Coates, William R. *A History of Cuyahoga County and the City of Cleveland.* 3 vols. Chicago: American Historical Society, 1924.

Colquitt, Harriet Ross, ed. *The Savannah Cookbook: A Collection of the Old Fashioned Receipts from Colonial Kitchens.* Charleston, SC: Colonial, 1933.

Commire, Anne, and Deborah Klezmer, eds. *Dictionary of Women Worldwide: 25,000 Women through the Ages.* 3 vols. Farmington Hills, MI: Yorkin Publications/Gale, 2007.

"Communication: New Name Wanted," *The Survey*, 37 (Dec. 16, 1916): 316.

Cooper, William J. *The Conservative Regime: South Carolina, 1877–1890.* Columbia: University of South Carolina Press, 2005.

Crellin, J. K., Jane Philpott, and A. L. Tommie Bass. *Herbal Medicine Past and Present: A Reference Guide to Medicinal Plants.* Durham: Duke University Press, 1990.

Dagbovie, Pero Gaglo. "Black Women, Carter G. Woodson, and the Association for the Study of Negro Life and History, 1915–1950." *Journal of African American History* 88, no. 1 (2003): 21–42.

Dana, James D., and Edward S. Dana, eds. "Obituary: Charles Upham Shepard." *American Journal of Science* 31, nos. 181–86 (1886): 482–83.

Daniel, Sadie Iola. *Women Builders.* Washington, DC: Associated Publishers, 1931.

Davis, Russell H. *Black Americans in Cleveland: George Peake, to Carl B. Stokes, 1796–1969.* Association for the Study of Negro Life and History in Cooperation with the Western Reserve Historical Society. Washington, DC: Associated Publishers, 1972.

Dills, R. S. *History of Fayette County, Together with Historic Notes on the Northwest, and the State of Ohio.* Dayton, OH: Odell & Mayer, 1881.

Dodworth, Allen. *Dancing and Its Relation to Education and Social Life, With a New Method of Instruction.* New York: Harper, 1885.

Dorris, Anna Verona. *Visual Instruction in the Public Schools*. Boston: Ginn & Co., 1928.

Drago, Edmund L., and W. Marvin Dulaney, eds. *Charleston's Avery Center: from Education and Civil Rights to Preserving the African American Experience*. Charleston: History Press, 1990.

Durham, Richard, and J. Fred Macdonald. *Richard Durham's Destination Freedom: Scripts from Radio's Black Legacy, 1948–50*. New York: Praeger Publishers, 1989.

Edwards, James T., ed. *Notable American Women, 1607–1950: A Biographical Dictionary*. 3 vols. Cambridge, MA: Belknap Press of Harvard University Press, 1971.

Ellis, Joseph. *After the Revolution*. New York: Norton, 2002.

Embree, Edwin Rogers, and Julia Waxman. *Investment in People: The Story of the Julius Rosenwald Fund*. 1st ed. New York: Harper & Brothers, 1949.

Encyclopedia of Cleveland History. Compiled by David D. VanTassel and John J. Grabowski. Western Reserve Historical Society and Case Western University, http://ech.case.edu/index.html.

Fairchild, James H. *Oberlin, its Origin, Progress and Results: An Address, Prepared for the Alumni of Oberlin College, Assembled August 22, 1860*. Oberlin, OH: Shankland and Harmon, 1871.

Ferris, William. *Blues from the Delta*. Rev. ed. New York: Da Capo, 1984.

Forbes, Jack D. *Africans and Native Americans: The Language of Race and the Evolution of Red-Black Peoples*, 2nd ed. Urbana: University of Illinois Press, 1993.

Fosdick, Raymond Blaine. *John D. Rockefeller, Jr., a Portrait*. New York: Harper, 1956.

———. *The Story of the Rockefeller Foundation*, 1st ed. New York: Harper & Bros., 1952.

Fought, Leigh. *Southern Womanhood and Slavery: A Biography of Louisa S. McCord*. Columbia: University of Missouri Press, 2003.

Fradenburgh, Jason Nelson. *History of Erie Conference*. Oil City, PA: Derick, 1907.

Franklin, Paul M., and Nancy Mikula. *South Carolina's Plantations and Historic Homes*. Osceola, WI: Voyageur Press, 2006.

Gates, Henry Louis Jr., and Evelyn Brooks Higginbotham, eds. *African American National Biography*. 8 vols. New York: Oxford University Press, 2008.

Gerber, Albrecht. *Deissmann the Philologist*. Berlin; New York: Walter de Gruyter, 2010.

Geber, David A. *Black Ohio and the Color Line, 1860-1915*. Urbana: University of Illinois Press, 1976.

Giffin, William W. *African Americans and the Color Line in Ohio: 1950–1930*. Columbus: Ohio State University Press, 2005.

Goldberg, Vicki. *Margaret Bourke-White: A Biography*. New York: HarperCollins, 1986.

Gorham, Barlow Weed, and John Bray. *Camp Meeting Manual, a Practical Book for the Camp Ground; in Two Parts*. Boston: H. V. Degen, 1854.

Greene, Harlan. *Mr. Skylark: John Bennett and the Charleston Renaissance*. Athens: University of Georgia Press, 2001.

Harlan, Louis R. *Booker T. Washington: The Wizard of Tuskegee, 1901–1915*. New York: Oxford University Press, 1983.

Holder, Frederick C. *Historic Sites of Oconee County, South Carolina*. 2nd ed. Oconee, SC: Oconee County Historical Society, 1991.

Hartley, Cecil B. *Heroes and Patriots of the South, Comprising the Lives of General Francis Marion, General William Moultrie, General Andrew Pickens, and Governor John Rutledge*. Philadelphia: G. G. Evans, 1860.

Harter, H. M. *World Railways of the Nineteenth Century*. Baltimore: Johns Hopkins University Press, 2005.

Hawthorne, Nathaniel. *Our Old Home: A Series of English Sketches*. Boston: Houghton, Mifflin, 1863.

Hazzard-Gordon, Katrina. *Jookin: The Rise of Social Dance Clubs in African-American Culture*. Philadelphia: Temple University Press, 1990.

Herdman, F. Cleland. "The Black Belt of Alabama." *Geographical Review* 10 (1920): 375–87.

Herrick, John Middlemist, and Paul H. Stuart, eds. *Encyclopedia of Social Welfare History in North America*. Thousand Oaks, CA: Sage, 2005.

Hess, Karen, and Samuel G. Stoney. *The Carolina Rice Kitchen: The African Connection*. Columbia: University of South Carolina Press, 1992.

Hine, Darlene Clark. *Hine-Sight: Black Women and the Re-Construction of American History*. Bloomington: Indiana University Press, 1997.

———. *Black Women in America*. 2 vols. New York: Oxford University Press, 2005.

History of Delaware County and Ohio. Chicago: O.L. Baskin & Co., 1880.

Hollen, Norma R., and Jane Saddler. *Textiles*. 3rd ed. New York: MacMillan, 1955.

Holt, Rackham. *Mary McLeod Bethune: A Biography*. Garden City, NY: Doubleday, 1964.

———. *George Washington Carver*. Garden City, NY: Doubleday, Doran & Co., 1943.

Hopkins, Charles Howard. *History of the Y.M.C.A. in North America*. New York: Association Press, 1951.

Hoyle, Edmond. *Hoyle's Games*. New York: McClure, 1938.

Huff, Archie Vernon, Jr. *Greenville: The History of the City and County in the South Carolina Piedmont*. Columbia: University of South Carolina Press, 1995.

Hunter, Jane Edna. *A Nickel and a Prayer*. Jane E. Hunter Scholarship Committee, 1984.

———. *A Nickel and a Prayer*. Nashville: Elli Kani Publishing Company/Parthenon Press, 1940.

———. *A Nickel and a Prayer*. 2nd printing. Nashville: Elli Kani Publishing Company/Parthenon Press, 1941.

Husband, Joseph. *The Story of the Pullman Car*. Chicago: A.C. McClurg & Co., 1917.

Jones, Adrienne Lash. *Jane Edna Hunter: A Case Study in Leadership, 1910–1950*. Vol. 12, *Black Women in United States History*, edited by Darlene Clark Hine. Brooklyn: Carlson, 1990.

Jones, Jacqueline. *Labor of Love, Labor of Sorrow: Black Women, Work, and the Family from Slavery to the Present*. New York: Basic Books, 1985.

Jones, Thomas Jesse, ed. "Negro Education: A Study of the Private and Higher Schools for Colored People in the United States. Vol. 2," *Department of the Interior, Bureau of Education: Bulletin, 1916*, no. 39 (1917).

Jones, Trina. "Shades of Brown: The Law of Skin Color." *Duke Law Journal* 49, no. 6 (2000): 1487–557.

Jones-Wilson, Faustine C., Charles A. Asbury, Margo Okazawa-Rey, D. Kamili Anderson, Sylvia M. Jacobs, and Michael Fultz, eds. *Encyclopedia of African American Education*. Westport, CT: Greenwood, 1996.

King, William Harvey. *History of Homeopathy and its Institutions in America*. New York: Lewis, 1905.

Korges, James. *Erskine Caldwell*. No. 78 of University of Minnesota Pamphlets on American Writers. Minneapolis: University of Minnesota Press, 2009.

Kusmer, Kenneth L. *A Ghetto Takes Shape: Black Cleveland 1870–1930*. Urbana: University of Illinois Press, 1976.

Longfellow, Henry Wadsworth. "The Village Blacksmith." *Ballads and Other Poems*. 4th ed. Cambridge, MA: J. Owen, 1842.

Loth, David Goldsmith. *A Long Way Forward: the Biography of Congresswoman Frances P. Bolton*. 1st ed. New York: Longmans, Green, 1957.

Mather, Fred. *Modern Fish Culture in Fresh and Salt Water*. New York: Forest & Stream, 1900.

Maxey, Chester C. "The Cleveland Election and the New Charter." *American Political Science Review* 16, no. 1 (1922): 83.

McCall, Ruth E., and Cathee M. Tankersley. *Phlebotomy Essentials*. Philadelphia: Lippincott Williams & Wilkins, 2007.

McCray, R. Y., ed. *Representative Clevelanders: A Biographical Directory of Leading Men and Women in Present-Day Cleveland Community*. Cleveland: Cleveland Topics, 1926.

McDermott, Kathleen, and Davis Dyer. *America's Paint Company: A History of Sherwin-Williams*. Cambridge, MA: Winthrop Group, 1991.

McLaughlin, J. Michael. *Insiders' Guide to Charleston: Including Mt. Pleasant, Summerville, Kiawah, and Other Islands*.11th ed. Guilford, CT: Globe Pequot Press, 2000.

McMaster, Sharon. *The Telecommunications Industry*. Westport, CT: Greenwood, 2002.

McNamara, Margaret E. "What Ohio is Doing for Delinquent Girls." *Ohio State Institution Journal* 1, no. 1 (1918): 33–35.

Megginson, W. J. *African American Life in South Carolina's Upper Piedmont, 1780–1900*. Columbia: University of South Carolina Press, 2006.

Men of Ohio in Nineteen Hundred. Cleveland: Benesch Art Publishing Co., 1901.

Mendenhall, Thomas C., ed. *Addresses and Proceedings of the Semicentennial Celebration October 13–16, 1920, History of the Ohio State University*. 8 vols. Columbus: Ohio State University Press, 1922.

Miller, Robert Moats. *Harry Emerson Fosdick: Preacher, Pastor, Prophet*. New York: Oxford University Press, 1985.

Mjagkij, Nina, ed. *Organizing Black America: An Encyclopedia of African*

American Associations. Florence, KY: Routledge, Taylor & Francis, 2001.

Moore, Jacqueline M. *Booker T. Washington, W.E.B. Du Bois, and the Struggle for Racial Uplift*. Wilmington, DE: Scholarly Resources, 2003.

Morgan, Marion J. *Women in Cleveland: An Illustrated History*. Bloomington: Indiana University Press, 1995.

Morning, Ann. "New Faces, Old Faces: Counting the Multiracial Population Past and Present." In *New Faces in a Changing America: Multiracial Identity in the 21st Century*, edited by Loretta I. Winters and Herman L. De Bose. Thousand Oaks, CA: Sage. 2003.

Morton, Marian J. *Women in Cleveland: An Illustrated History*. Bloomington, IN: Indiana University Press, 1995.

National Foreign Trade Council. *Official Report of the Second National Foreign Trade Convention*. Cambridge, MA: Harvard University, 1922.

Nelson, Timothy J. *Every Time I Feel the Spirit: Religious Experience and Ritual in an African American Church*. New York: New York University Press, 2004.

Newman, Richard S. *Freedom's Prophet: Bishop Richard Allen, the AME Church, and the Black Founding Fathers*. New York: New York University Press, 2008.

Norrell, Robert J. *Up from History: The Life of Booker T. Washington*. Cambridge, MA: Belknap of Harvard University Press, 2009.

Ohio Medical Society. "Dudley P. Allen." *Transactions of the Forty-Eighth Annual Meeting Held at Put-in Bay, June 28, 29, and 30, 1893*. Cincinnati: Earhart & Richardson, 1893.

Pardee, Richard Gay. *The Sabbath School Index: Pointing Out the History and Progress of Sunday-Schools*. Philadelphia: J. C. Garrigues, 1868.

Patterson, Frederick D. *Chronicles of Faith: The Autobiography of Frederick D. Patterson*. Edited by Martha Graham Goodson. Tuscaloosa: University Of Alabama Press, 1991.

Penn, Irvine Garland. *The Afro-American Press and Its Editors*. 1891. Reprint, New York: Arno, 1969.

Perrin, W. H., and J. H. Battle. *History of Delaware County and Ohio*. Chicago: O. L. Baskin, 1880.

Pastras, Phil. *Dead Man Blues: Jelly Roll Morton Way out West*. Berkeley: University of California Press, 2001.

Phillips, Kimberley L. "'But It is a Fine Place to Make Money': Migration and

African-American Families in Cleveland, 1915–1929." *Journal of Social History* 30, no. 2 (1996): 393–413.

Porter, Philip W. *Cleveland: Confused City on a Seesaw*. Columbus: Ohio State University Press, 1976.

Pyatt, Sherman E. *Burke High School, 1894–2006*. Mt. Pleasant, SC: Arcadia Publishing, 2007.

Randall, Emilius O., and Daniel Joseph Ryan. *History of Ohio: The Rise and Progress of an American State*. 6 vols. New York: Century History, 1912.

"Religious Mission and Politics," *Journal of Women's History* 19, no. 2 (Summer 2007): 85–110.

Reynolds, David S. *John Brown Abolitionist: The Man who Killed Slavery, Sparked the Civil War, and Seeded Civil Rights*. New York: Knopf, 2005.

Richings, G. F. *Evidences of Progress Among Colored People*. Philadelphia: Geo. S. Ferguson, 1905.

Roberts, Edward A. *Official Report of the Centennial Celebration of the Founding of the City of Cleveland and the Settlement of the Western Reserve*. Cleveland: Cleveland Printing and Publishing, 1896.

Roberts, Richard. *Florence Simms: A Biography*. New York: Women's Press, 1925.

Robinson, David. *The Unitarians and the Universalists*. Westport, CT: Greenwood, 1985.

Rodriguez, Junius P. *Slavery in the United States: a Social, Political and Historical Encyclopedia*. 2 vols. Santa Barbara, CA: ABC-CLIO, 2007.

Roebuck, Julian B., and Komanduri S. Murty. *Historically Black Colleges and Universities: Their Place in American Higher Education*. Westport, CT: Praeger, 1993.

Rose, William Ganson. *Cleveland: The Making of a City*. Cleveland: World, 1950.

Roster, Jacqueline Jones. *Profiles of Ohio Women 1803–2003*. Athens: Ohio University Press, 2003.

Ross, Lawrence C., Jr. *The Divine Nine: The History of African American Fraternities and Sororities*. New York: Kensington, 2000.

Rudwick, Elliott M. *Race Riot at East St. Louis: July 2, 1917*. Champaign: University of Illinois Press, 1982.

Safire, William. *Safire's Political Dictionary*. New York: Oxford University Press, 2008.

Salem, Dorothy C. *To Better our World: Black Women in Organized Reform,*

1890–1920. Black Women in United States History, vol. 14. Brooklyn: Carlson, 1990.

Samuelson, Dale, and Wendy Yegoiants. *The American Amusement Park*. St. Paul: MBI, 2001.

Sass, Herbert Ravenel. *The History of the South Carolina Lowcountry*. West Columbia, SC: J. F. Heyer, 1956.

Savage, Beth L., Carol D. Shull, United States National Park Service, National Conference of State Historic Preservation Officers, and National Register of Historic Places, eds. *African American Historic Places*. Hoboken, NJ: John Wiley and Sons, 1994.

Scott, Anne Firor. "Most Invisible of All: Black Women's Voluntary Associations." *Journal of Southern History* 56, no. 1 (1990): 3–22.

Scroop, Daniel. *Mr. Democrat: Jim Farley, the New Deal, and the Making of Modern American Politics*. Ann Arbor: University of Michigan Press, 2006.

Sewell, George A., and Margaret L. Dwight. *Mississippi Black History Makers*. revised and enlarged edition. Jackson: University Press of Mississippi, 1984.

Simkins, Francis Butler. *Pitchfork Ben Tillman: South Carolinian*. Baton Rouge: Louisiana State University Press, 1944.

Simpson, R. W. *History of Old Pendleton District: With a Genealogy of the Leading Families of the District*. Greenville, S.C.: Southern Historical Press, 1996.

Sims, Mary S. *The Natural History of a Social Institution: the Young Women's Christian Association*. New York: Woman's Press, 1936.

"Sketch of Charles Upham Shepard." *Popular Science Monthly* 47, no. 35 (1895): 548–53.

Smith, Jessie Carney, Millicent Lownes Jackson, and Linda T. Wynn. *Encyclopedia of African American Business*. 2 vols. Santa Barbara, CA: Greenwood, 1999.

Smith, Jessie Carney, ed. *Notable Black Women, Book II*. New York: Gale, 1996.

Smith, Suzanne E. *To Serve the Living: Funeral Directors and the African American Way of Death*. Cambridge, MA: Belknap Press of Harvard University Press, 2010.

Smyth, Thomas. *Autobiographical Notes, Letters and Reflections*. Edited by Louisa Cheves Smythe Stoney. Charleston: Walker, Evans & Cogswell, 1914.

Snowden, Yates, ed. *History of South Carolina*. 5 vols. Chicago: Lewis Publishing, 1920.

Soldan, Frank Louis. *The Century and the School and Other Educational Essays*. New York: MacMillan, 1912.

Spain, Daphne. "Safe Havens for Cleveland's Virtuous Women, 1868–1928." *Journal of Planning History* 3, no. 4 (2004): 267–91.

———. *How Women Saved the City*. Minneapolis: University of Minnesota Press, 2001.

State Historic Preservation Office. *African American Historic Places in South Carolina*. Columbia: South Carolina Department of Archives and History, 2007.

Tennyson, Alfred. *The May Queen*. London: Sampson Low, 1861.

Thomas, Richard Walter. *Life is What We Make It: Building Black Community in Detroit, 1915–1945*. Bloomington: Indiana University Press, 1992.

Tindall, George Brown. *South Carolina Negroes, 1877–1900*. Columbia: University of South Carolina Press, 2003.

Tuennerman-Kaplan, Laura. *Helping Others, Helping Ourselves: Power, Giving and Community Identity in Cleveland, Ohio, 1880–1930*. Kent, OH: Kent State University Press, 2001.

United States Department of Commerce, Bureau of the Census. *Negroes in the United States, 1920–32*. Washington, DC: Government Printing Office, 1935.

United States Industrial Commission. "Testimony of Mr. Charles U. Shephard." *Report of the U.S. Industrial Commission on Agriculture and Agricultural Labor*, vol. 10. Washington, DC: Government Printing Office, 1901.

Upton, Harriet Taylor. *History of the Western Reserve*. 3 vols. Chicago: Lewis, 1910.

Van Tine, Warren R., and Michael Dale Pierce, eds. *Builders of Ohio: A Biographical History*. Columbus: Ohio State University Press, 2003.

Venezky, Richard L. *The American Way of Spelling: The Structure and Origins of American English Orthography*. New York: Guilford, 1999.

Wade, Louise Carroll. *Graham Taylor: Pioneer for Social Justice, 1851–1938*. Chicago: University of Chicago Press, 1964.

Ware, Lowry. *Old Abbeville: Scenes of the Past of a Town Where Old Time Things are not Forgotten* Columbia, SC: SCMAR, 1992.

Washington, Booker T. *Tuskegee: Its Story and Its Work*. Boston: Small, Maynard, 1900.

Weems, Robert E., and Lewis A. Randolph. *Business in Black and White:*

American Presidents and Black Entrepreneurs in the Twentieth Century. New York: New York University Press, 2009.

Weinburg, Meyer. *A Chance to Learn: the History of Education and Race in the United States*. 2nd ed. Long Beach: California State University Press, 1995.

Whipple, Guy Montrose. "Communications and Discussions: Continuation Schools for Girls." *Journal of Educational Psychology*, no. 3 (1912): 158–59.

White, John H., Jr. *The American Railroad Passenger Car.* Baltimore: Johns Hopkins University Press, 1985.

Wiggins, William H. *"Free at Last": a Study of Afro-American Emancipation Day Celebrations*. PhD diss., University of Indiana, 1974.

Wiles, Beth Ann. "Pinckney Home Built Soon after Revolutionary War is Still Standing," *Anderson Daily Mail*, March 11, 1932.

Winter, Nevin Otto. *A History of Northwest Ohio: a Narrative Account of its Historical Progress and Development from the First European Exploration of the Maumee and Sandusky Valleys and the Adjacent Shores of Lake Erie, Down to the Present Time*. Vol. 2. Chicago: Lewis, 1917.

Wordsworth, William. "The Solitary Reaper." *The Poetical Works of Wordsworth*. New York: John Wurtele Lovell, 1881.

Wright, George Frederick. *Representative Citizens of Ohio: Memorial-Genealogical*. Cleveland: Memorial, 1913.

Young, Jeffrey Robert. *Domesticating Slavery: The Master Class in Georgia and South Carolina, 1670–1837*. Chapel Hill: University of North Carolina Press, 1999.

INDEX

Adams, Beatrice Gaines, 74

Adams, Charles, 102, 224

Addams, Jane, 23, 27, 166, 198–99

Adger, Joseph Ellison, 45, 160, 207

African Methodist Church, South
Carolina, 80

Allen University, 5

Allen, Florence E., 142, 236

Allen, Richard, 153, 239

Alpha Kappa Alpha Sorority, 5,
158–59, 242

American Association of Social
Workers, 142, 237

Anderson, South Carolina, 43, 59, 207

Antioch Baptist Church, 89, 108,
220–21

Arter, Charles K., 102, 224

Arter, Eliza Kingsley, 133–34, 232

Arter, Frank Asbury, 134, 232–33

Arter, Mrs. Frank A. See Arter, Eliza
Kingsley

Aunt Nan. See English, Nancy
Milliner

Avery Institute, 162, 244

Bailey, Bertha L., 138, 234

Baldwin, Arthur D., 102, 225

Baldwin, Mrs. Arthur D. See Baldwin,
Reba Williams

Baldwin, Reba Williams, 102, 225

Baldwin-Wallace Law School, 142,
234, 236

Beason, Mr. and Mrs. James, 198,
220–21

Bell, Catherine, 118

Bellamy, George A., 28, 199

Bennett, John, 16–17, 18–19, 20, 30,
47, 162, 179–83, 201

Bennett, Susan Smythe, 16–18, 46,
162, 208

Bethune, Mary McLeod, 9, 10, 158,
185, 189, 191, 241–42

Bethune-Cookman College, 9,
241–42

Biggar Sr., Hamilton Fisk, 72, 214

Bishop Jr., Robert H., 7, 100–101,
171–73, 200, 225

Bishop, Constance Mather, 29, 98,
101, 200

Bishop, Mrs. Robert H. *See* Bishop, Constance Mather

Black Belt of Alabama, 239

black vernacular expressivity, xiii

black women's club movement, 4, 218

Blue, Charles, 95

Bolton Presbyterian Church, 72, 214

Bolton, Chester C., 137, 234

Bolton, Frances P., 137, 234

Booker T. Washington Trade Association, 148

Boulevard Presbyterian Church, 87, 220

Bourke-White, Margaret, 31, 202

Boyd, Albert "Starlight", 12–14, 70, 104–11, 214, 227

death and funeral, 110–11

Woodluff Hall, 69–70, 214

Boyd, Cora Stuart, 92, 94, 221

Boyd, Mrs. Elmer F. *See* Boyd, Cora Stuart

Boyd, Olive Azaler, 105–6, 227

Boyton, Virginia, 11

Bradley, Anna A., 136, 234

Bradley, Morris A., 136, 233

Braxton, Joanne M., xiii, 10

Brown, George A., 156

Brown, Hallie Quinn, 18, 157, 241

Tales My Father Told, 18

Brown, John, 134, 233

buck-dancer, 46, 208

Buell, Viola Smith, 141, 235

Bundy, Rev. Mr. Charles, 86, 219

Burke Industrial School, 162, 245

Burke, Ella M., 97, 101, 222

Burke, Mrs. Edwin, 101

Burke, Mrs. Stevenson. *See* Burke, Ella M.

Burroughs, Nannie Helen, 9–10, 19, 185, 187–88, 190

National Training School for Women and Girls, 9

Butler, Susan Dart, 162, 244

Caldwell, Erskine, 31, 201

Calhoun family, 43, 207

Camp Merriman, 115

Camp Mueller, 194

Cannon Street Hospital and Training School for Nurses, 60–61, 180, 211

Carby, Hazel, 11, 12

Carey Farm, 41, 206

Carver, George Washington, 148, 239

Central High School, 114–15, 118, 141, 143, 229

Central State University, 5

Champney Sr., Mrs. W. P. *See* Champney, Clara P.

Champney, Clara P., 141, 236

Charleston City Hospital, 62, 212

Charleston, South Carolina, 3, 17, 44, 46, 57, 59, 63, 65, 69, 77, 161–62, 177–78, 180, 207–08, 213

Chesnutt, Charles W., 6, 222

Church of the Covenant, 126, 222, 232

Civil War, 19, 31, 45, 134, 201, 205

Clapp, Raymond, 135, 233

Clemson College, 12, 41, 160, 206, 243

Clemson, South Carolina, 43–45, 47, 77, 160

Cleveland Board of Education, 125, 129, 143, 152

Cleveland Chamber of Commerce, 164

Cleveland Foundation, 115, 132, 229–30

Cleveland Library Board, 144

Cleveland Trust Company, 96, 222

Cleveland, Ohio, 67–68

  Arthur Avenue, 70, 73

  black belt, 104, 152, 181, 227

  black elite, xi, 2, 5, 19, 84

  Central Avenue, 68–69, 90, 98, 110, 213–14

  Chamber of Commerce, 1

  Euclid Avenue, 72

  Euclid Beach, 81, 217–18

  Hamilton Avenue district, 69, 70

  housing for African American migrants, 70, 81

  impact of great migration on population, 104, 181, 218, 227

  JEH migrates to, 68

  racial segregation, schools, 125, 152

  Roaring Third, 107, 227

  Sheriff Street Market, 73

  the Heights, 102, 224

  Third District, 111

Cohen, Amy, 80, 82, 94

Coleman, Mr. and Mrs. William, 67

color prejudice, 61, 211

Community Fund of Cleveland, 135, 233

Cutler, James Elbert, 139, 235

Daniel, Sadie Iola, 14–15

  Women Builders, 14

Delta Sigma Theta Sorority, 158–59, 242

Democratic Party, 107

Dillard, James H., 73, 215

Director of Public Welfare, 90–91

"Dixie", 201

Dixie Hospital and Training School for Nurses, 66–67, 80, 213

domestic service, 2, 45, 59, 124, 129, 131, 174

DuBois, W. E. B., 4, 166, 199

Dunbar-Nelson, Alice, 6

education for black Americans, 150

Ellison, Ralph, xiii

English, Nancy Milliner, 157, 185–86, 241

equality of opportunity, 124

Evans, Florence, 80, 82

Everett, Syble Ethel Byrd, 11

Fant Plantation, 40–41, 91, 205

Feger, Hattie, 191

Ferguson and Williams College, 3, 12, 49–54, 60, 208–9

Fisk University, 5

Flagman, Tim. *See* Fleming, Thomas W.

Fleming, Thomas W., 107, 228

Fosdick, Harry Emerson, 98, 222–23

Frackelton, David Waddell, 30, 200

Frackelton, Fannie Pitcairn, 30, 100, 127, 200

Frackelton, Mr. and Mrs. D. W. *See* Frackelton, David Waddell *and* Frackelton, Fannie Pitcairn

Fuller, Mrs. Ralph. *See* Fuller, Thalia Reese

Fuller, Thalia Reese, 142, 236

Garrett, Zuleime, 30, 200

Garvin, Charles H., 144, 237

Gates, Marie Taylor, 72

Gilkey, Mary Virginia King, 72, 215

Gilkey, Mrs. W. S. *See* Gilkey, Mary Virginia King

Girl Reserves, 4, 99, 118, 121, 223

Gleason, Eugene F., 19

Goodhue, Laura S., 93, 221–22

grandmother, maternal. *See* Milliner, Pauline "Polly"

Graves, Charles H., 220

great migrations, xii–xiii, 5, 96

Greater Cleveland Federation of Women, 115, 229

Great-grandmother Cumber. *See* Hamilton, Cumber

Green, David E., 102, 225

Green, John P., 93, 222

Halle, Samuel H., 156, 240

Hamilton, Cumber, 35–36, 161, 204

Hampton Institute, 4, 66–67, 80, 213

Hanckel Place, 32, 202

Harlem Hospital, 115, 229

Harper, Hattie, 80–83

Harris Jr., Benjamin Bonneau, 207

Harris, Edward, 3, 14, 31–34, 36–38, 40–41, 43, 47, 55, 76, 155, 180, 202

death and funeral, 42, 206

desire for his children to receive education, 39, 77

marriage to Harriet Milliner, 32

Harris, Harriet Milliner, 3–4, 11–12, 30, 32–34, 36–41, 43, 45, 49, 52, 57–58, 94, 176, 178, 180, 202

her death as inspiration for JEH's life work, 79

JEH's attempt to reconcile with, 76–77

remarriage after Edward Harris's death, 44

sudden death of, 78

Harris, Orpha G., 46, 208

Harris, Rebecca, 32, 38, 43, 56, 60, 202

Harris, Rosa, 32, 42–43, 60, 202

Harris, Rose, 81, 83

Harris, Winston, 22, 32, 41–43, 46, 202

Hawthorne, Nathaniel, 225–26

Haynes, Rebecca, 81

Henderson, Emma, 95

Henderson, Tom, 32–33, 37

Hills, Mrs. Adin T. *See* Hills, Sarah C.
Hills, Sarah C., 87–88, 93, 221
Home for Aged Colored People, 74,
    214, 216
Hughes, Everett C., 19
Hunt, Ella, 60, 211
Hunter, Edward, 57
    JEH's brief marriage to, 3, 57–58,
        176–78, 210
Huron Road Hospital, 72–73, 215
Hurston, Zora Neale, 11
hymns, 21, 42, 75, 160, 162, 206, 209,
    210, 216, 243, 245

Imes, G. Lake, 15
Interdenominational Ministerial
    Alliance, 6, 85–86, 219
International Convention on Moral
    Rearmament, 22, 198
interracial cooperation, 87, 93, 113,
    154, 163
Iota Phi Lambda Sorority, 159,
    242–43

Jackson, Ellen, 101
Jacobs, Harriet, 13–14
Jane Addams School, 125, 129, 231
Jane E. Hunter Scholarship
    Committee, xiv, 20
Jefferson, Lucy C., 157, 241
Jones, Adrienne Lash, 11, 17, 176
Journal of the National Medical
    Association, 5
Judd, Mary Rathburn, 106, 227

Kepke, Mrs. John T., 71
King's Chapel African Methodist
    Episcopal Church, 37, 39, 47, 204
Kohler, Josephine B., 137, 230, 234

Lake View Cemetery, 22
Lewis, Robert E., 93, 222
library schools, 124, 231
life insurance companies, 148
Lincoln Hospital, 80, 217
Lincoln, Abraham, 32, 201
Longfellow, Henry Wadsworth, 76,
    216
Longwood School, 125, 231–32

Martin, Mary B., 237
Maschke, Maurice, 136, 234
Maschke, Minnie Rice, 137, 234
May Company, 95, 222
McC. Black, Mrs. T., 126, 232
McClellan, Alonzo Clifton, 62, 212
McCrary, Jane, 32
McCulloch, Rhoda E., 19, 30, 179,
    184, 201
McCullough, Rhoda E.. *See*
    McCulloch, Rhoda E.
McGaffin, Anna DeYoe, 126, 232
McGaffin, Mrs. Alexander H. *See*
    McGaffin, Anna DeYoe
Meldrum, Andrew Barclay, 89, 220
Men of the Cleveland Bar
    Association, 103
Merriam, Cliffe Updegraff, 118, 230
Merriam, Mrs. Walter H. *See*
    Merriam, Cliffe Updegraff

Methodist Churchwomen, Cleveland, 133

Miller, Emma, 157

Milliken, Mrs. Benjamin L. *See* Millikin, Julia W. Severance

Millikin, Benjamin L., 233

Millikin, Julia W. Severance, 135–136, 233

Milliner, Abe, 46–47, 49, 208
  barely escapes lynching, 47

Milliner, Anna, 44, 207

Milliner, Caroline, 12, 45, 47, 49, 54, 177–78, 207

Milliner, Flora, 43, 186, 207

Milliner, Neat, 40, 186, 205

Milliner, Parris John, 57, 67, 178, 210

Milliner, Pauline "Polly", 20, 32, 34–35, 37, 39, 41–42, 51, 56–57, 98, 160, 203

Milliner, William, 32, 202

Morris, Mrs. C. T., 193

Mother Rich, 101

Moton, Jennie Dee Booth, 8, 158, 242

Moton, Mrs. Robert R. *See* Moton, Jennie Dee Booth

Moton, Robert R., 6, 15, 103, 225

Mottley, Christian LaTrobe, 71, 214

Murrell, Howard E., 110, 228

Myers, George A., 1, 2, 5, 164–70, 246

National Association of Colored Women, 8, 91, 157, 182, 221
  Phillis Wheatley Department, 8, 91, 182, 221
  Thirteenth Biennial Convention, 157

National Conference of Social Work, 143, 237

National Federation of Colored Women's Clubs, 9

National Housewives' League, 238

Negro National Anthem, 159, 243

Negro spirituals, 16, 21, 35, 40, 47, 49, 56, 67, 79, 91, 122, 155, 157, 159, 161, 163, 204–205, 231, 244

Nickel and a Prayer, A xiv
  book reviews, 18, 179–84
  copyright registration, 17
  difficulties in finding a publisher, 16
  editorial assistance, 15–17, 20
  Elli Kani Publishing Company, 17, 20, 199
  manuscript preparation, 15, 176
  new final chapter entitled "Fireside Musings", xv, 20, 198
  Parthenon Press, 18, 20
  three extant versions, xiv, 20

Nickens, Cornelia F., 72, 214

normal schools, 124, 231

Oberlin College, 138, 234–35

Ohio Department of Job and Family Services, 23

Ohio State Federation of Colored Women's Clubs, 8, 144, 237

Ohio State School at Delaware, 143, 237

Ohio State University, 118, 230

Ohio Women's Hall of Fame, 23

Old Stone Church, Cleveland, 89, 220

Old Stone Church, South Carolina, 160, 243
Open Door, The 4, 9, 15, 20
Osie. *See* Boyd, Olive Azaler

Parker, Thomas F., 139, 235
Parks, Mabel, 114
Patterson, Frederick D., 142, 236
Peck, Fannie B., 147, 238
  National Housewives' League, 147–48
Peck, William H., 148, 239
Pendleton County School, 49, 208
Pendleton Historic Foundation, xv
Pendleton, South Carolina, xii, 3, 26, 39, 45, 53, 75, 77, 155, 160–161, 179, 185, 204
Phillis Wheatley Association, 198
  adoption of new name for, 91
  begun as Working Girls' Home Association, xii, 4, 83
  Board of Trustees, 6, 89–90, 92, 93, 95–97, 128, 131, 145
  Camp Merriam, 118, 229
  Camp Mueller, 22
  capital campaign, 2, 100, 171
  contents of cornerstone, 102, 225
  criticism by *Cleveland Gazette*, 86, 219
  drafting the constitution, 91
  Ella Ford Finishing House, 123, 132, 231
  Employment Bureau, 131, 174
  endowment established for, 146
  first building opened for, 94

Fiscal Board of Trustees, 146, 238
  functions as community center, 100
  initial opposition by black club women, 84, 218
  interracial co-operation, 112
  JEH's resignation from, 21, 191–94
  Josephine Kohler Pre-School, 121, 230
  Junior Board, 116
  Junior Mothers' Club, 121, 230–31
  Kingsley-Arter Center, 134, 233
  move to make subsidiary of Y.W.C.A., 97
  music department, 100, 223
  new nine-story building, 102, 223
  purpose, 123
  recreational hall, 106
  Sarah C. Hills Training School, 87, 123, 126–32, 137, 174, 219
  second building purchased, 98, 223
Phillis Wheatley Association of Greenville, 139, 235
Phillis Wheatley Foundation, 14, 22
Pickens Jr., Thomas, 35, 41, 180, 203
Pickens, Andrew, 160, 243
Pilgrim's Progress, 13, 104, 226
Pine Hurst Inn, 63
Pomeroy, Harlan, 72–73, 215
Pomeroy, Lawrence A., 72, 215
Popular Lady Contest, 74, 215
Presbyterian Board of Missions for Freedmen, 53, 209
Presbyterian Missionary Society of Cuyahoga County, 87

Presbyterian Missionary Society of
  Cuyahoga County, 220
Progressive Negro Business League,
  148
Pullman Service, 57, 63, 210

Quadrille, 77, 216

race leadership for black Americans,
  149
race pride, 58, 85
racial discrimination, employment,
  71, 73, 125, 147
racial segregation, how to combat,
  150–54
Radke, Frank, 103
Radke, Kaney, 103
reels, 40, 205
Republican Party, 1, 9, 164
  black vote, 107, 227–28
Richardson, Williard S., 30, 200
Richman Brothers Company, 146, 238
Richman, Charles L., 145, 238
Richman, Henry C., 145, 238
Rockefeller Jr., John D., 8, 101, 103,
  224
  makes $100,000 pledge to PWA,
    101
Rockefeller Sr., John D., 72, 215
  Laura Spelman Foundation, 101, 224
  Rockefeller Foundation, 101, 224
Roosevelt, Eleanor, 9
Rosenwald, Julius, 156, 240
  Rosenwald Fund, 156, 240

Ruffin, Josephine St. Pierre, 157, 241
Rutledge, Benjamin H., 59, 180, 211
Rutledge, Emma Blake, 59, 211
Rutledge, Major and Mrs. Benjamin.
  See Rutledge, Benjamin H. and
  Rutledge, Emma Blake

salary inequity for black Americans,
  149
salary inequity for black and white
  Americans, 149
Sands, Ruby, 39, 43–44, 205
Scofield, Elizabeth, 7, 30, 86, 89–90,
  93, 200
Scofield, Mrs. Levi T. See Scofield,
  Elizabeth
Second Presbyterian Church, 87
  Women's Missionary Board, 87,
    219–20
settlement movement, 4, 5, 27, 82,
  218. Also see Addams, Jane;
  Belamy, George; and Taylor,
  Graham.
Severance, Emily C., 102, 134, 136,
  225
Severance, Mrs. Solon. See Severance,
  Emily C.
Severance, Solon L., 134, 225
Shepard, Charles Upham, 63–64,
  212–13
Sherwin, Henry A., 8, 90, 93, 220
Sieglestein, L. E., 71, 214
Silver Spring Baptist Church, 39, 205
Silver Spring School, 41, 43, 49, 205

Simms, Daisy Florence, 141, 235–36

Simons, Thomas Grange, 62, 66, 180, 211–12

slavery, 38, 160

Emancipation Proclamation, 32, 161

happier circumstances, 37, 204

JEH's paternal grandmother, 31, 202

Market House, Charleston, 162

Smythe III, Augustine T., 16, 208

Smythe Sr., Augustine T., 45–46, 162, 207–08

Southernaires, 159, 243

Spain, Daphne, 12

St. John's AME Church, 72, 108, 134, 165, 214

St. John's Baptist Church, 41

St. Michael's Church, 162, 245

St. Phillip's Church, 162, 245

Stecher, Lue Morgan, 138, 235

Stecher, Mrs. F. See Stecher, Lue Morgan

stepfather of JEH, 52

Stephens, Patrick, 90, 220

Stewart, Maria W., 13

Stewart, Sallie W., 158, 242

Street Railway Company, 107, 227

Strickland, Ruth, 80, 82

Studebaker, Edna M., 115, 229

Stuphen, Bertha B., 95, 222

Stuphen, Paul F., 95, 100, 102, 222

Summerville, South Carolina, 62–64, 161

Sutphen, Dr. and Mrs. Paul F. See

Sutphen, Paul F. and Sutphen, Bertha B.

Taylor, Graham, 27, 199

Taylor, Rebecca Stiles, 157, 241

Terrell, Mary Church, 11

Thomas H. White Trust Fund, 132, 232

Thompson, Era Belle, 11

Tillman, Benjamin, 161, 244

Traveler's Aid, The, 119, 230

Tubbs, Jeanette, 80

Tuskegee Institute, 5, 6, 15, 103, 142, 153, 156, 158, 164, 182–83, 240

two schools of thought, 150

Uncle Abe. See Milliner, Abe

Unemployment Sewing Circle, The, 126, 232

Unitarian Church, 136, 234

Virginia Reel, 77, 216

Wagner Sleeping Car Company, 63, 212

Wagner, Webster, 63

Walker Jr., Legare, 64, 213

Waring, Mary F., 8, 158, 242

Washington, Booker T., 1–2, 7, 15, 85, 142, 153, 164–69, 183, 199, 219

Welfare Federation of Cleveland, 21, 135–36, 194, 233

Wendell Phillips High School, 157, 241

Werner Place, 39

Western Reserve University, 114–15, 139, 142, 229

Wheatley, Phillis, 91, 221
  US Postal stamp, JEH's support of, 10

Wilberforce University, 5, 142, 236

Williams, Ella, 3, 12, 51–53, 208

Williams, Emory, 3, 208

Williams, Rev. Mr. E. W. and wife. *See* Williams, Emory and Williams, Ella

Williamson, Mollie, 66

Willoughby Methodist Church, 142, 236

Wills Sr., Jay Walter, 224

Wilson, James, 43

Wilson, Woodrow, 97

Wings Over Jordan Singers, 159, 243

Winston, Tenus, 78, 217

Woodburn Farm, 3, 5, 12, 14, 16–17, 26, 31–32, 36, 38–39, 45–47, 54, 98, 104, 162, 179, 180, 201
  JEH's birthplace, 32, 179

Woodson, Carter G., 6, 15, 19

Wooley, Edna Kay, 19

Wordsworth, William, 76, 216

World War I, 96–97

Wright, Hannah Smythe, 20, 46, 208

Wright, Richard, xiii

Wylie, J. R., 93, 221

Young Men's Christian Association (YWCA), 5, 156, 240

Young Women's Christian Association (YWCA), 1, 4, 5–7, 82, 84, 86, 89, 106, 141, 218
  Girls' Industrial Conference, 141, 236

Zeta Phi Beta Sorority, 159, 242

Jane Edna Hunter (1882-1971) founded the Phillis Wheatley Association (PWA), an organization that offered housing, job training, and recreational activities to thousands of black women and girls who sought better opportunities in the North during the Great Migration. She gained recognition through her work at the PWA, National Association of Colored Women, National Association for the Advancement of Colored People, Ohio Federation of Colored Women's Clubs, and the Republican Party.

Rhondda Robinson Thomas is Assistant Professor in the Department of English at Clemson University in Clemson, South Carolina, where she teaches African American and Early American Literature.